AF263244

USER INTERFACE PROGRAMMING FOR GAMES

LUIS SEMPÉ

To Gaby, the most beautiful and loving human being, you have given me such wondrous gifts.

To Luka, Joseph, Emma and Ethan, you are my source of inspiration and wonder, the sky is not the limit!

CONTENTS

FOREWORD

More than ever, gamers these days can be fickle and impatient. If the game you just spent months or years creating doesn't boot up almost instantly, and allow the player to jump right into the action, his or her interest may be lost, and your game might never be turned on again. The player's experience with your game starts---and ends---with your game's user interface. It is the first thing the player sees when the game starts. And it is the primary means by which the player interacts with your game's universe. It is also one of the primary means by which the player judges the quality of your game as a whole. As such, more than for any other kind of software product, games are expected to have incredibly intuitive, effective, and attractive user interfaces.

Certainly many educational resources exist to aid an aspiring user interface programmer. However, these resources are almost entirely aimed at developers of desktop, web and mobile apps. Sadly, very few educational materials are targeted specifically toward the creation of graphical user interfaces for interactive entertainment.

Thankfully for game programmers everywhere, Luis Sempé has taken it upon himself to rectify the situation. The book you see before you fills this gaping hole in game programming pedagogy, and does so extremely well. *"User Interface Programming for Games"* covers all the key topics, from laying all of the necessary foundations, all the way to illustrating how to put the finishing touches on your game's UI. And it does so in an accessible and easy-to-understand manner.

This is no surprise to me, given Luis' excellent track record in the games industry. I first met Luis when we worked together on *Medal of Honor: Pacific Assault* (MOHPA) at Electronic Arts, Los Angeles. Even during these relatively early days of his career, Luis always brought with him an infectious enthusiasm and a thirst for learning, as well as a keen knack for solving problems and a strong sense of professionalism and follow-through. I recall being particularly impressed with Luis' game development skills when he implemented an entire flight-based mini-game for MOHPA, including the aircraft's diegetic user interface (i.e., a user interface which exists within the game world, rather than being overlaid in 2D over top of the 3D display). He also worked on numerous other tools and engine systems for MOHPA, including implementing various runtime visual effects and helping to develop a powerful terrain editor for the team.

Since then, Luis has continued to amass a great deal of expertise, both as a game programmer in general, and in the art of creating graphical user interfaces for games in particular. He was in charge of the UI in *Army of Two* at Electronic Arts, Montreal, and handled the core UI technology for *Deus Ex Human Revolution* at Eidos, Montreal. He now has ten years of experience in game programming, and numerous commercially-successful games under his belt. I'm confident you'll see Luis' experience and expertise shining through as you read this book.

It is a great time to be learning the craft of game development. A wide range of tools are available to you, as you undertake this exciting educational journey: from online tutorials to sample code to a host of articles and books. But until now, information on user interface programming for games had been sorely lacking. The book you have in front of you expertly fills this gap, and it will undoubtedly become an invaluable tool in your game programming toolkit.

Jason Gregory
Lead Programmer, Naughty Dog Inc.
Author of *Game Engine Architecture*
www.gameenginebook.com

ABOUT THE AUTHOR

Luis Sempé has had the privilege of developing AAA games professionally as a software engineer for the past ten years. His passion for game development has driven him to develop expertise in many disciplines. During his career he has developed systems and features in 3D graphics, created gameplay features and authoring tools, developed artificial intelligence systems to simulate flight combat and character behaviors, developed user interface systems for many games and integrated, supported and extended user interface middleware. He has also developed systems for video streaming, localization, and general game engine and tools.

User interface development has been a staple of his career, designing and implementing user interface systems for *Medal of Honor: Pacific Assault*, *Army of Two* and in particular, the critically acclaimed *Deus Ex Human Revolution*.

In the June/July 2010 issue of *Game Developer Magazine* he shared his design for the technology that drives the conversation system and character social interactions in *Deus Ex Human Revolution* in the article *Machina Ex – Creating a State-driven gameplay system for Deus Ex: Human Revolution*.

When he is not developing games professionally he is researching and prototyping game features in C++, XNA, Unity and any new technologies that seem interesting. He has a deep appreciation for independent and hobbyist games and sometimes participates in the indie games community discussions.

ABOUT THE CODE

The goal of this book is to provide you with a good conceptual and practical understanding of user interface programming applied to games. Most examples provide code that works "out of the box", however, it is impossible to anticipate every use case, readers are encouraged to use the code as a starting point towards developing their own UI systems or to implement their own features.

Code organization is a complex topic in itself within a project's structure, presenting code on paper has its own challenges, for example, in C++ we often write code such that the declarations exist in a header file (.h), while the actual operating code will be written in a code file (.cpp). The examples in print use a more concise presentation that highlights the relevant parts of the code and may not always reflect the same organization as it is in the live code repository.

In many cases, this book will use the simplest implementation of many data structures with the goal of illustrating the concepts and use cases without delving into complexity that may result from code that should generally be optimized, when appropriate code optimization suggestions are given.

Many of the classes and data structures used in this book have been made deliberately verbose with the intention that if you are working on an existing or proprietary code base, you should be able to find the respective objects or functions within your own technology.

The coding style is meant to be simple and concise, some choices are practical for illustration purposes, while others are subjective.

The code is presented in C++11 and the examples use Direct3D 11 and the DirectX Toolkit. http://directxtk.codeplex.com/

For more information about the source code please visit http://uipg.sempemedia.com

PREFACE

Style matters.

The development of fluid, visually pleasing and efficient user interfaces is a complex endeavor. The goal is to find an elegant way to display useful and time critical information to players in a way that is intuitive. Players need to make split second decisions without thought or hesitation. A good user interface will become an indispensable aid.

As software developers, our instinct is to create and develop something that works, and we stop at nothing until it does. Once our feature works, we feel excited and we want to show off our accomplishment to the world.

But the world may not be ready to see our creation, more pointedly, our creation may not be yet ready to be seen. *Style matters*.

When we develop a feature, before we share it with the team, before we submit it into version control and commit it into the project's history, we need to be confident not only that it works, but that it looks good, good enough to be understood and appreciated. Spend the extra time to make sure the user interface elements are properly aligned, scaled, colored. Make certain that text fields are in the right place, font sizes are correct. Make screens and images fade, rather than pop.

When developing a user interface, everything we do will be seen first by the development team. Just as players eventually will, developers rely on the user interface to gain more information about the game world as they develop their own features.

Strive to make the gap from placeholder to production quality as small as possible, be mindful of the art direction and make placeholders conform to the style and colors set by the artists. Attention to detail and a working and visually pleasing user interface will make a significant difference during the game's production.

ACKNOWLEDGEMENTS

Writing this book was a fun and exciting experience and I owe much of it to my family. My wonderful wife Gaby who always motivated me to keep going, always bought me those few extra minutes I needed for writing or developing the sample code during the day or night and even proofreading portions to make sure I wasn't rambling on. I am also very grateful to my kids Luka and Joseph whose excitement and curiosity has been a constant source of fuel for my motivation. And to my twin babies, Emma and Ethan whom I often held in my arms while I scribbled down notes, algorithms and ideas for this book. And to my mom Mirtha and my dad Jorge who raised me around computers and bought me my first game programming book when I was 14 years old, I have not stopped making games since!

The inspiration from this book was born during my time at *Eidos Montréal* where I had the distinct pleasure of creating *Deus Ex Human Revolution* alongside many talented engineers and some of the most creative and passionate artists, musicians and writers I have ever met. I learned so much from every single one of them and much of this book was written with them in mind. In particular I am grateful to Daniel Fortier for his patience and trust, many chapters of this book were born from conversations we had or problems we faced and how we solved them. He showed me that *programmer art* does not mean it has to be *bad* art, style matters. I am also grateful to Alexandre Richer and Fernando Secco, together, the four of us developed the vast majority of the UI for *DHXR*. I could probably fill a few chapters with anecdotes of our often spirited discussions.

I also want to thank Shawn Guzzo for his advice and design feedback, I may have done a few design *faux pas* were it not for him.

A special thanks to Jason Gregory for his very kind words and taking the time from finishing up his own book to write a bit on mine!

INTRODUCTION

Modern games have complex user interface development needs and require skilled game programmers capable of communicating and interfacing with different game systems efficiently. Nowadays, many gameplay and development features are presented as part of the user interface, from mini-games that allow players to complete smaller challenges to unlock and navigate the game universe, to complex statistical models that need to be presented to players, developers or even studio executives.

The *user interface* is the name given to a broad set of systems that provide players with a bidirectional flow of information. Players need to see the status of the game in real-time, the player's health, ammo, energy, stamina, and many properties that are changing as often as the game is updated. Visual feedback systems are crucial for players to make decisions about how they navigate the game world, as well as interacting with the game world through a variety of well-known controls and features.

User interface programming is often associated with the development of menus that allow players to configure their gaming experience, while this is true, this is a small part of the big picture. The user interface programmer's work goes beyond what is seen and perceived by players, user interface developers provide tools to developers to make their development and debugging experience more efficient. We develop systems to show developers a view of the game universe players don't get to see, hidden enemies, secret rooms, an NPC's vision cone, the AI's goal tree, and many more properties that developers need to visualize to understand at a glance what the code is doing underneath the hood.

Whether a dedicated user interface programmer or a game programmer that finds himself doing user interface work, the goal of this book is to provide you with the core knowledge needed to develop user interfaces efficiently and to provide development teams with useful tools that will make their daily work more efficient.

1 MATHEMATICS FOR GAMES

The most important skill you can develop if you want to develop user interfaces for games or other media, is mathematics. The range of mathematics used in user interfaces is incredibly broad in 2D space alone, once you take your user interface into your game's 3D space the amount of mathematics you will encounter grows significantly. A clear understanding of the math means less time spent trying to solve a complex problem through a brute force or a trial and error approach and more time creating interesting and efficient features. One of the most important trait you gain from investing time in understanding the math, is the intuition you develop that often leads you to find and apply reusable mathematical patterns, oftentimes a complex set of if/else conditions can be reduced to a single mathematical formula.

1.1 NOTATION

In this book and the example code we will use a left-handed coordinate system, with the viewer is looking down the Z axis. We will generally refer to the Z axis as the *forward* axis, the positive Y axis as the *up* axis, and the positive X axis as the *right*.

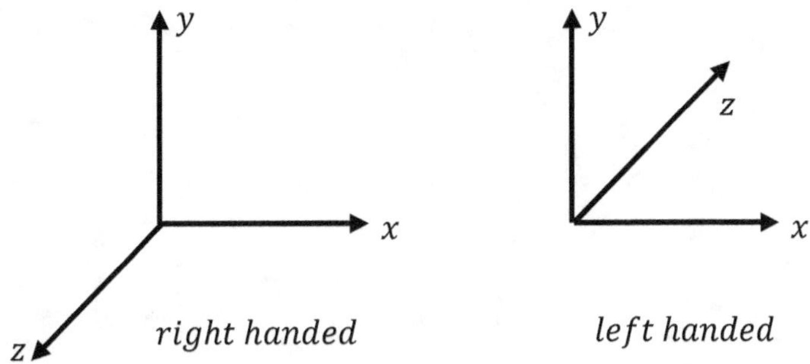

Figure 1- Left and right handed coordinate systems

Vectors will be presented in column-major form,

$$v = \begin{bmatrix} v_0 \\ v_1 \\ v_2 \end{bmatrix}$$

Matrices will be also in column major form

$$M = \begin{bmatrix} m_{00} & m_{10} & m_{20} \\ m_{01} & m_{11} & m_{21} \\ m_{02} & m_{12} & m_{22} \end{bmatrix}$$

The following table lists the conventions used in this book.

v	A vector.
$\lvert v \rvert$	A vector's magnitude (length).
$\hat{v}$	A unit vector.
$\cdot$	Dot product between vectors.
$\times$	Cross product between vectors.
$\perp$	Denotes that two vectors are perpendicular.
$\parallel$	Denotes that two vectors are parallel.
M	A matrix.
Θ	Theta, used to represent angles, in radians.

1.2 Linear Algebra

When it comes to game development, a powerful tool at our disposal is a good understanding of a few concepts in linear algebra. We will discuss linear algebra in a way in which is applicable to game development, but in particular with an emphasis towards user interfaces.

1.2.1 Vectors

For computer graphics, we are interested in a vector as a geometrical object that contains both a direction and a magnitude (length). Vectors are of great importance in games, you can imagine that every object in every game, whether 2D or 3D has an arrow that starts from its center and points in the direction it is traveling. This arrow, is a vector, and the length of this vector means how fast this object is traveling. This is perhaps the easiest way to picture what a vector is, vectors and the mathematical operations we can perform on them are useful in a very large number of situations.

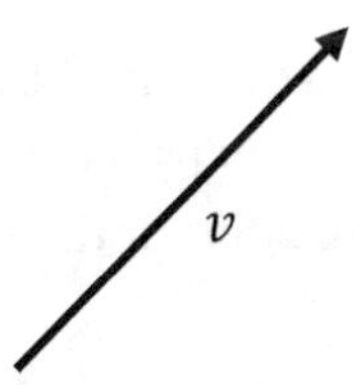

Figure 2- A vector denoted by the letter "v"

Vectors have a number of mathematical operations that can be performed on them, here we will discuss the most common uses and the meaning behind them.

An essential part of any game engine is a comprehensive vector class that offers all the facilities and often used functions in an intuitive way. The goal of this book is to present concepts in a straightforward manner and avoid adding complexity by presenting highly optimized code. We will use different classes *vector2*, *vector3* and *vector4* to explicitly state the kind of vector a problem requires, and we will forego some optimizations (such as parallelizing vector hardware) because optimized interfaces are typically more verbose and would distract us from our goal.

Note: The Direct3D example code provides conversion operators between the vector classes and the optimized XMVECTOR, it foregoes the optimization in favor of a more readable and straightforward interface, at the same time this compatibility allows optimized operations to be used in high performance situations and the vector classes used for local storage.

1.2.1.1   Vector Addition

Vector addition is the straightforward operation of adding all the components of one vector to the components of another.

$$v + u = \begin{bmatrix} v_0 + u_0 \\ v_1 + u_1 \\ v_2 + u_2 \end{bmatrix}$$

Geometrically, the result can be visualized by placing the second vector at the end point of the first, then drawing a vector between the starting point of the first vector to the ending point of the second.

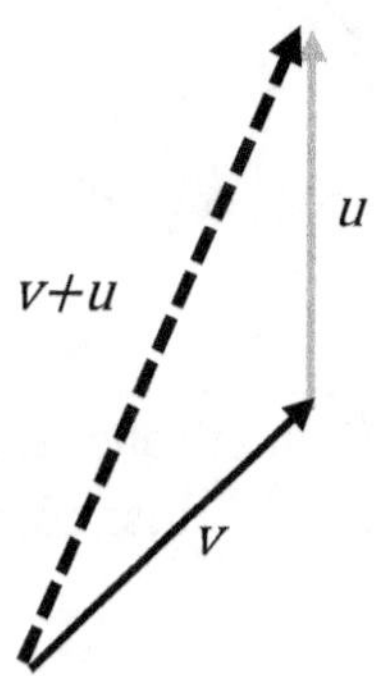

Figure 3 - Vector addition

The code to add two vectors together is equally straightforward, it is useful to implement the addition operators in the vector class.

```cpp
const vector4 vector4::operator + (const vector4 &rhs) const
{
    vector4 r;
    r.x() = x() + rhs.x();
    r.y() = y() + rhs.y();
    r.z() = z() + rhs.z();
    r.w() = w() + rhs.w();
    return r;
}

vector4 &vector4::operator += (const vector4 &rhs)
{
    x() += rhs.x();
    y() += rhs.y();
    z() += rhs.z();
    w() += rhs.w();
    return *this;
}
```

1.2.1.2 Vector Subtraction

Just as addition, subtraction is the straightforward operation of subtracting each of the vector's components.

$$u - v = \begin{bmatrix} u_0 - v_0 \\ u_1 - v_1 \\ u_2 - v_2 \end{bmatrix}$$

Vector subtraction is an operation we will find often when working in games, it allows us to calculate a vector between the end points of two other vectors.

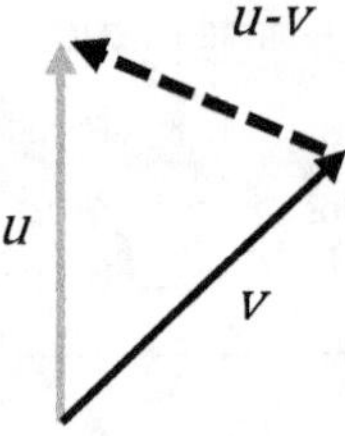

Figure 4 - Vector subtraction

This means that if we have two vectors $\mathbf{u}, \mathbf{v}$ in space representing two points in space, by performing a vector subtraction of $\mathbf{u} - \mathbf{v}$ we get the vector between these two points. From this vector we can determine the direction and we are also able to calculate the distance between the two points. One situation in which we may want to do this is to calculate the direction we want to aim the camera in order to look at some point in space. By performing vector subtraction from the point of interest and the camera's position, we get the direction vector to which we should orient the camera.

1.2.1.3 Vector Length

A vector represents both a direction and a magnitude, often we need to measure the length (magnitude) of a vector. The length of a vector will be denoted by:

$$\|v\|$$

Given a vector

$$v = \begin{bmatrix} x \\ y \\ z \end{bmatrix}$$

The length of the vector is computed with the Euclidean norm:

$$\|v\| = \sqrt{x^2 + y^2 + z^2}$$

Which as we will see, happens to be the square root of the dot product of the vector against itself.

$$\|v\| = \sqrt{v \cdot v}$$

It is not always necessary to calculate the precise length of a vector, particularly when what is necessary is only to know if a vector is longer than another vector. In this case we can skip computing the square root and use the squared length for comparison. Most math libraries provide two length functions.

```cpp
float vector3::Length() const
{
    return sqrt(x()*x() + y()*y() + z()*z());
}

float vector3::LengthSquared() const
{
    return x()*x() + y()*y() + z()*z();
}
```

1.2.1.4 Vector Normalization

A *unit vector* is a vector whose magnitude is one. It is often desirable to remove the magnitude component of a vector but preserve its direction. We can do this by converting a vector into a *unit vector*.

$$\hat{v} = \frac{v}{\|v\|}$$

The vector is normalized by dividing the vector by its length.

```cpp
vector4& vector4::Normalize()
{
    const float inverseLength = 1.0f / Length();
    return ((*this) *= inverseLength);
}
```

The *Normalize* function will multiply the components of the vector by the reciprocal of the vector's magnitude. This has the effect of scaling the components of the vector so that the overall vector magnitude becomes one. It will apply the normalization and return a reference to itself.

1.2.1.5 Dot Product

In graphics and game development, the dot product is one of the most useful operations we can perform on a pair of vectors. Given two unit vectors **u** and **v** the dot product is defined as:

$$\mathbf{u} \cdot \mathbf{v} = \|\mathbf{u}\|\,\|\mathbf{v}\|\,\cos\theta$$

The result is a scalar value that holds valuable information about the angular relationship between the vectors **u** and **v**. The key things to remember are that if the angle between **u** and **v** is $\frac{\pi}{2}$ (90°) then the dot product will be 0. If the dot product is greater than zero, the angle will be less than $\frac{\pi}{2}$. If the dot product is less than zero, the angle between the vectors will be greater than $\frac{\pi}{2}$.

$$\mathbf{u} \cdot \mathbf{v} = 0 \;\rightarrow\; \mathbf{u} \perp \mathbf{v} \;\rightarrow\; \theta = \frac{\pi}{2}$$

$$\mathbf{u} \cdot \mathbf{v} < 0 \;\rightarrow\; \frac{\pi}{2} > \theta \le \pi$$

$$\mathbf{u} \cdot \mathbf{v} > 0 \;\rightarrow\; 0 \le \theta < \frac{\pi}{2}$$

This operation will be useful anytime we wish to test whether two vectors align towards the same direction, this situation comes up often and we rely on the dot product to help us understand what is going on in the game. For example, if we want to know if an enemy is in front of the player, we would compute a direction vector towards each enemy **v**, then compute the dot product against the player's forward direction **f**, if the dot product is less than zero ($\mathbf{v} \cdot \mathbf{f} < 0$), the enemy is behind the player.

In another example, say we want to display a message on the UI when the player has been spotted by a guard. During the game update we would compute the direction from each guard to the player, then using the dot product against the guard's view direction. If the dot product is greater than zero, meaning that the angle between the enemy's view direction and the direction in which the player is at, is less than 90 degrees, then the player has been spotted by this guard.

At times we may want to compute precisely what the angle is between two vectors, we can use the dot product to find the angle. Recall the definition of the dot product:

$$\mathbf{u} \cdot \mathbf{v} = \|\mathbf{u}\| \, \|\mathbf{v}\| \, \cos \theta$$

We can solve for the angle θ

$$\cos \theta = \frac{\mathbf{u} \cdot \mathbf{v}}{\|\mathbf{u}\| \, \|\mathbf{v}\|}$$

Then solve the inverse cosine:

$$\theta = \cos^{-1}\left(\frac{\mathbf{u} \cdot \mathbf{v}}{\|\mathbf{u}\| \, \|\mathbf{v}\|}\right)$$

If the vectors are unit vectors it can be simplified to:

$$\theta = \cos^{-1}(\hat{\mathbf{u}} \cdot \hat{\mathbf{v}})$$

Which will return the angle θ in radians. One important thing to understand is that getting the angle through the dot product will always give us the most interior angle, that is, the angle will be in the range $0..\pi/2$. If we don't pay attention to this we would undoubtedly see some unexpected results when using the angle between vectors.

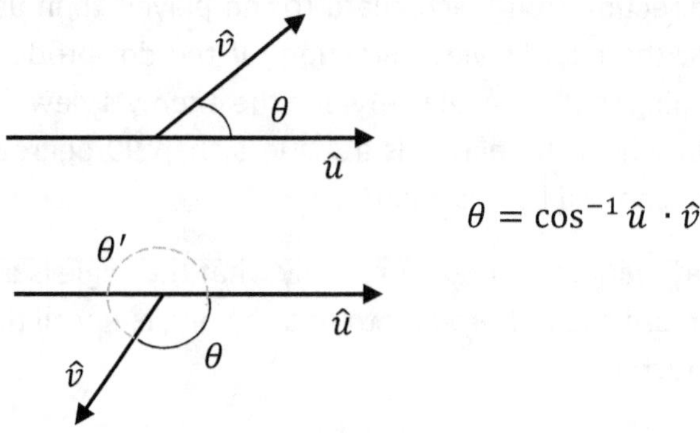

$$\theta = \cos^{-1} \hat{u} \cdot \hat{v}$$

Figure 5 - The angle from the dot product yields an angle in the range $0..\pi$

If what we are really looking for is the exterior angle (θ') then we can use a *cross product* to determine the direction of the angle. The operation thus becomes:

$$\hat{q} = \hat{u} \times \hat{v}$$

$$\theta = \cos^{-1} \hat{u} \cdot \hat{v} * sign(\hat{q}.z)$$

In this case we are still using the angle we computed but we extend the range to be $-\pi..0..\pi$ depending on the use case rather than multiplying by the sign we may want to add π when the sign is negative in order to get the exterior angle which would be in the range $0..2\pi$.

The next important use of the dot product is as the projection of a vector **u** onto a vector **v**.

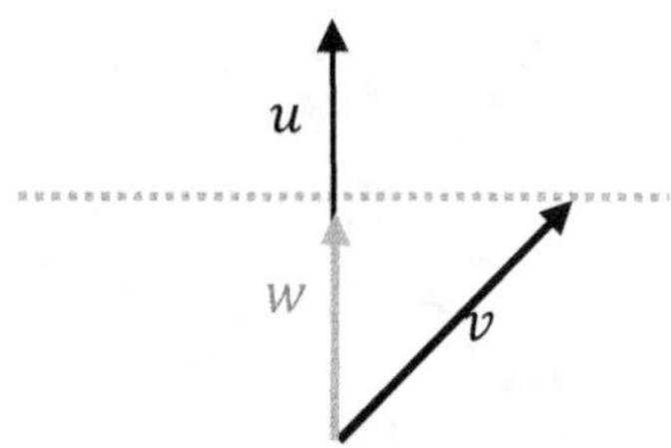

Figure 6 - Geometric representation of the dot product as the projection of u onto the vector v.

The projection of an arbitrary vector **u** onto a vector **v** is defined by:

$$w = \left(\frac{u \cdot v}{\|v\|^2}\right) v$$

If **v** is a normalized vector $\hat{v}$, then the projection can be simplified to

$$w = (u \cdot \hat{v})\hat{v}$$

A useful thing to note is that this will be the part of **u** that is parallel to **v**, we can use this fact to compute the part of **u** that is perpendicular to **v** by subtracting the projection from **u**.

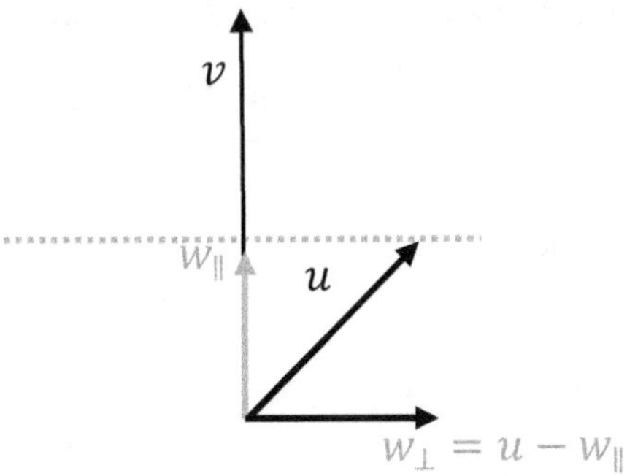

Figure 7 - Using the dot product to compute a perpendicular vector.

This fact is useful when calculating the distance from a point to a line. Given a point **p** and a line defined by two points $\mathbf{p_0}, \mathbf{p_1}$ we can define two vectors,

$$\hat{v} = \frac{p_1 - p_0}{\|p_1 - p_0\|}$$

$$u = p - p_0$$

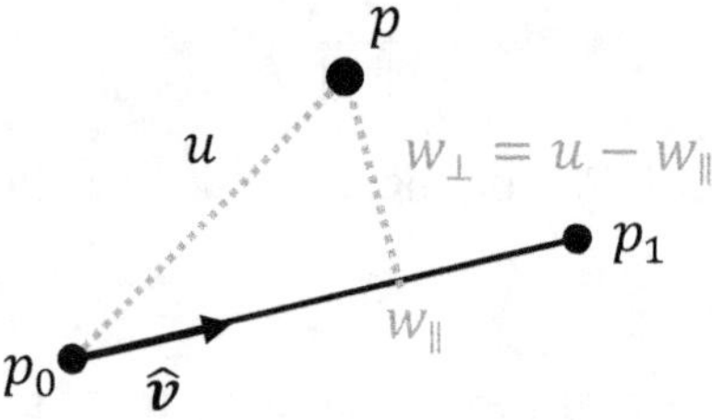

Figure 8 - Calculating the distance from a point to a line.

We can then compute the projection and perpendicular component,

$$w_{\parallel} = (u \cdot \hat{v})\hat{v}$$
$$w_{\perp} = u - w_{\parallel}$$

The distance to the point is then given by $\|w_{\perp}\|$.

1.2.1.6 Cross Product

The cross product between two vectors yields a vector that is perpendicular to both. In game development the cross product is a very useful tool, we will see use it when we construct geometry procedurally as it will help us in calculating and orthographic basis from a direction vector.

The cross product is defined as a vector w which is perpendicular to the vectors $v \times u$

$$w = v \times u$$

It is important to remember that the cross product of two vectors of the same direction, or if one of the vectors has a zero magnitude the result will be a *zero vector*.

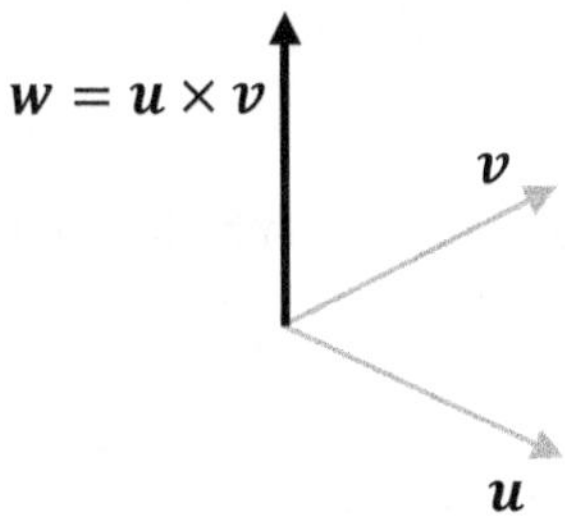

Figure 9 - Cross product between u and v yields a perpendicular vector w.

The direction of the resulting vector w is given by the *right hand rule*, this means that by using your right hand, if you aim your forefinger in the direction of u and the middle finger in the direction of v, the vector formed by extending your thumb will be the direction of w.

The cross product has the property of being anticommutative, this means that swapping the position of any of the two arguments will negate the result.

$$v \times u = -u \times v$$

This will yield a negated w' vector, which will have the opposite direction as w. We can confirm this by applying the right hand rule in the same way we did before.

1.2.2 Matrices

Matrices are a tool used to solve systems of linear equations, and in our case, transform geometric objects, among many other uses. A matrix is represented by a grid, or array of numbers arranged in rows and columns.

$$M = \begin{bmatrix} m_{00} & m_{10} & m_{20} \\ m_{01} & m_{11} & m_{21} \\ m_{02} & m_{12} & m_{22} \end{bmatrix}$$

Arrays may have different numbers of rows and columns, different sizes of matrices can be used to solve problems either in two dimensional space or three dimensional space, at least these are the uses we are interested in.

The size of a matrix is usually described by $m \times n$, where m is the number of rows and n the number of columns.

We can index individual elements in a matrix. This is usually described as getting the $(i, j)^{th}$ element of the matrix, that is the element located at the ith row and j^{th} column.

The *identity* matrix is a matrix that has the property that any matrix multiplied by the identity will be equal to the matrix.

Given a matrix M and the *identity matrix I:*

$$M \times I = I \times M \equiv M$$

The identity matrix consists of 1's down the diagonal starting at (0,0).

$$I = \begin{bmatrix} 1 & 0 & 0 \\ 0 & 1 & 0 \\ 0 & 0 & 1 \end{bmatrix}$$

There are many useful operations that we will be using when working with matrices, perhaps the most important one is *matrix multiplication*.

Matrix multiplication of linear transformations corresponds to the *composition* of linear transformations. Given two linear transformations, the product of their multiplication is a linear transformation that is the composition of the matrices.

To put it into context, we will often create the composition of three different transformations, *rotation, scale* and *position.* The multiplication of these matrices will yield a matrix that will perform all three transformations in the order in which they were multiplied.

We will not delve too deeply into the proof or inner implementation of the different matrix operations that we will use (e.g. matrix multiplication, inversion). The scope of implementing these operations usually falls outside of the field of user interface programming. We will focus on the applicability of the different matrix operations in the context of graphics and user interface development. That said, it is of great value to understand why these operations work; you are highly encouraged to dig deeper and see for yourself what is going on underneath the hood.

There are excellent resources that cover matrix operation implementation in detail (James M. Van Verth, 2004), (Tomas Akenine-Moller, 2008), (Gregory, 2009).

1.2.3 Positions

Positions in 2D space are represented by 2 decimal numbers, defined by the X and Y variables. The simplest representation of this in code is

```
point p = new point(10.f, 5.f);
```

A point, represents a position in some space, in our case this is either a 2D space or a 3D space. If we wish to move this point, we can change its position by changing its X and/or Y values, we can also add a value to either X or Y and this will translate the point into a new position. The arithmetic for points is the same as for vectors, this is why often vectors are used to represent points.

1.3 ROTATION

When talking about rotations, we usually think about angles in degrees, it's intuitive to say that we'll rotate an object by 45 degrees, we can visualize this. In reality, most angular operations are performed in radians, you should only use degrees as user input, this is simpler for the person that is entering the data, but internally you should always perform angular calculations in radians. If you decide to ignore this advice and work in degrees, you will find that you will end up with many unnecessary calls to functions that convert from degrees to radians and vice-versa.

```
constexpr float DegreesToRadians(float degrees)
{
    return degrees * ( 180.f / Pi );
```

```
}

constexpr float RadiansToDegrees(float radians)
{
    return radians * ( Pi / 180.f );
}
```

We can use C++11's *constexpr* keyword to perform the evaluation of the calculation to compile-time, at least for the calls in which the compiler receives a constant value as input. Otherwise, it will perform the calculation at runtime as expected.

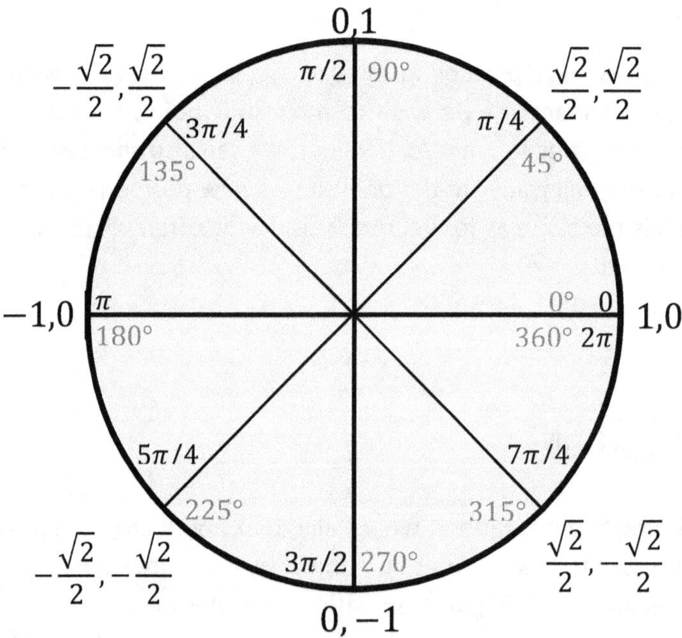

Figure 10 - Helpful chart showing angles in radians and degrees, as well as the X,Y coordinates of a circle.

Figure *10* is a good reference to have handy when working with rotations, it shows the angles in degrees and radians as well as the value for the x, y coordinates at each of the primary angles.

1.3.1 Rotation Demystified

It is important to understand how rotations are done in two dimensions, later we will use these same concepts when we discuss rotations in 3D space.

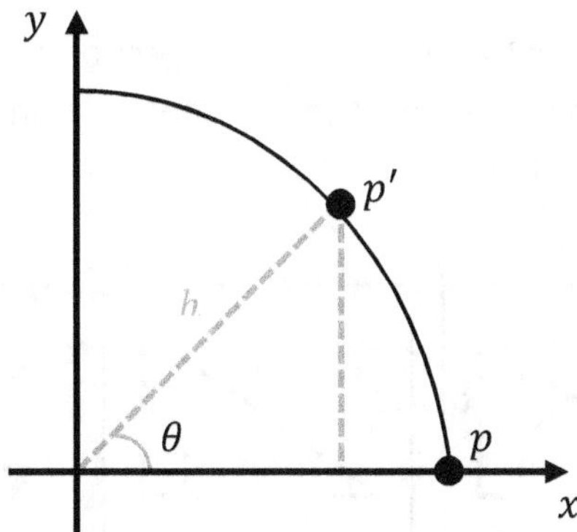

Figure 11 - Rotation around the origin of a point in 2D space.

Our goal is to rotate the point p which is defined as $p \rightarrow \{x, y\}$ to a new position p' defined as $p' \rightarrow \{x', y'\}$. For this we will turn to trigonometry, which is the study of angles and the angular relationships of figures in two or three dimensions.

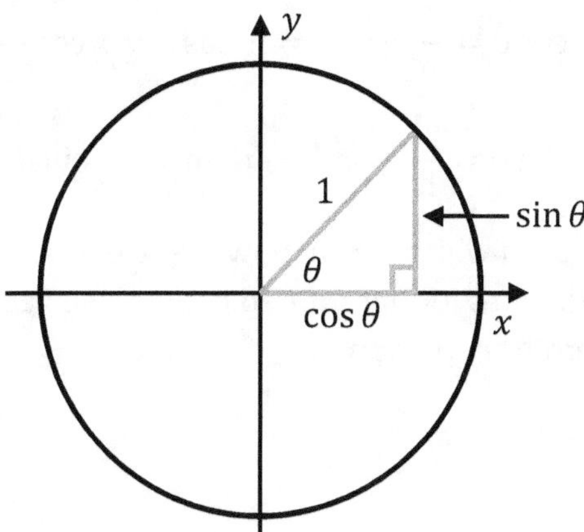

Figure 12 - Trigonometric properties of a unit circle.

To best understand these relationships, we will consider the simplest case, a **unit circle**.

The angle θ is measured starting on the x axis counterclockwise along the circumference of the circle. The trigonometric function $\cos\theta$ represents the horizontal coordinate of our point $x \mid x \in p$, and $\sin\theta$ is the vertical coordinate $y \mid y \in p$. The ratio of $\sin\theta / \cos\theta$ is defined as $\tan\theta$.

The right triangle has three sides, the longest of which is the hypotenuse, the side next to the angle θ is the adjacent side and the opposing side is known as the opposite θ.

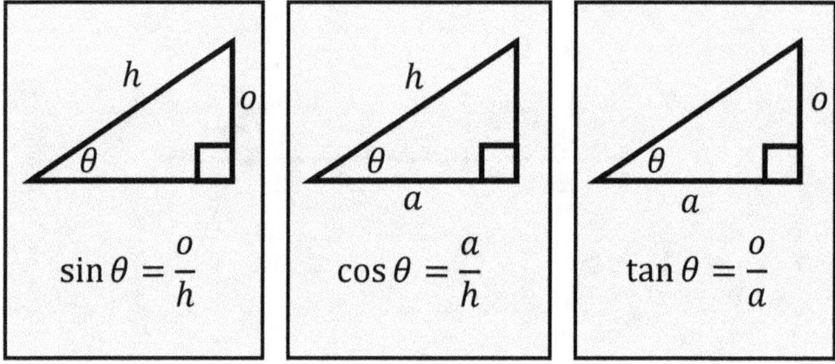

Figure 13- Trigonometric relationships of a right triangle.

With these relationships established, we can see that for our point p'.

$$\cos\theta = \frac{x'}{h} \rightarrow x' = h\,\cos\theta = x\cos\theta$$

$$\sin\theta = \frac{y'}{h} \rightarrow y' = h\,\sin\theta = x\sin\theta$$

This is the basic case in which $x = h$, now that we have established how to calculate the coordinates for our rotated point p' we need to consider how to do it given an arbitrary point p.

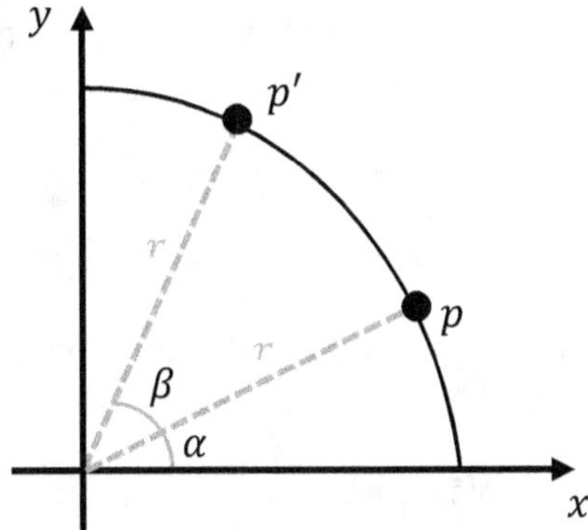

Figure 14 - Rotation about an arbitrary angle.

As we determined earlier,

$$x = r \cos \alpha$$

$$y = r \sin \alpha$$

To calculate p', we can use the same calculation as we did for p by adding β to the angle α.

$$x' = r \cos(\alpha + \beta)$$

$$y' = r \sin(\alpha + \beta)$$

Using the trigonometric identities that state

$$\sin u \pm v = \sin u \cos v \pm \cos u \sin v$$

$$\cos u \pm v = \cos u \cos v \pm \sin u \sin v$$

We can expand the calculation of the rotate point x' to

$$x' = r \cos \alpha \, \cos \beta - r \, \sin \alpha \sin \beta$$

$$y' = r \cos \alpha \, \sin \beta + r \, \sin \alpha \cos \beta$$

We had previously determined that $x = r\cos\alpha$ and $y = r\sin\beta$ we substitute them to get

$$x' = x\cos\beta - y\,\sin\beta$$

$$y' = x\sin\beta + y\,\cos\beta$$

At this point, we can rotate any arbitrary point p by an angle β, and the result will be the point p'.

Now we could implement this equation in code as a function that receives a point and an angle and use it to perform the rotations we need. While this may work well enough for very simple cases, it often results in sub-optimal or difficult to maintain code. There is a more versatile tool we can use that will allow us to build a mechanism by which we can perform rotations, as well as chain together multiple rotations; it is the standard method used in graphics programming, for this we turn to linear algebra.

In linear algebra, we can represent the rotation equation we derived previously using a matrix.

$$\begin{bmatrix} \cos\beta & -\sin\beta \\ \sin\beta & \cos\beta \end{bmatrix}$$

This matrix will rotate any point represented by a column vector v containing the coordinates of the point.

$$v = \begin{bmatrix} x \\ y \end{bmatrix} \qquad R = \begin{bmatrix} \cos\beta & -\sin\beta \\ \sin\beta & \cos\beta \end{bmatrix}$$

We obtain the rotated vector v' by multiplying the vector v by the rotation matrix.

$$v' = vR = \begin{bmatrix} x \\ y \end{bmatrix}\begin{bmatrix} \cos\beta & -\sin\beta \\ \sin\beta & \cos\beta \end{bmatrix}$$

Rotation matrices can only be used to perform rotations about the origin of the coordinate system. This means that in order to rotate any point about a position that is not the origin of the coordinate system, we will need to first translate this point into a position relative to the origin, perform the rotation and then translate the point back to its previous position.

1.3.2 Object Rotation

We now can apply these concepts to perform rotation on an image mapped onto a polygon. For simplicity we'll rotate quad with a spaceship texture mapped onto it.

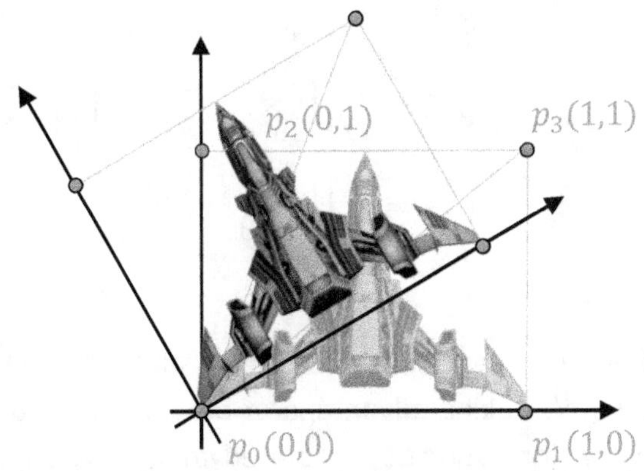

Figure 15 - Rotation of a texture mapped quad.

A unit quad consists of four vertices defined by the positions:

$$p_0 = (0,0)$$

$$p_1 = (1,0)$$

$$p_2 = (0,1)$$

$$p_3 = (1,1)$$

We construct it by ordering the vertices into two triangles built in counter clockwise order, the triangles would be defined by the vertices indexed such that:

$$\Delta_0 \rightarrow [0,1,2]$$

$$\Delta_1 \rightarrow [2,1,3].$$

In order to rotate the quad by an angle θ we transform each vertex by a rotation matrix R.

$$R = \begin{bmatrix} \cos\theta & -\sin\theta \\ \sin\theta & \cos\theta \end{bmatrix}$$

For each vertex we perform the transformation such that:

$$p_0' = p_0 R = \begin{bmatrix} x \\ y \end{bmatrix} \begin{bmatrix} \cos\theta & -\sin\theta \\ \sin\theta & \cos\theta \end{bmatrix}$$

$$p_1' = p_1 R = \begin{bmatrix} x \\ y \end{bmatrix} \begin{bmatrix} \cos\theta & -\sin\theta \\ \sin\theta & \cos\theta \end{bmatrix}$$

$$p_2' = p_2 R = \begin{bmatrix} x \\ y \end{bmatrix} \begin{bmatrix} \cos\theta & -\sin\theta \\ \sin\theta & \cos\theta \end{bmatrix}$$

$$p_3' = p_3 R = \begin{bmatrix} x \\ y \end{bmatrix} \begin{bmatrix} \cos\theta & -\sin\theta \\ \sin\theta & \cos\theta \end{bmatrix}$$

Notice that we are working at an object level rather than at a pixel level, this is because we are taking advantage of modern GPUs to perform the actual per-pixel transformation of the rotated image. Typically we wouldn't perform the vertex transformations by hand as described here (doing so is possible, but would be done on the running thread on the CPU rather than taking advantage of the GPU), instead we would build our transformation matrix that may include translation, rotation and/or scale then we will send it to the GPU when we are about to render our object, then each vertex will be transformed in the vertex shader.

1.3.2.1 Bitmap Rotation

The rotation as described so far, will work to rotate images at the pixel level if we were to transform each pixel position by the matrix R. However, in this case, it would not give good enough results as it would introduce aliasing due to the fact that pixels on the screen are represented as integral coordinates, while rotations are floating point operations. Errors creep in when we round off the results causing pixels to land on the same destination as neighboring source pixels, or to miss their target altogether, causing gaps or tears in the resulting image.

One approach to solve aliasing problems when rotating bitmaps is to apply an area mapping algorithm, for each rotated pixel we find four source pixels that partially cover it, then compute the rotated pixel as the area weighted average of those four pixels.

1.3.2.2 Rotation by Shear

There is an approach to rotation that works by performing three shear transformations on a bitmap. A horizontal shear transformation will move a row of pixels by a distance that is proportional to its vertical distance from some reference point. By doing three shear operations alternating between horizontal and vertical shears we can achieve a perfect rotation by any angle (Paeth, 1986).

The shear matrix along the x axis has the form:

$$x_{shear} = \begin{bmatrix} 1 & \alpha \\ 0 & 1 \end{bmatrix}$$

And along the y axis:

$$y_{shear} = \begin{bmatrix} 1 & 0 \\ \beta & 1 \end{bmatrix}$$

As mentioned above, rotation by shearing can be achieved by three successive shears along alternating axes. This implies that the product of the three shear matrices will be the same as the rotation matrix we had previously found.

$$\begin{bmatrix} 1 & \alpha \\ 0 & 1 \end{bmatrix} \begin{bmatrix} 1 & 0 \\ \beta & 1 \end{bmatrix} \begin{bmatrix} 1 & \gamma \\ 0 & 1 \end{bmatrix} = \begin{bmatrix} \cos\theta & -\sin\theta \\ \sin\theta & \cos\theta \end{bmatrix}$$

By solving this equation we can find the values α, β we need for a given angle θ.

$$\alpha = \gamma = -\tan\frac{\theta}{2}$$

$$\beta = \sin \theta$$

Each shear transformation is done on one axis at a time, displacing the pixels along the scanline, essentially transforming by translation rather than by an actual rotation; this ensures that there will be no gaps in the transformed bitmap.

Figure 16 - 30 degree rotation by applying three shear transforms.

On the first shear the image is skewed vertically around the center point, each side relative to one another. The second shear skews the image horizontally, always around the center. And finally, the third shear is the same as the first shear, which brings the image into its final rotation.

It is important to understand how rotation works, however given that we will be taking advantage of modern graphics hardware, it is unlikely we will need to implement these rotation algorithms ourselves, most of the time we will use the GPU's interpolators by passing in a rotation transform to the device.

1.3.3 Rotation in 3D

Modern user interfaces in games are not constrained to a 2D plane on the screen, most recent games are applying user interface elements directly within the game world, it is important for this reason to understand how transformations in 3D space work.

Now that we are able to perform a rotation in $\mathbb{R}^2$, we can extend this concept to $\mathbb{R}^3$, the idea is that we are able to perform a rotation as we have described so far about each of the axes in $\mathbb{R}^3$. In other words, if we want to rotate in $\mathbb{R}^3$ about the z axis we need to keep the z axis unchanged.

$$x' = x \cos \beta - y \sin \beta$$

$$y' = x \sin \beta + y \cos \beta$$

$$z' = z$$

Similarly, we can derive the rotation equations for the other axes, always keeping the angle you want to rotate about unchanged.

Rotation about the y axis:

$$x' = x \cos \beta - z \sin \beta$$

$$y' = y$$

$$z' = x \sin \beta + z \cos \beta$$

Rotation about the x axis:

$$x' = x$$

$$y' = y \cos \beta - z \sin \beta$$

$$z' = y \sin \beta + z \cos \beta$$

So far we have used a matrix in $\mathbb{R}^2$ to represent our rotation, what we need now is to represent the rotations about each of the axes in $\mathbb{R}^3$, the matrix in $\mathbb{R}^3$ for each of the axes are given by the following:

$$R_x(\alpha) = \begin{bmatrix} x \\ y \\ z \end{bmatrix} \begin{bmatrix} \cos \alpha & \sin \alpha & 0 \\ -\sin \alpha & \cos \alpha & 0 \\ 0 & 0 & 1 \end{bmatrix}$$

$$R_y(\beta) = \begin{bmatrix} x \\ y \\ z \end{bmatrix} \begin{bmatrix} 1 & 0 & 0 \\ 0 & \cos \beta & \sin \beta \\ 0 & -\sin \beta & \cos \beta \end{bmatrix}$$

$$R_z(\gamma) = \begin{bmatrix} x \\ y \\ z \end{bmatrix} \begin{bmatrix} \cos \gamma & 0 & -\sin \gamma \\ 0 & 1 & 0 \\ \sin \gamma & 0 & \cos \gamma \end{bmatrix}$$

These matrices are orthonormal, this means that the vectors are orthogonal, in other words, the vectors are perpendicular with respect to each other. Also, each of the vectors in the matrix has unit length; we know this to be true because from the beginning we derived all our equations off of a unit circle. This property implies that the product of two orthonormal matrices will be an orthonormal matrix, therefore the product of a series or rotation matrices will also result in a rotation matrix.

We can derive a general rotation matrix by concatenating a series of rotation matrices, namely the rotation matrix for each of the axes. The order in which the matrices are concatenated will define the order in which the rotations are applied, thus:

$$R = R_x R_y R_z =$$

$$\begin{bmatrix} \cos\alpha & \sin\alpha & 0 \\ -\sin\alpha & \cos\alpha & 0 \\ 0 & 0 & 1 \end{bmatrix} \begin{bmatrix} 1 & 0 & 0 \\ 0 & \cos\beta & \sin\beta \\ 0 & -\sin\beta & \cos\beta \end{bmatrix} \begin{bmatrix} \cos\gamma & 0 & -\sin\gamma \\ 0 & 1 & 0 \\ \sin\gamma & 0 & \cos\gamma \end{bmatrix}$$

Where R is general rotation matrix that will rotate about the x axis, then the y axis and finally about the z axis.

At this point we are able to rotate any point about any (or all) axes in $\mathbb{R}^3$, provided that the points are rotated around the origin. What we will need is the ability to rotate any points around an arbitrary origin.

```
matrix CreateRotationX(float radians)
{
    const float cosine = cosf(radians);
    const float sine = sinf(radians);

    return matrix(
            1.0, 0.0,   0.0,   0.0,
            0.0, cosine, -sine,  0.0,
            0.0, sine,   cosine, 0.0,
            0.0, 0.0,   0.0,   1.0);
}

matrix CreateRotationY(float radians)
{
    const float cosine = cosf(radians);
    const float sine = sinf(radians);

    return matrix(
            cosine, 0.0, -sine, 0.0,
```

```
            0.0,   1.0, 0.0,   0.0,
            sine,  0.0, cosine, 0.0,
            0.0,   0.0, 0.0,   1.0);
}

matrix CreateRotationZ(float radians)
{
    const float cosine = cosf(radians);
    const float sine = sinf(radians);

    return matrix(
            cosine,  sine,  0.0, 0.0,
            -sine,  cosine, 0.0, 0.0,
            0.0,   0.0,   1.0, 0.0,
            0.0,   0.0,   0.0, 1.0);
}
```

Before we delve into the details on how we will achieve this, let's talk about the next important transformation, translation. We will then come back and close our discussion about rotations.

1.3.4 Translation

Whenever we have points or objects in a given space and we wish to move them to a new position, we translate them. One way to think about translation is that given an arbitrary point, we add a constant vector to it.

$$p' = p + v$$

The resulting vector will be offset, or moved as a result of the vector addition, see **Vector Addition**.

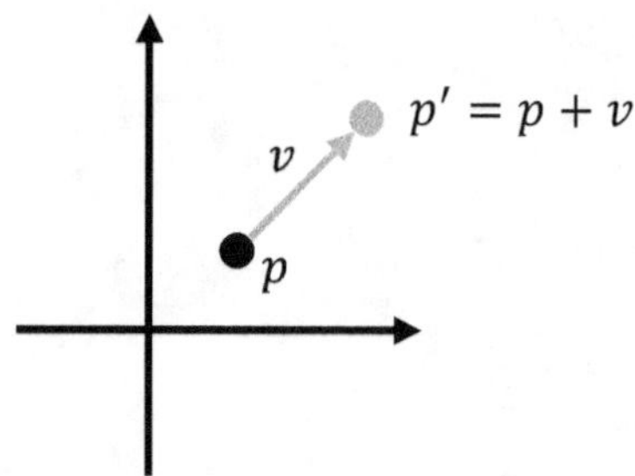

Figure 17 - Translation of a point in space.

Just as it is with rotations, it is useful to describe translation as an affine transformation matrix, however, recall that the rotation matrices we derived were all done around a fixed point, the origin. A translation has no fixed point which would make it impossible to perform using matrices were it not for homogeneous coordinates.

For a complete, and well written description of homogeneous coordinates, see (Chen, n.d.).

For our purposes we will limit the explanation on the part that is relevant for game transformations. Homogeneous coordinates add another dimension to a point, while initially our point in $\mathbb{R}^3$ was described by:

$$P = \begin{bmatrix} x \\ y \\ z \end{bmatrix}$$

Adding a new dimension, we introduce the w component

$$p = \begin{bmatrix} x \\ y \\ z \\ w \end{bmatrix}$$

We introduce homogeneous coordinates to allow us to represent translations as a matrix in the form:

$$T = \begin{bmatrix} 1 & 0 & 0 & 0 \\ 0 & 1 & 0 & 0 \\ 0 & 0 & 1 & 0 \\ T_x & T_y & T_z & 1 \end{bmatrix}$$

When multiplied by a point in homogeneous coordinates with the w component as 1, the resulting point will be translated.

$$Tp = \begin{bmatrix} p_x \\ p_y \\ p_z \\ 1 \end{bmatrix} \begin{bmatrix} 1 & 0 & 0 & 0 \\ 0 & 1 & 0 & 0 \\ 0 & 0 & 1 & 0 \\ T_x & T_y & T_z & 1 \end{bmatrix} = \begin{bmatrix} p_x + T_x \\ p_y + T_y \\ p_z + T_z \\ 1 \end{bmatrix} = p + v$$

This means that any point we multiply, or transform with this matrix will be translated by the vector T_x, T_y, T_z.

It's easy to see this with an example, say we have a point:

$$P = \begin{bmatrix} p_x \\ p_y \\ p_z \end{bmatrix} = \begin{bmatrix} 1 \\ 0 \\ -1 \end{bmatrix}$$

We will translate it with the matrix T such that:

$$T = \begin{bmatrix} 1 & 0 & 0 & 0 \\ 0 & 1 & 0 & 0 \\ 0 & 0 & 1 & 0 \\ 2 & 0 & -2 & 1 \end{bmatrix}$$

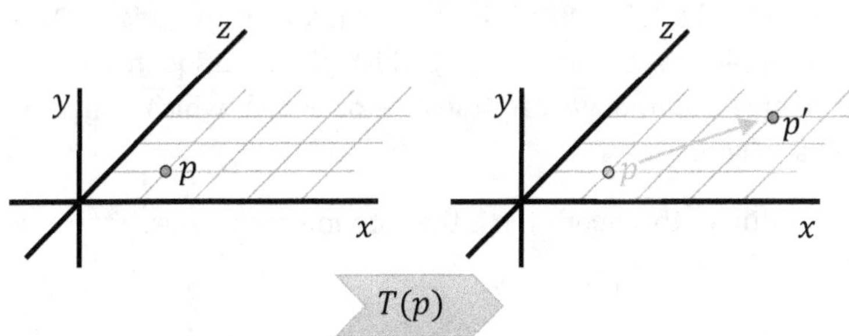

Figure 18 - Translation of a point in 3D space.

$$Tp = \begin{bmatrix} 1 \\ 0 \\ -1 \\ 1 \end{bmatrix}\begin{bmatrix} 1 & 0 & 0 & 0 \\ 0 & 1 & 0 & 0 \\ 0 & 0 & 1 & 0 \\ 2 & 0 & -2 & 1 \end{bmatrix} = \begin{bmatrix} 1+2 \\ 0+0 \\ -1+-2 \\ 1 \end{bmatrix} = p' = \begin{bmatrix} 3 \\ 0 \\ -3 \\ 1 \end{bmatrix}$$

1.3.5 Wrapping up Rotations

Remember that so far we are able to perform rotations around the origin, however, often we want to rotate points around an arbitrary point. To do this, we start by translating the point around which we wish to rotate to the origin, once there, we apply the rotation to the points we wish to transform and finally we translate them back to their original point.

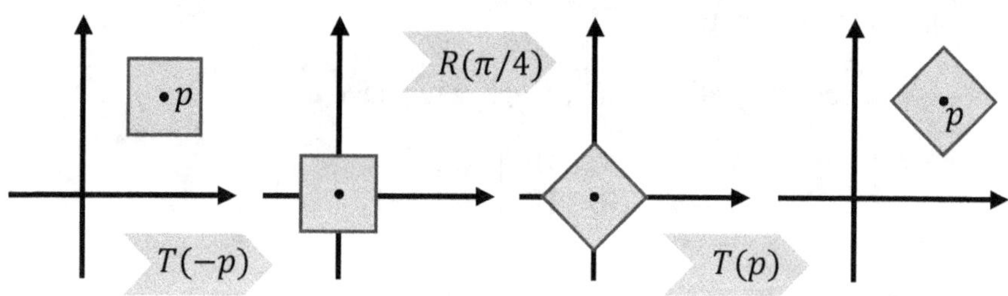

Figure 19- Rotation must be done relative to the object's local space.

The first step is to translate **p** to the origin, we can do this be translating by the negated value of **p**, this brings the square to the origin. Once at the origin we apply the rotation R(π/4) which gives the square a 45°clockwise rotation, once rotated, we can translate back by **p** which brings us back to our initial origin.

The end result of this operation is the rotation about an arbitrary axis as we needed.

1.3.6 Scale

When discussing scale, it's easier to imagine a shape rather than a single point. Scale refers to a factor by which we can grow or shrink the given shape. We can do it uniformly across all axes, this means the scaling factor is the same for every axis whether in $\mathbb{R}^2$ or $\mathbb{R}^3$, this is known as uniform scale.

$$S_x = S_y = S_z$$

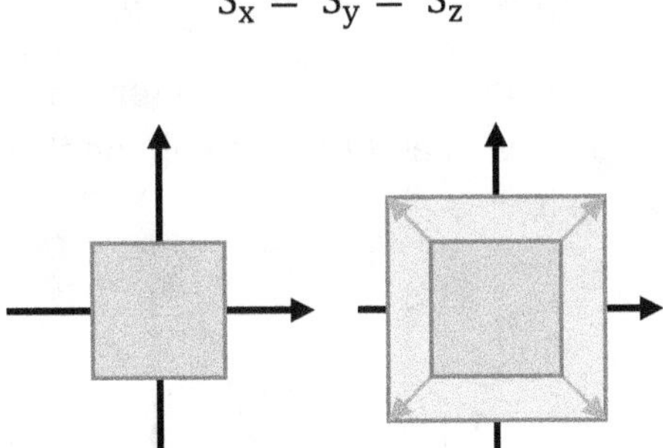

Figure 20- Uniform scaling in $\mathbb{R}^2$

A scale factor of 1, means that the shape will retain its original size. While uniform scaling preserves the shape of the object, non-uniform scale will change it by stretching towards a side, or shrinking the shape disproportionately.

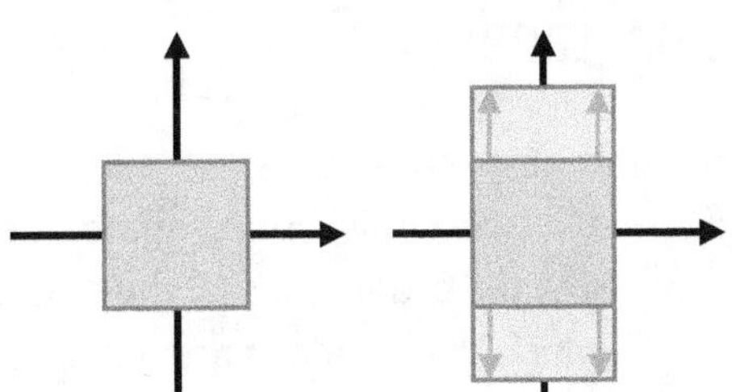

Figure 21 - Non-uniform scaling in $\mathbb{R}^2$

Scale is a linear transformation and can also be represented in matrix form.

$$S = \begin{bmatrix} S_x & 0 & 0 \\ 0 & S_y & 0 \\ 0 & 0 & S_z \end{bmatrix}$$

Such that a point transformed by this scaling matrix would have the expected result.

$$S = \begin{bmatrix} p_x \\ p_y \\ p_z \end{bmatrix} \begin{bmatrix} S_x & 0 & 0 \\ 0 & S_y & 0 \\ 0 & 0 & S_z \end{bmatrix} = \begin{bmatrix} p_x S_x \\ p_y S_y \\ p_z S_z \end{bmatrix}$$

Scale transformations can also be represented in homogeneous coordinates which allows us to add the w component to the scale vector, giving us a matrix of the form.

$$S = \begin{bmatrix} S_x & 0 & 0 & 0 \\ 0 & S_y & 0 & 0 \\ 0 & 0 & S_z & 0 \\ 0 & 0 & 0 & 1 \end{bmatrix}$$

Now in this form, the scale matrix is in the same form as the translation matrix we described earlier. This is useful because now we are able to combine all the transformations we have developed giving us the ability to scale, translate and rotate a point or a collection of points across any axis we may need.

1.3.7 Matrix Concatenation

When we discussed rotations, we established that in order to create a generalized rotation matrix we could concatenate the rotation matrix around each axes in $\mathbb{R}^3$. How the order in which the matrices are multiplied determined the order in which the rotations are applied. This is due to the non-commutativity property of matrix multiplication.

$$M_0 = \begin{bmatrix} 1 & 1 \\ 0 & 1 \end{bmatrix}$$

$$M_1 = \begin{bmatrix} 0 & 1 \\ 0 & 1 \end{bmatrix}$$

$$M_0 M_1 = \begin{bmatrix} 0 & 2 \\ 0 & 1 \end{bmatrix} \neq M_1 M_0 = \begin{bmatrix} 0 & 1 \\ 0 & 1 \end{bmatrix}$$

It is important to remember this because the results of your transformations will be substantially different depending on the order in which they are applied as illustrated in Figure *22*.

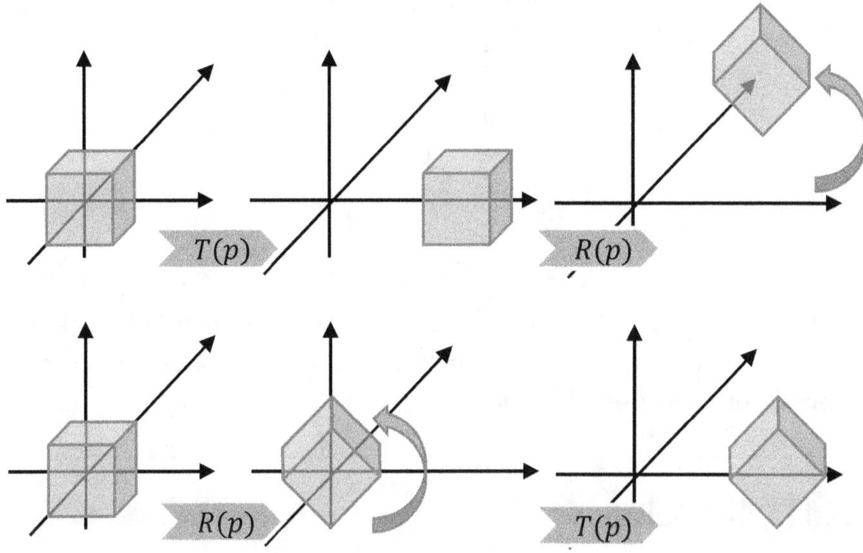

Figure 22 - The order of operations is important when concatenating transformation matrices.

1.3.8 Euler Angles

Euler angles are often used to describe rotations. They represent an orientation in three parameters, angles commonly referred to as yaw, pitch and roll. Euler angles apply rotations sequentially over the axes of a coordinate system, each axes will be rotated by its respective angle such that the roll will be applied in z, the pitch will be applied in x and finally the yaw will be applied in y.

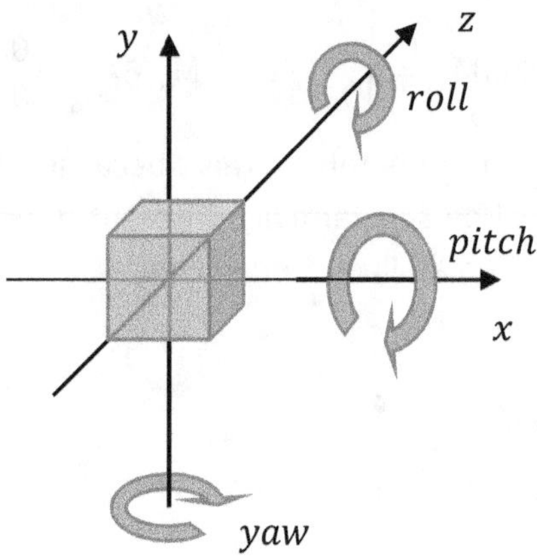

Figure 23 - Euler angles, yaw, pitch and roll.

Euler angles are useful in some situations but their use needs to be carefully controlled as they can result in a condition called *gimbal lock* which occurs when we lose a degree of freedom.

1.3.8.1 Gimbal Lock

Gimbal lock is the loss of one degree of freedom that happens when two of the rotation axes become parallel, this "locks" the rotation into an unrecoverable state where the rotation is only possible along two axes.

A solution to avoid gimbal lock is to represent rotations using matrices or quaternions, these rotation representations are numerically more stable.

1.3.9 Quaternions

Quaternions seem to inspire fear in many programmers; they are perceived as these wildly complex mathematical entities that appear to be so difficult to comprehend, it is best to avoid them entirely. The problem may stem from the way quaternions are usually presented, the fact is most programmers in a game team will not be tasked with implementing a high performance math library. The majority of programmers will be the client of an existing library, either some in-house library or as part of some existing game engine like Unity or Unreal. So rather than focusing on how quaternions work on the inside (which is not as scary as it seems!), we will focus on how to use quaternions and what we can do with them.

Most complete quaternion libraries will have a good number of functions available that will allow us to create quaternions for different kinds of values we have, we can create quaternions from Euler angles or from an axis and an angle or from a rotation matrix.

A good quaternion class should provide the following functions:

```
quaternion CreateFromRotationMatrix(const matrix& m)
```

Given a rotation matrix, this function will create a quaternion and return it.

```
quaternion CreateFromAxisAngle(const vector3& axis, float angle)
```

Given an axis $\hat{v}$, create a quaternion that will rotate by some angle θ in radians.

```
quaternion CreateFromDirection(const vector3& axis)
```

Given a direction vector $\hat{v}$, it will return a quaternion rotated towards the axis (the angle is calculated against the standard basis).

```
quaternion CreateFromEuler(float yaw, float pitch, float roll)
```

Given a set of Euler Angles, yaw, pitch and roll (in radians), it will return a quaternion rotated towards those angles. Euler angles are susceptible to gimbal lock, even when using them to create quaternions. That does not mean this function is useless, we just need to be mindful of the angles we pass in to prevent losing a degree of freedom.

Quaternions, like rotation matrices may be concatenated to create complex rotations.

```
quaternion x_rotation = quaternion::CreateFromAxisAngle(vector3::UnitX, Pi/4);

quaternion y_rotation = quaternion::CreateFromAxisAngle(vector3::UnitY, Pi/4);

quaternion z_rotation = quaternion::CreateFromAxisAngle(vector3::UnitZ, Pi/4);

quaternion rotation = x_rotation * y_rotation * z_rotation;
```

The quaternion rotation is the concatenation of the individual rotations on each axis, we can convert this quaternion into a rotation matrix that we can then use to transform any vertex.

```
matrix result = matrix::CreateFromQuaternion(rotation);
```

Another useful trait of quaternions is the ability to perform spherical linear interpolation, *slerp*. A *slerp* allows us to perform smooth animation of rotations in 3D, essentially, interpolate from one quaternion to another. A *slerp* will give us the shortest and straightest path between the starting quaternion and the ending quaternion.

```
quaternion start_rotation = quaternion::CreateFromAxisAngle(vector3::UnitX, Pi/4);

quaternion end_rotation = quaternion::CreateFromAxisAngle(vector3::UnitZ, Pi/4);

quaternion result = start_rotation;

float t = 0.0;
while ( t < 1.0 )
{
    result = quaternion::Slerp(start_rotation, end_rotation, t);
    object.SetRotation(result);
    t += 1.0 / 30.0;
}
```

This very simple example shows how we can interpolate between some starting rotation represented with a quaternion towards an ending rotation, in the loop we simulate 30 frames per second, each frame we advance the interpolation forward storing it in result which we then use to transform some object. What we would see is an object smoothly animating between facing 45° in x towards facing 45° in z.

Programmers should shed the irrational fear of quaternions, while a good understanding of what they do and how they do it is expected, do not start by spending hours learning the intricate details of how to multiply them, or how to implement your own slerp function. Instead learn to use them first, grab an object and rotate it, then multiply another quaternion in and watch the result. Once you understand how to use them properly and when they are appropriate, invest the time to learn why they work, they are fascinating all the way down to how they were first conceived.

1.4 Geometry

In this section we will review some geometry concepts that are often used when developing user interfaces. We will develop a library of classes that give us access to different geometrical shapes in an easy to use way.

1.4.1 Shapes

During development of user interfaces we will rely on different shapes to create visual effects, but also as tools that help us constrain elements within areas and perform intersection testing to see if elements overlap.

We primarily will focus on the geometrical representation of shapes and the mathematical formulas to model them and implement some of the most commonly used operations in the context of user interface development.

1.4.1.1 Points

A point is the most atomic geometrical shape we have, it represents a position in space, for our cases we are only concerned with 2D and 3D space, so points will be represented by X,Y coordinates for 2 dimensional space (R^2)

$$x, y \in \mathbb{R}^2$$

X,Y,Z for 3 dimensional space ($\mathbb{R}^3$).

$$x, y, z \in \mathbb{R}^3$$

It is often the case that developers take advantage of the fact that the representation of points and vectors are the same. For simplicity when a point is required, the vector class is used. While there may be some valid reasons to use the vector class to represent points (such as an optimized vector class that takes advantage of hardware accelerated floating point operations), it is preferable to provide a distinction between the two. The key advantage of making distinct types for points and vectors is that the code becomes self-documenting, as we saw in the Linear Algebra section, a vector is an entity that represents both a direction and a magnitude, while a point is a fixed position in space. If you keep this in mind, you can see how using vectors to represent points may lead to ambiguous functions.

```
// Ambiguous function that uses vectors to represent points, we rely on the named
argument to know that this function expects two positions in space.
void DrawLine(const vector& pointA, const vector& pointB)
{
    ...
}


// Non-ambigous function declaration clearly states that this function expects two points
or positions in space to draw a line.
void DrawLine(const point& a, const point& b)
{
    ...
}
```

```
// This function shows that it expects to draw a line from the provided point, in the
direction of the vector, using the direction vector's magnitude to determine the length of
the line.
void DrawLine(const point& origin, const vector& direction)
{
    ...
}
```

That said, it may be the case that the software architecture you are using does not provide a point representation and uses a vectors, in this case, do your best to make it clear to the caller of a function what parameters are expected and what the function's result will be.

1.4.1.2 Lines

We consider a line to be the collection of all the points within two extreme points, in some cases a line may have one point and extend to infinity. We will not go into much detail regarding line rasterization as most modern graphics hardware and software APIs already provide efficient line rasterization features. Instead we will focus on the use of lines for user interfaces, there are many uses for lines that may not always be necessary for a shipping product, but that are great tools during development and debugging. Often during development, we may need to display more information about the world, such as the surface normals of a geometrical model, or the velocity of an object or sprite, the trajectory of a projectile, there are countless situations in which drawing lines comes in handy.

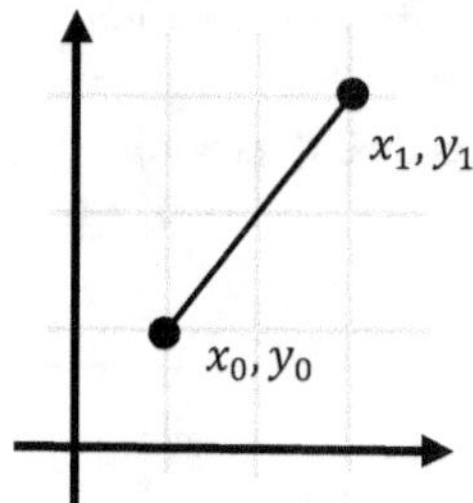

Figure 24- A line in 2D space.

A single line will at a minimum have 2 points, in the context of rendering, if we want to draw two or more continuous lines we can achieve it by adding successive points, each new point generates a new line, this is known as a line strip.

While lines are often represented with the slope-intercept form:

$$y = mx + b$$

This form cannot represent vertical lines, a vertical line's slope is undefined. It is far more useful for our needs to represent lines using the parametric line equation.

$$x = p + t\hat{v}$$

Where p is the starting point of the line, and $\hat{v}$ the direction vector of the line, finally, t is the parameter it defines how far along the vector $\hat{v}$ the line will go.

Point to Line Distance

If we happen to find ourselves in a situation in which we have a line, this line could have many possible meanings, it could be the representation of some world boundary, it could be a simplification of the game world's geometry, it could represent the finish line in a racing game, whatever the case, we may want to calculate the distance of a point to the line, this distance can be useful information for the player that we may wish to present, perhaps the player is equipped with a proximity sensor and any time he gets near any two points, we display a warning by projecting some UI over the line.

We start from the parametric equation of the line, which as we saw is given by:

$$x = p + t\hat{v}$$

The distance to an arbitrary point q is given by

$$d = \left\| (p - q) - ((p - q) \cdot \hat{v})\hat{v} \right\|$$

The first part $(p - q)$ is a vector from the point q to the starting point of the line p, we then use this to with the dot product of $(p - q) \cdot \hat{v}$ is which is the projection of the length of the line from the point onto $\hat{v}$.

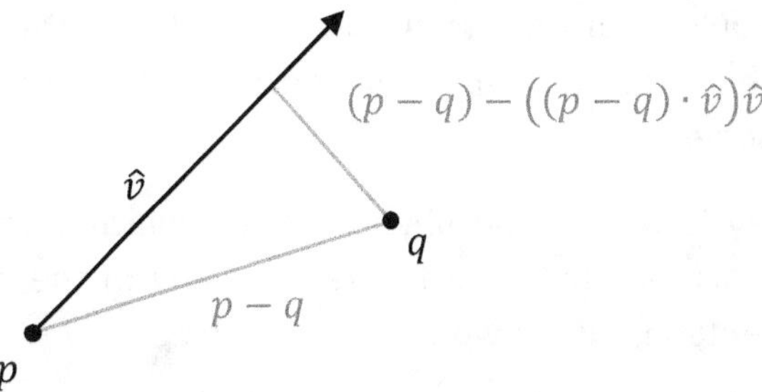

Figure 25 - Distance from a point to a line.

The distance from the point to the line is the length of the resulting vector.

```
float PointToLineDistance(const point& a, const point& b, const point& p)
{
    vector2 v = b - a;
    vector2 n = v.Normalize();
    vector2 m = a - p;
    vector2 r = m - (m * m.Dot(n));
    return r.Length();
}
```

1.4.1.3 Ray

A ray, unlike a line is not represented by two points in space but rather by a single point and a direction. The ray may extend infinitely and is often used when we are interested in finding any objects that may be down the path of the ray.

Rays are important in UI programming, they provide the mechanism by which the player interacts with a 3D world. When the player performs an action on a 2D display, we calculate a ray starting at the screen position, projected into world space in a direction into the world, with this point and direction we can build a ray, a ray that we then use to query other systems for information that we may be interested in, such as, has the player selected an object? If we find that we have indeed intersected our ray with an object or multiple objects in the game world. The system we queried with the ray should return the world space position of the objects it has intersected with, we can then use this information to project information back onto the screen.

Typically the ray is sent to the physics system which is responsible for detecting any collisions between the ray and any of the objects in the physical representation of the world.

```
auto p0 = viewport.Unproject(vector3(mouse.x(), mouse.y(), 0.f), camera.View(),
camera.Projection(), matrix::Identity);

auto p1 = viewport.Unproject(vector3(mouse.x(), mouse.y(), 1.f), camera.View(),
camera.Projection(), matrix::Identity);

auto position = p0;
auto direction = p1 - p0;
direction.Normalize();

QueryResult qr = PhysicsSystem()->Query(ray(position, direction));
if ( qr.Contacts().size() > 0 )
{
    for (auto contact : qr.Contacts())
    {
        // Our ray has intersected with the physical representation of an object
        // the contact typically will have a reference or pointer to the game object
```

```
        // that we have touched.
    }
}
```

This example shows how a ray can be constructed by a mouse press in screen space. We *Unproject* the mouse coordinates at the near and far planes, we use these world space positions to determine a direction vector. We can then use the world space position and direction vector to create a ray which we pass into our physics system. If there are any intersections with game objects we will know as a result of this query. This code will undoubtedly vary depending on the game engine, some engines may call the *Query* function by some other name such as *RayCast* or *LineProbe*, more advanced engines will likely provide an asynchronous method for receiving the results which will change the structure of the code, generally the concept will be the same.

1.4.1.4 Triangles

Triangles are one of the most important rendering primitive, most video hardware expects data to be organized into triangles prior to rendering, some platforms and frameworks also use quads, but triangles are more commonly used.

In the context of UI programming it is important to understand how geometry is represented at its most basic level, whenever we are faced with the need to generate geometry procedurally, it is through triangles that we will create or approximate other shapes.

It is also important to understand how we can use triangle data to interact with the game world's geometry. There are a number of tests we can do to understand more the game world.

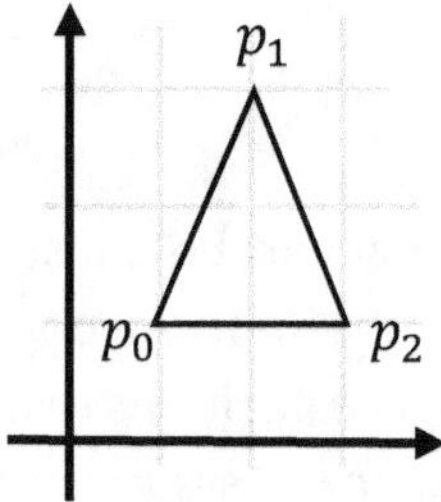

Figure 26 - A triangle is given by 3 vertices.

Triangles, in Euclidian geometry have the property of being planar as long as its vertices are not collinear, this means we can use a triangle to define a plane. In rare occasions when rendering, it may happen that the vertices of a triangle are collinear, this results in a degenerate triangle.

Given a triangle we can calculate the plane defined by its vertices.

$$\mathbf{u} = p_1 - p_0$$

$$\mathbf{v} = p_2 - p_0$$

$$\hat{\mathbf{n}} = \mathbf{u} \times \mathbf{v}$$

Where $\hat{\mathbf{n}}$ is the triangle's surface normal, the direction in which the triangle is facing.

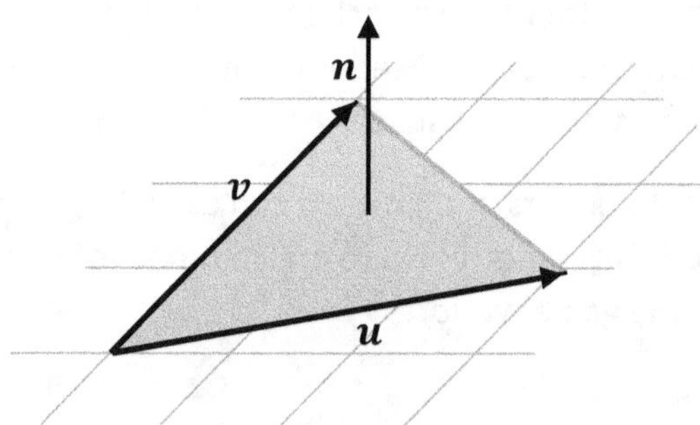

Figure 27 – A triangle's surface normal is given by the cross product of the vectors formed by its vertices.

As we will see when we discuss **Rendering Primitives**, we can use the surface normal of a triangle as one of the basis vectors to define a transformation. A transformation from which we can procedurally generate the geometry for a quad. This is a useful technique that can be used to procedurally generate geometry used by user interface systems such as *augmented reality*.

1.4.1.5 Rectangles

Rectangles are very useful when developing user interfaces, they are often the shape used to create containers within which any number of UI elements reside, we also use this rectangle shape as boundaries within which the user interface, a collection of buttons, labels, etc. must exist; this could mean we do not allow these elements to leave said boundaries, or we may decide to clip these UI elements against the rectangle, leaving them partially visible within.

At the time of this writing, computer screens are still rectangular, therefore our work is already bound within a rectangle. An axis aligned rectangle is described by a point and a size. The point represents the top left corner of the rectangle, the size consists of scalars for width and height. It is convenient to represent rectangles in this manner because with this information we can calculate the right and bottom coordinates, and simplify some calculations down the line.

An oriented rectangle is one which may contain an orientation parameter, this parameter is an angle in radians that represents how much to rotate the rectangle by. In addition to an orientation parameter it is also useful to specify the pivot of the rectangle, this is the point around which the rotation will be computed. The pivot point does not have to be a point within the rectangle, a pivot outside of the rectangle will cause the rectangle to rotate with an amount of translation defined by the distance from the pivot to the rectangle.

Some systems such as Unity actually represent the display using the bottom left corner, this approach is consistent with the Cartesian coordinate system in which the origin (0,0) is located on the bottom left corner of the screen. In this book, we will place the origin at the top left corner of the rectangle, with the x axis moving to the right and the y axis moving down.

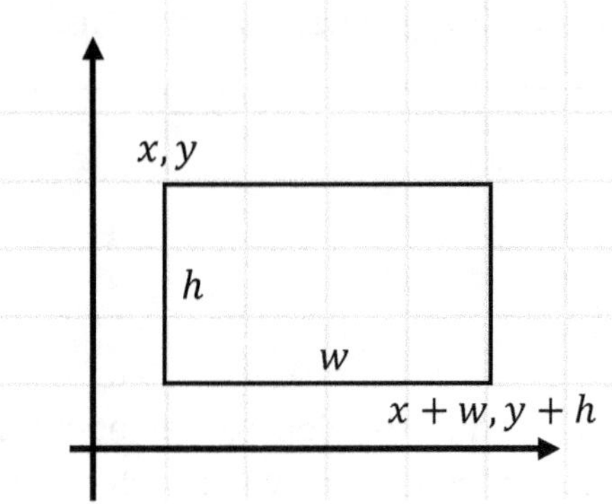

Figure *28* - A rectangle represented by x, y and width, height.

The interface provided by a rectangle class should be versatile to allow rectangles to be used in a wide variety of contexts.

```cpp
class rectangle
{
public:

    rectangle();
    rectangle(float left, float top, float width, float height);

    static rectangle MakeRectangle(float left, float top, float right, float bottom);

    float Top() const { return m_top; }
    float Left() const { return m_left; }
    float Width() const { return m_width; }
    float Height() const { return m_height; }

    float& Top() { return m_top; }
    float& Left() { return m_left; }
    float& Width() { return m_width; }
    float& Height() { return m_height; }
```

```cpp
float Right() const { return m_left + m_width; }
float Bottom() const { return m_top + m_height; }

void Right(float right);
void Bottom(float bottom);

const vector2 Position() const;
const vector2 Size() const;
const vector4 Extents() const;

void SetPosition(const vector2& position);
void SetSize(const vector2& size);
void SetExtents(const vector4 extents);

bool operator == (const rectangle& r);
bool operator != (const rectangle& r);

bool IsEmpty() const;
const point Center() const;

virtual bool Contains(float x, float y) const;
virtual bool Intersects(const rectangle& rect) const;

bool Contains(const vector2& position) const;
bool Contains(const rectangle& rect) const;
bool Contains(const point& point) const;

void Inflate(float x, float y);
void Contract(float x, float y);
void Offset(float x, float y);
void Offset(const point& point);

rectangle& operator + (const rectangle& rhs);
rectangle operator + (const rectangle& rhs) const;

void Constrain(point& p, const point& size = point::Zero) const;
void ClipTo(const rectangle& clipping_rectangle);

operator RECT () const
{
    RECT rc;
    rc.left = static_cast<LONG>( m_left );
    rc.top = static_cast<LONG>( m_top );
    rc.right = static_cast<LONG>( Right() );
```

```
        rc.bottom = static_cast<LONG>( Bottom() );
        return rc;
    }

    static rectangle Zero;

protected:

    float m_left;
    float m_top;

    float m_width;
    float m_height;
};
```

Given the importance of the *rectangle* class during user interface development we will see the implementation of the useful operations we can perform on rectangles.

Point in Rectangle

If the rectangle is axis aligned, the test to determine if a point is within it is trivial, we need to compare the point in question against the boundaries of the rectangle and verify that if the point is within all of the rectangle's edges, then it cannot possibly be outside of it.

$$P = (x, y)$$

$$R = (x_1, y_1)(x_2, y_2)$$

$$\left(P_x \geq R_{x_1}\right) \wedge \left(P_x \leq R_{x_2}\right) \wedge \left(P_y \geq R_{y_1}\right) \wedge \left(P_y \leq R_{y_2}\right) \Rightarrow P \text{ is inside } R$$

Which translates into the following code:

```
bool rectangle::Contains(float x, float y)
{
    return (x >= Left() && x <= Right() && y >= Top() && y <= Bottom());
}
```

Less trivial cases arise when the rectangle in question is not axis aligned, one interesting approach to this problem is to create four triangles, using two points in the rectangle and the point in question. Then calculate the area of each triangle and sum them, if the total area is greater than the area of the rectangle, we can conclude that the point lies outside of the rectangle, if however, the area is precisely the area of the rectangle, then it is inside.

$$P = (x, y)$$

$$R = A(x1, y1), B(x2, y2), C(x3, y3), D(x4, y4)$$

$$\Delta R = (x2 - x1) * (y2 - y1)$$

$$\Delta APD + \Delta DPC + \Delta CPB + \Delta PBA \begin{cases} \equiv \Delta R \Rightarrow P \text{ is inside } R \\ > \Delta R \Rightarrow P \text{ is outside } R \end{cases}$$

This method has the benefit that it's valid for any convex polygon, the downside is the number of operations required to calculate the areas, and the fact that we need to test for equality to know if the point is inside, means that care must be taken to ensure that floating point precision does not affect the result of our calculation.

Another approach that is less computationally demanding but limited to rectangles is to rotate the point into the rectangle's local space, then do the point in rectangle test.

```cpp
bool rectangle_oriented::Contains(float x, float y)
{
    float cosine = cos(m_angle);
    float sine = sin(m_angle);

    const auto center = Center();
    float rx = center.x() + cosine * ( x - center.x() ) - sine * ( y - center.y() );
    float ry = center.y() + sine * ( x - center.y() ) + cosine * (y - center.y() );

    return rectangle::Contains(rx, ry);
}
```

Rectangle Intersection

The test for rectangle overlap is straightforward, given two rectangles, a and b respectively, to test if a intersects with b we test whether a is completely outside of b, if it is, then it is impossible for an intersection to exist, otherwise the rectangles intersect in some way.

```cpp
bool rectangle::Intersects(const rectangle& rect) const
{
    return (Left() < rect.Right() && Right() > rect.Left() &&
        Top() < rect.Bottom() && Bottom() > rect.Top());
}
```

Clipping

It is often useful to clip or cut a rectangle to be within another, the rectangle being clipped takes on the characteristics of the clipping rectangle wherever it intersects.

If the left edge of the rectangle is less than the clipping rectangle's left edge, we need to reduce the width of the rectangle to cut off the portion that is outside of the clipping rectangle and then we clamp the left coordinate to the clipping rectangle's left coordinate. Clipping the top coordinate is done in the same way using the top and heights respectively.

Clipping from the right side only requires decreasing the width of the rectangle by the portion of the rectangle that extrudes the clipping rectangle, the left coordinate remains unaffected as it is guaranteed to be within the clipping rectangle.

```cpp
void rectangle::ClipTo(const rectangle& clipping_rectangle)
{
    if ( m_left < clipping_rectangle.Left() )
    {
        m_width -= clipping_rectangle.Left() - m_left;
        m_left = clipping_rectangle.Left();
    }

    if ( m_top < clipping_rectangle.Top() )
    {
        m_height -= clipping_rectangle.Top() - m_top;
        m_top = clipping_rectangle.Top();
    }
```

```
    if ( Right() > clipping_rectangle.Right()  )
    {
        m_width -= ( Right() - clipping_rectangle.Right() );
    }

    if ( Bottom() > clipping_rectangle.Bottom() )
    {
        m_height -= ( Bottom() - clipping_rectangle.Bottom() );
    }
}
```

Constraining

Similar to clipping, in some cases we want to guarantee that some point cannot leave the boundary defined by the rectangle. The same test can be applied whether we intend to constrain a point or another rectangle. The tests are straightforward, if the point minus half of the optional width parameter is less than the rectangle's left boundary, we will clamp the left point to the left boundary. If the point plus half of the optional width is beyond the right boundary, we clamp the point to the right boundary minus the optional width. This will ensure that the rectangle (or point, if the width is zero) is constrained. The tests are the same for the top and bottom coordinates.

```
void rectangle::Constrain(point& p, const point& size/*=point::Zero*/) const
{
    float halfWidth = size.x() * 0.5f;
    float halfHeight = size.y() * 0.5f;

    if ( p.x() - halfWidth < m_left )
    {
        p.x() = m_left;
    }

    if ( p.x() + halfWidth > Right() )
    {
        p.x() = Right() - size.x();
    }
```

```
    if ( p.y() - halfHeight < m_top )
    {
        p.y() = m_top;
    }

    if ( p.y() + halfHeight >= Bottom() )
    {
        p.y() = Bottom() - size.y();
    }
}
```

1.4.1.6 Ellipses

Ellipses can be very useful primitives, even if our intention is not necessarily to draw ellipses or circles. One common use for ellipses in user interfaces is to create constraints for dynamic elements that move on the screen.

Ellipses are defined by two axes, the larger axis is called the major axis often referred to with the letter a, and the smaller the minor axis referred to with the letter b, the semi-major axis represents half the major axis and respectively the semi-minor axis represents half the minor axis. The center of the ellipse is given by C.

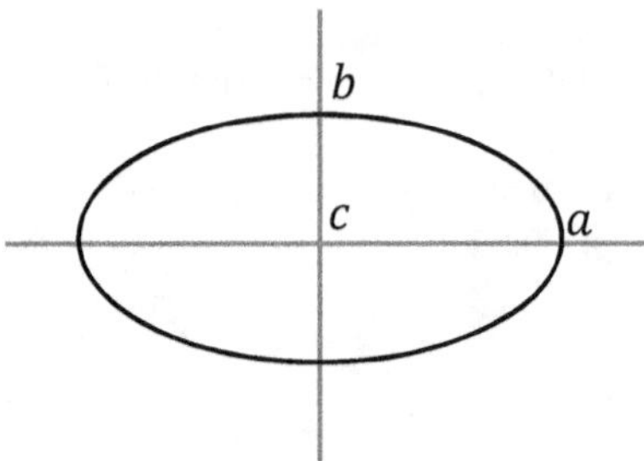

Figure 29 – Ellipse centered at point c, defined by its axes a,b.

For our purposes, it's easier to see the ellipse using trigonometry, in its parametrical form, such that:

$$X(\alpha) = X_c + a\cos\alpha\cos\beta - b\sin\alpha\sin\beta$$
$$Y(\alpha) = Y_c + a\cos\alpha\sin\beta + b\sin\alpha\cos\beta$$

Where β is the angle between the x axis and the major axis of the ellipse, $C = \{X_c, Y_c\}$ and α is the parameter that varies from $0..2\pi$.

With this definition we can implement an ellipse in code.

```
class ellipse
{
public:
    point GetPointOnEllipse(float angle);
    point GetPointOnEllipse(const vector2& direction);
    void GetPoints(int count, std::vector<point>& points);

private:

    vector2 m_axes; // the semi axes
    float m_angle; // angle of the ellipse
    vector2 m_center;
};
```

Get Point on Ellipse

When using an ellipse as a means to constrain some element, it's useful to request a point that lies directly on the ellipse given an α angle.

```
vector2 GetPointOnEllipse(float angle)
{
    float sinAlpha = sin(angle);
    float cosAlpha = cos(angle);

    float beta = -m_angle;
    float sinBeta = sin(beta);
    float cosBeta = cos(beta);

    float X = (m_axes.x() * cosAlpha * cosBeta - m_axes.y() * sinAlpha * sinBeta);
    float Y = (m_axes.x() * cosAlpha * sinBeta + m_axes.y() * sinAlpha * cosBeta);

    return m_center + vector2(X,Y);
```

```
}
```

Often in graphics and gameplay systems we use vectors to represent directions rather than working with angles, it's useful to provide a function that given a direction vector will also return a point on the ellipse.

```
point GetPointOnEllipse(const vector2& direction)
{
    float alpha = -atan2(direction.x(), direction.y()) + HalfPi;
    return GetPointOnEllipse(alpha);
}
```

Get Point in Ellipse

Another useful function will let us query a point within the ellipse, but constrained by it, we pass a point to the ellipse, if the point is within the ellipse's boundaries we return it, otherwise we will return the point on the ellipse. This will become useful when we implement elements such as world markers that we want visible on screen even if they're behind the player or a radar that constrains out of range elements at the border of an ellipse.

```
vector2 GetPointInEllipse(const vector2& position)
{
    vector2 p1 = GetPointOnEllipse(position);
    vector2 v1 = p1 - m_center;

    if (position.LengthSquared() < v1.LengthSquared())
        return m_center + position;

    return p1;
}
```

Drawing an Ellipse

Finally, we may want to draw an ellipse, for this we can create a list of points, we can take advantage of the function *GetPointOnEllipse* by iterating in the range $[0..2\pi]$.

```
void GetPoints(int count, std::vector<point>& points)
{
    for (int angle = 0; angle < 360; angle += 360 / count)
    {
     point p = GetPointOnEllipse(static_cast<float>(angle));
     points.push_back(p);
    }
}
```

This list of points can then be used to render sprites or to connect line segments to form an ellipse.

1.5 ALIGNMENT

When working in user interfaces, one thing that comes up often is the need to align elements to one another. This functionality is driven by a set of straightforward equations that modify the position and size of one element to that of another, yet all too often in practice, many programmers write the alignment code in-place as needed, don't do this! Any time we implement well defined solutions to problems, we need to provide these solutions as tools that are available to anyone that may need them, including our future selves.

We will implement alignment of rectangles, as most, if not all of our user interface elements may be bound by a rectangle.

1.5.1 Alignment of Two Rectangles

Given two rectangles, we will define one to be the fixed rectangle, this is the rectangle we will align other rectangles to. And a floating rectangle, or several, these are the rectangles that will be moved in relation to the fixed one.

We will create a class that will provide all the different types of alignment, we will construct this class with the two rectangles, the invariable "fixed" rectangle, and one or more "floating" rectangles that we will move to align. A good way to implement this class is using enum flags that will allow us to combine different alignments when needed, in order to get a rectangle that is aligned to the bottom right, we would combine the flags Bottom | Right.

The class will work directly using references to the rectangles we wish to affect, we keep a reference to a list of floating rectangles and a constant fixed rectangle. The main part of the align object is the Apply function in which we apply the alignment to the rectangles.

1.5.1.1   Top

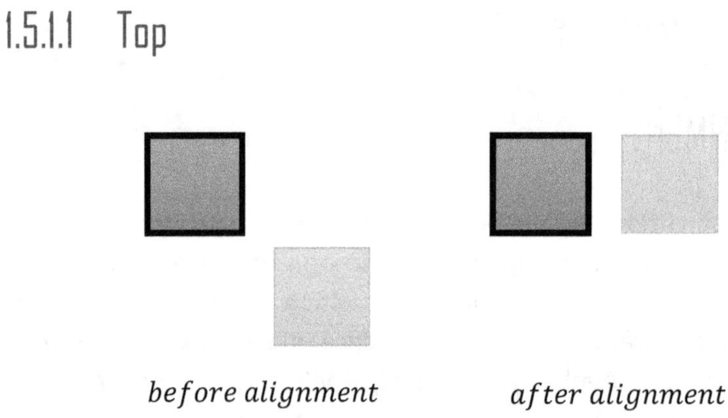

before alignment   *after alignment*

```
result.Top() = m_to.Top();
```

Aligning to top is a straightforward case in which we assign the Top coordinate to the moving rectangle.

1.5.1.2 Bottom

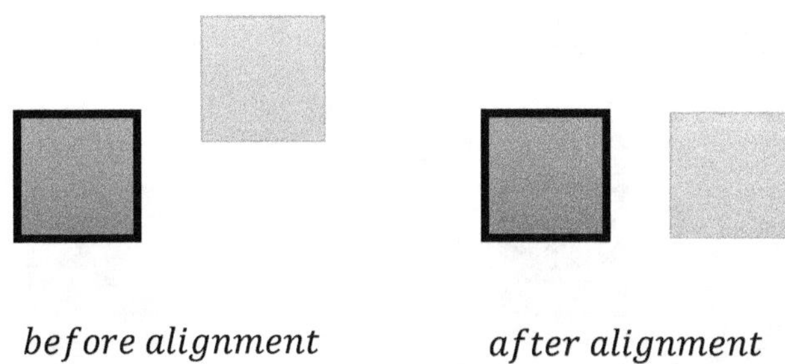

before alignment   *after alignment*

```
result.Top() = m_to.Bottom() – m_from.Height();
```

To align to the bottom of a rectangle, we set the top of our floating rectangle to the bottom of the fixed rectangle minus the height of the floating rectangle.

1.5.1.3 Left

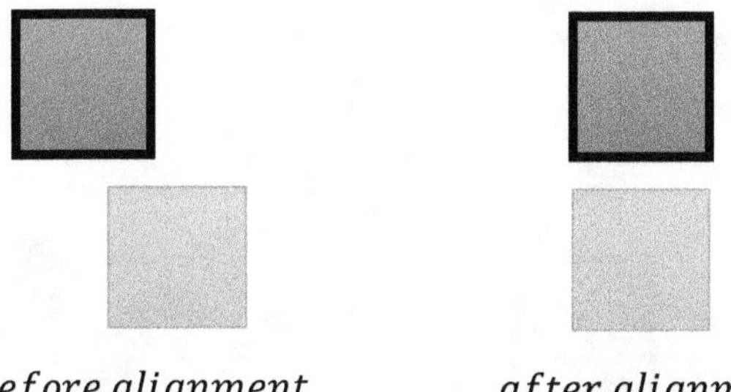

before alignment   *after alignment*

```
result.Left() = m_to.Left();
```

The left alignment is trivial, we match the Left coordinate of the floating rectangle to the Left of the fixed rectangle.

1.5.1.4 Right

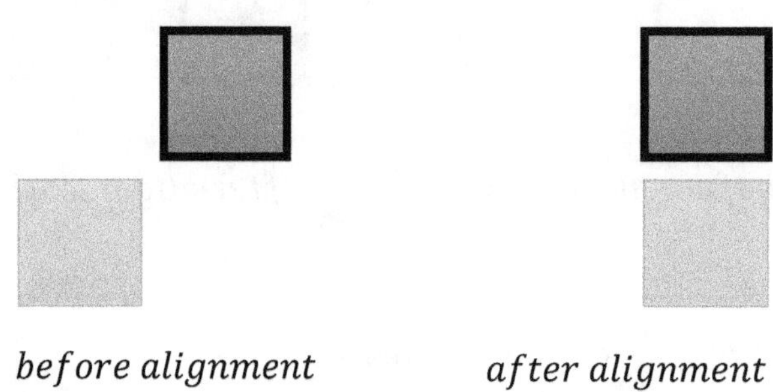

before alignment   *after alignment*

```
auto offset = to.Right() - from.Left();
result.Left() += (offset - result.Width());
```

To align to the right, we first need to calculate how much we should move the floating rectangle's Left coordinate so that it is right aligned, then we subtract the floating rectangle's width.

1.5.1.5 Center

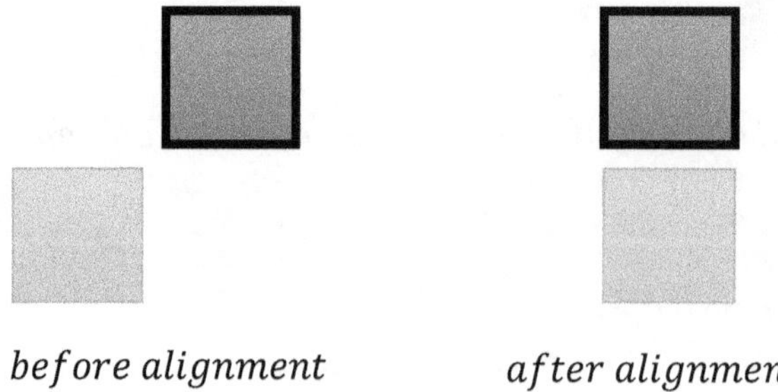

before alignment   *after alignment*

```
result.Left() = to.Center().x() - ( from.Width() / 2 );
```

The center alignment refers to the horizontal alignment, to align the centers by taking the center of the fixed rectangle and subtracting half the width of our floating rectangle.

1.5.1.6 Middle

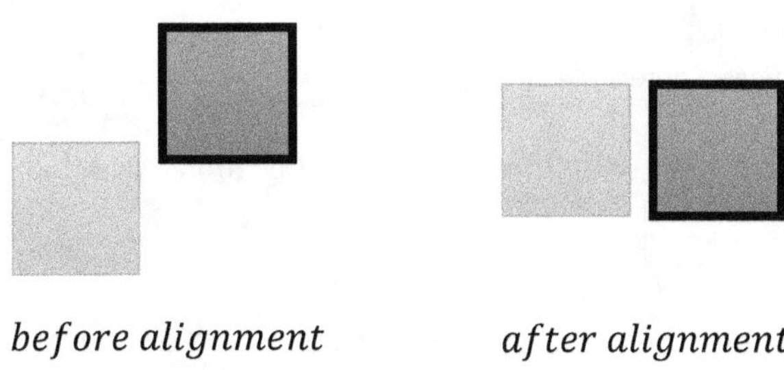

before alignment   *after alignment*

```
result.Top() = to.Center().y() - (from.Height() / 2);
```

The middle refers to the vertical center of the rectangles, to align the centers vertically, we use the fixed rectangle's center and subtract half of our floating rectangle's height.

The full alignment function works in a way that it supports the combination of multiple flags, with the exception of combining *Top/Bottom* and *Left/Right* which don't make sense.

```cpp
void Apply(unsigned int flags, math::rectangle& from, const math::rectangle& to)
{
    if ( IsSet(flags, Top) )
    {
        from.Top() = m_to.Top();
    }
    else
    if ( IsSet(flags, Bottom) )
```

```
        {
            from.Top() = to.Bottom() - from.Height();
        }

        if ( IsSet(flags, Left) )
        {
            from.Left() = m_to.Left();
        }
        else
        if ( IsSet(flags, Right) )
        {
            auto offset = to.Right() - from.Left();
            from.Left() += (offset - from.Width());
        }

        if ( IsSet(flags, Center) )
        {
            from.Left() = m_to.Left() + (m_to.Width()/2) - (from.Width()/2);
        }

        if ( IsSet(flags, Middle) )
        {
            from.Top() = m_to.Top() + (m_to.Height()/2) - (from.Height()/4);
        }
    }
```

To align multiple rectangles to a fixed rectangle we can call the Apply function to a reference to a list of rectangles.

```
void Apply(unsigned int flags, std::list<math::rectangle>& from, const math::rectangle& to)
    {
        for ( auto& rectangle : from )
        {
            Apply(flags, rectangle, to);
        }
    }
```

The goal of any helper class such as the align class is to provide an easy way to do actions that we may want to do often, and to do this, we must design the class to provide the facilities we need in an intuitive, unobtrusive way. The align class implements a constructor that allows us to do an immediate alignment in a single line.

```
align a(floatingRectangle, fixedRectangle, ui::align::Center | ui::align::Middle);
```

This single line of code will modify *floatingRectangle* to be aligned vertically and horizontally with *fixedRectangle*. However, there may be situations in which we may wish to defer the alignment, the align class also allows this, if the alignment flags are not provided in the constructor, it is the responsibility of the user to call Apply at the desired moment and provide the alignment flags. The important thing to remember is that classes such as align should not keep a copy of the data they are working upon, they should work on references and should not need to be dynamically allocated in order to be used.

2 User Interface Models

There are two significant paradigms when it comes to creating user interface systems, each with its own strengths and drawbacks, it's important to understand the difference and when each pattern is useful.

The goal of this book is to present user interface techniques and how they pertain to game development and does not focus on the creation of general purpose user interface toolkits.

2.1 Retained Mode

A retained mode user interface is one in which the components of the UI system are objects capable of retaining a state. What this means is that an element of the UI can be created as an object, kept around for as long as it's necessary and eventually released when no longer needed.

Let's dissect a simple UI element to see what makes it a retained.

```
std::shared_ptr<Label> exampleLabel = UI.CreateLabel("Example Label");
```

Here, *exampleLabel* will exist until it no more shared pointers to it exist, it also will have an internal string member in which it keeps the text for the label "Example Label", this means that each label has a memory cost. If we track the amount of memory used by each active UI element, we can calculate the memory cost of the entire UI at any given moment.

Retained mode UIs are common in games because they're intuitive to develop in terms of object oriented design and lend themselves well for the creation of UI authoring tools, but more importantly, game designs vary greatly and we need the ability to create completely customized behaviors that go beyond simple user interface components such as labels and simple buttons, the ability to create custom elements is crucial.

There can be substantial overhead in terms of code management using a retained mode system, we need to be careful with the lifetime of all the UI objects; it puts a lot of responsibility on the users to understand the model, in particular the lifetime and ownership of the objects.

Modern UIs continue to become complex and reactive and for this it has become important to multithread portions of UI code, a retained mode system lends itself well for multithreading as we can cache and prepare data, tick animations and process the frame during the game's update thread then the render thread may capture a snapshot of the user interface data at the moment when it's ready to display it.

2.1.1 Callbacks

For our purposes, a callback is a function that we provide to a system with the expectation that it will call our function at some specific time. There are a few ways to provide callbacks to a system, very often we rely on function pointers, another useful construct we can use is a functor which is an object on which we override the function call operator, and C++11 gives us the opportunity to use Lambda Expressions as well.

2.1.1.1   Function Pointers

Function pointers have been one of the most popular ways to implement callback mechanisms in games, they work well but have cumbersome syntax. C++11 has better mechanisms to implement callbacks, but many existing systems will already implement function pointers in a way similar to what is described here, so it is worth understanding how these work. The example code in this section is for demonstration only.

We start by defining a new type that will have the signature of the function pointer.

```cpp
typedef bool (*fnInputCallback)(std::shared_ptr<input_device> device);
```

This rather confusing syntax means that we are defining a type called *fnInputCallback* and that this type will be a pointer to a function that receives a shader pointer to an input device as an argument.

Now that *fnInputCallback* is a type, we can use it as a member of a class, or as an argument to a function or in our case, both, by keeping it as a member of an object we make it possible for us to invoke it in the future, and we provide a function that allows us to install this callback into our system.

```cpp
class input_system
{
public:

typedef bool (*fnInputCallback)(std::shared_ptr<input_device> device);

void InstallInputCallback(const fnInputCallback& callback)
{
        m_inputCallback = callback;
}

private:

fnInputCallback m_inputCallback;
};
```

Naturally, we need a function body to which we will point, in this case we will provide a very simple function that determines if the "move forward" input was entered by the user, and if so, move the player.

```cpp
bool game::OnInput(std::shared_ptr<input_device> device)
{
    if ( device->Active(eInput::Forward) )
    {
        // move forward
```

```
        m_player->MoveForward();
    }
}
```

And of course, we need to install our function pointer at some point during initialization, or during construction, where we do this may depend on many factors.

```
void game::Init()
{
    ...
    m_inputSystem.InstallInputCallback(game::OnInput);
    ...
}
```

Finally, we are able to invoke the callback whenever an input from the user is received.

```
void input_system::Update()
{
    if ( keyboard->IsKeyPressed() )
    {
        if (m_inputCallback != nullptr )
        {
            m_inputCallback(keyboard);
        }
    }
}
```

Notice that we check if the pointer is valid, it's doesn't always need to be required, as the system should be able to run even if we are not interested in providing a callback.

The biggest problem with this example is that it is applying a solution to a general problem within a specific feature, the danger of doing this is that we can end up applying the same solution in different parts of the code, creating code that is duplicated and difficult to maintain.

To find a more general way to solve this problem, we can draw inspiration from the way C# implements delegates to create reusable, general purpose callbacks.

2.1.1.2 Event Handling

The good news is that C++11 has introduced two very useful constructs that will greatly simplify this system, *std::function* and *std::bind*. The definition of *std::function* is a general-purpose polymorphic function wrapper; it allows us to store, copy and invoke any function, including lambda expressions and function objects.

std::function is a general-purpose wrapper that can store, copy and invoke any callable target.

```cpp
template <typename T>
class event_handler
{
public:

typedef std::function<void(void*, T)> signature_t;
typedef std::list<signature_t> functionList_t;

typename functionList_t::iterator operator += (signature_t callback)
{
    m_callbacks.emplace_front(callback);
    return m_callbacks.begin();
}

void operator -= (typename functionList_t::iterator& it)
{
    m_callbacks.erase(it);
}

void Invoke(void* sender, T data)
{
    for (auto& callback : m_callbacks )
    {
        callback(sender, data);
```

```
    }
}
private:
    functionList_t m_callbacks;
};
```

The *event_handler* class keeps a list of callbacks, this means that we can register any number of functions to be invoked should the event occur, conversely we have the ability to unregister a callback should one of the owners of a callback goes out of scope or gets released, we need to avoid calling a function on an object that has been destroyed.

As we mentioned, the *std::function* is a wrapper that supports anything that behaves as a callable function, including lambda expressions as you can see in the following code:

```
event_handler<int> handler;
handler += [](void*, int data)
{ std::cout << "Callback: " << data << std::endl; }
```

When the event is invoked by calling *handler.Invoke(this, n);* (where n is any int), the lambda function will be called and we would see the output "Callback: n" in the standard output.

It's possible to use *std::function* in conjunction with *std::bind*, which allows us to create functions for which certain arguments are already bound to some value to bind a function object to a member function of an object.

```
using std::placeholders;

event_handler<wchar_t> inputEventHandler;

keyboard keyb;

auto onInputFunction =
std::bind(&keyboard::OnInput, &keyb, _1, _2);

inputEventHandler += onInputFunction;
```

In this example, we know that an event handler expects a callback function with the signature (void*, T), where T is defined by the template argument, these parameters are represented by the placeholder values _1, _2 and *std::bind* returns a function pointer to the *OnInput* member function in the object keyb. This is one possible use of *std::bind*, however it can also be used for argument reordering, binding to member data as well as functions and of course, creating functions with bound arguments.

Static functions may also be provided as callbacks:

```
static void onEvent(void* sender, int d)
{
    std::cout << "Callback: " << data << std::endl;
}

event_hander<int> handler;
handler += onEvent;
```

In short, it's possible to bind any callable object to an event handler, which one you choose will depend entirely on the game's code architecture or a particular feature.

2.2 IMMEDIATE MODE

An immediate mode user interface does not keep any state, the code must be executed every frame and the information displayed will be in real-time. This means than rather than creating objects for labels, buttons and such, we do function calls and we pass into them the information on how they need to be drawn precisely at that moment.

```
std::string itemNames[] = { "a", "b", "c", "d" };
int selectedItem = -1;
for ( int i = 0; i < 4; ++i )
{
    if ( radio(selectedItem == i, layout, itemNames[i]) )
    {
```

```
        // if true, we update the selected item's index
        selectedItem = i;
    }
    layout.y += layout.height;
}
```

For example, if we need to draw a group of radio buttons.

```
rectangle layout { width=40, height=10, x=0, y=0 }
```

Where the radio function may take the form,

```
bool radio( bool selected, const rectangle& rect, const std::string& text)
{
    drawRectangle(layout, selected ? SELECTED_COLOR : INACTIVE_COLOR);
    drawText(layout, text);
    return isSelected(layout);
}
```

The benefit of this approach is that the user does not have to worry about object creation or lifetime, information passing or synchronization, essentially, the data is owned by the application and not the user interface.

On the other hand, there is a performance cost incurred per-frame for every function call, complex UIs may require more function calls per frame possibly tying the performance cost to the complexity.

This approach holds well for modest UI needs, in particular if memory is tight, however, as the complexity of the UI rises, this UI code becomes more difficult to maintain. We can imagine having a set of flags that control the visibility of UI components, if not done with care and forethought the code may end up with many complicated if-else conditions that test multiple flags, creating edge cases and complex relationships.

Finally this method may pose certain challenges when integrating to different game engines as their rendering systems vary, in particular there may be some complexity involved in threaded environments, as the game data may be processed and updated in one thread, but the rendering will occur in a separate thread, in this situation we end up needing some form of caching or synchronization system to pass the data from one thread to another, ultimately removing one of the key advantages of this method.

2.2.1 Polling

Polling refers to the action of sampling the status of a system over time. In games, this means that we sample game data every frame for as long as we are interested in capturing or displaying it. A good example is the player's health, the user interface does not and should not keep the health of the player; it should only retrieve it directly from the player and display it.

The game engine must provide the interfaces for the UI to be able to poll the data we need to display. One approach is to create interfaces for the data that must be polled.

```cpp
class IUIPlayerData
{
    float GetHealth() const = 0;
    float GetStamina() const = 0;
    IUIWeaponData* GetWeaponData() const = 0;
}

class Player : public IUIPlayerData
{
    ...
    float GetHealth() const { return m_health + m_bonusHealth; }
    float GetStamina() const { return m_stamina; }
    IUIWeaponData* GetWeaponData() const { return m_activeWeapon; }
    ...
};
```

In this way, it is the responsibility of the Player class to provide the implementation of the interface that will allow the UI code to poll for the data.

2.2.2 Rendering Passes

Breaking up the UI rendering into passes is very important in modern games, not all user interface elements should be rendered at the same time. The organization of passes depends on the type of game and the game engine's architecture, but there are at least three passes that are important.

The first pass is for all the user interface elements that are displayed directly on the screen, but that may be affected by the game's post processing effects. In this pass we would render any user interface elements that we want to be in the frame buffer at the time the post processing system applies the effects. When would we want to do this? In many games the HUD is part of the game's immersion, it's a part of the player somehow, as a helmet's interior or a cybernetic eye, some post process effects may impair visibility or create an effect when the player takes damage; it's important to understand your game's rendering goals and how post processes are used to make sure this pass is done at the right moment.

The next pass is for anything that should NOT be affected by the post processing effects, this could very well be the HUD if the game's design calls for the HUD to be "always on top" or it can be used to display menus when the game is paused, anything that requires direct player interaction should not be affected by post processes, after all the player needs to be able to read and interact with the UI.

There is another pass, this one is interleaved with the game rendering pass as it is usually dependent on some game mechanic, a camera for example. This is a pass in which we may render any sort of interface into a render target, and then use this render target to display the interface "in-world". This is a special case, and not every game requires it. The reason why this should be considered a separate pass is that by coupling the rendering of the UI with a related world object, we ensure that we can render the UI to a render target, then use this render target directly within the object that owns it. This can be used to render the UI for game objects, keypads, computer displays, basically anything you can imagine with a UI that exists as part of the game's universe.

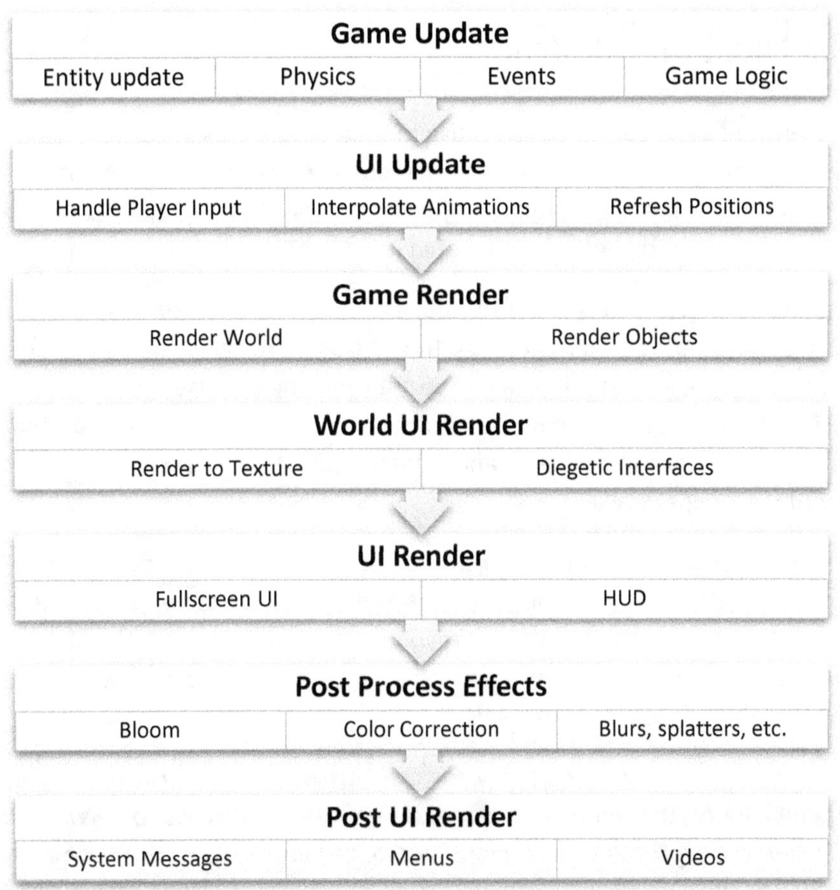

Figure *30* - Example of single threaded game loop with multiple UI passes

In a multithreaded game loop many of these passes would run in parallel and would need to have certain a synchronization strategy where the rendering thread receives a snapshot of the state of the UI.

2.3 Diegetic Interfaces

The term diegetic comes from its use in film, where it is used to describe the internal world that the film's characters experience, for example, a diegetic sound refers to a sound, or perhaps, music that the characters can hear, while a non-diegetic sound would not be relevant to the action.

In games, the term diegetic also applies, it can be used to describe the game's universe as experienced by the character in the game. When we talk about a diegetic user interface, we are referring to a user interface that exists within the game's universe and that it supports the immersion that the characters are able to see and interact with these user interfaces as part of their experience.

Diegetic interfaces are any in which the user interface is not bound to the two dimensional plane of the player's screen, but that can exist as part of game objects or the environment, keypads, computer screens, the interior of vehicles often use diegetic interfaces, in particular those in which the player is able to look around freely.

There is no real recipe to follow for creating diegetic interfaces as they depend a lot on the underlying game design. We will discuss some ways in which diegetic interfaces may be implemented and set a basic framework in place to support them.

2.3.1 Render To Texture

In very broad terms, when we render the game we are rendering it into a memory buffer, a buffer that will then be rasterized onto the screen by the graphics hardware. We have the ability to specify a different memory buffer into which to render, this is known as a render target. The render target is a type of texture that the graphics hardware knows may be used as an output for the rendering stage, but that also may be used as an input in a later part of the rendering stage.

Rendering to a texture, or to a render target is a common way to implement *diegetic interfaces*. At some moment in the rendering pipeline, we set the graphic's device render target from the frame buffer, to our own. We then proceed to render some user interface elements into it, progress bars, text displays, a radar, basically any user interface element we need. With the finished render target in hand, we can then provide it as an input texture when rendering a game model, such as a virtual computer display.

Another use of render targets is to render a part of the game world into our render target, then through composition, we can overlay user interface information on this render target which we then use as the input texture on one of our UI elements. We often see this when games implement cameras that the players can see through within the game.

One useful tool when developing a render to texture system is to create a *camera* object that when needed can capture what it sees into a render target. This allows us to place a camera anywhere in the world, and then capture what the camera can see and store this into a texture that we can later use for our game features.

```cpp
class camera_rt : public camera
{
public:

...

    void Capture(std::function<void(void)> renderFunction)
    {
        auto context = m_device->GetImmediateContext();

        // Set the render target active on the graphics device.
        auto* renderTargetView = m_renderTarget->GetRenderTargetView();
        context->OMSetRenderTargets(1, renderTargetView, nullptr );

        // Optionally, clear the render target
        if ( m_clear )
        {
            context->ClearRenderTargetView(*renderTargetView, m_clearColor);
        }

        auto& vp = m_device->GetViewport();
```

```cpp
        // Set this camera's viewport and view/projection transform
        m_device->SetViewport(m_viewport);
        m_device->SetViewMatrix(View());
        m_device->SetProjectionMatrix(Projection());

        // Invoke the provided render function
        renderFunction();

        // Reset the render target back to the default
        ID3D11RenderTargetView* nullRenderTargetView = nullptr;
        context->OMSetRenderTargets(1, &nullRenderTargetView, nullptr );

        // Restore the device's viewport
        m_device->SetViewport(vp);
    }
```

In this implementation, when we wish to capture what the camera can see, we can do so by providing a custom render function. This is useful because often when we render into a target we may not want to render the scene exactly as it is rendered during the rest of the game. Sometimes due to performance implications, sometimes by design and other times we want to render something else entirely.

```cpp
m_cameraRT->Capture(std::bind(&my_game::Draw, this) );
```

Where the *Draw* function may be the same render function as the rest of the game, or a simplified view of the world.

2.4 Augmented Reality

Augmented reality (AR) is a term that has in recent years become popular. Our powerful mobile devices are creating new ways for us to interface with users and with the world around us. As the name implies, reality is augmented, augmented with more information, images, sounds, and user provided details, such as reviews or comments by other people.

In games, forms of augmented reality have existed for many years, but it is until recently that user interfaces from games are converging with user interfaces we use in our daily lives and we see new and interesting applications for it.

To implement AR in games we need to spend some time deciding how the AR data will be assigned and retrieved. Game objects need to be marked and given the data that we wish to display. Some information may be calculated in real-time, such as the distance to the object, its angle in relation to the player, its world space coordinates. But the game specific information, its name, description and any other interesting information has to be stored and retrieved efficiently.

Once the data pipeline for an AR system is designed and implemented, we need to implement the AR display. Fortunately, in games, and unlike reality, we have very accurate information about the world and all the objects around us. We don't generally need to worry about algorithms that perform feature detection/recognition, edges, corners, image recognition or pattern matching. Instead, we usually will have an object's world space coordinates available, or we can generate a ray down the camera's center and if any object is hit, we use the contact data from the intersection to first, query the object's AR data from our game's database, and second to procedurally generate the geometry for the AR display, or project the user interface from the object's world space into the player's screen space. We will see many techniques that apply to augmented reality in the following chapters.

3 RENDERING

This section is a primer on rendering, it aims to explain the core concepts of graphics programming. Rendering systems are different depending on platforms and frameworks

3.1 VIEWPORTS

Viewports represent rectangular areas of a render target unto which the game world is rendered. A viewport consists of the properties top, left, width, height which describe the dimensions of the window into the render target; typically applications will use the entire size of the render target for fullscreen rendering, however, multiple viewports may be used to render the view from different cameras, or to achieve certain effects.

Viewports also have properties that specify how much of the projected depth they can map, these are a *MinDepth* and *MaxDepth* values that typically range from 0.0 to 1.0, meaning that the entire depth range can be used by the viewport. Some special effects can be achieved by using different depth ranges, for example setting both values to 0.0 would force objects to be rendered in the foreground, setting both values to 1.0 would force objects to be rendered in the background.

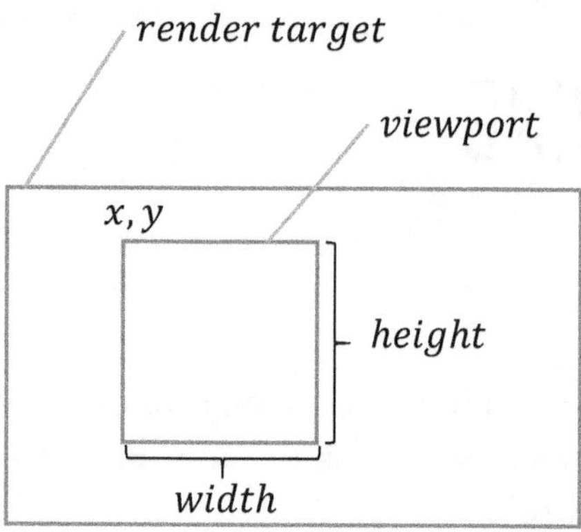

Figure *31* - A viewport defines an area of a render target.

3.2 TITLE SAFE AREA

On standard television sets, the area around the edges of the screen could become distorted or obscured, so any information that should be readable needs to be displayed within a title safe area. This is an area that represents a reduction of the viewport by 10 to 20%.

Newer displays such as flat panels, plasma, LCDs, are able to display most of the image outside the safe area, however, it still remains important if your game may run on a game console that needs to support a large variety of television displays and configurations. In fact, many console manufacturer's state in their guidelines that any critical text should be within the inner 80% of the game's viewport.

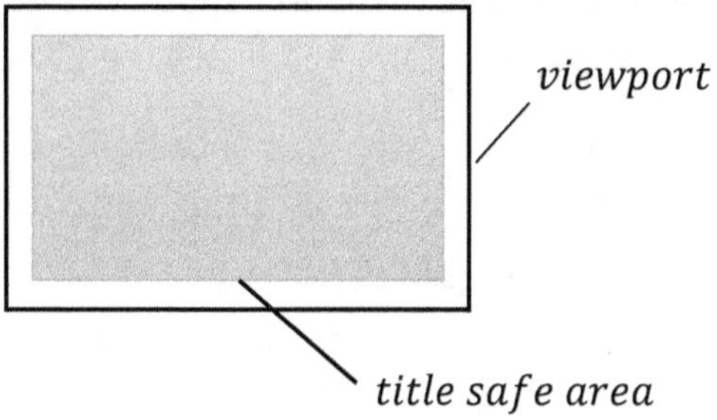

Figure 32 - The title safe area lies within the viewport, anything within this area is guaranteed to be visible even on old CRT displays.

We can calculate the title safe area of a viewport when we construct the viewport,

```
float safeAreaWidth = (Width * ( 1.0 – titleSafeRatio));
float safeAreaHeight = (Height * (1.0 – titleSafeRatio));

Rectangle titleSafeArea = Rectangle(Left + (safeAreaWidth * 0.5), Top + (safeAreaHeight * 0.5), Width – safeAreaWidth, Height – safeAreaHeight);
```

The calculated title safe area is accessible through the viewport by calling the function *viewport.TitleSafeArea()*, we will use it to be certain that when we display UI elements we constrain them within this area to ensure maximum compatibility with devices and compliance with certification requirements.

3.3 Project (World to Screen)

To *project* something unto a viewport means to bring a position that is somewhere within the view frustum and find it's respective position in the 2D-space of the viewport. We do this often in games to highlight objects in the game world, to display some information about an object in the world next to it such as a health bar, or a character's name.

A *project* function then expects a world space position, a world space transform, the view space transform and finally the projection transform.

The first step is to compute a concatenated matrix for the *World/View/Projection*, this will give us a single matrix by which we can transform the world space position.

$$M = WVP$$

$$p' = pM$$

As we saw earlier, the viewport contains a pair of scalars *MinDepth* and *MaxDepth*, these are used to map the viewport to a range of the view frustum's depth, typically these are 0.0 and 1.0 respectively, meaning that they will map the entire range of the frustum, that is from the near clipping plane to the far clipping plane of our projection matrix.

$$p'_z = p'_z * (\text{depth}_{max} - \text{depth}_{min})$$

This scales p'_z within the depth range, now we need to convert the position into non-homogenous coordinates by dividing p' by the homogenization factor in p'_w,

$$p' = \frac{p'}{p'_w}$$

Finally, we need to bring the x, y components of p' within the viewport's bounds, where x, y represents the top left corner of the viewport and w, h the width and height, we also need to ensure that the p'_z coordinate is within the depth range.

$$p'_x = x + (1 + p'_x) * \frac{w}{2}$$

$$p'_y = y + (1 - p'_y) * \frac{h}{2}$$

$$p'_z = p'_z + \text{depth}_{min}$$

```cpp
vector3 Project(vector3 worldPosition, matrix world, matrix view, matrix projection)
{
    matrix wvp = world * view * projection;
    vector4 result = vector4::Transform(worldPosition, wvp);

    result.z() = result.z() * (m_maxDepth - m_minDepth);
    result /= result.w();

    vector3 finalResult = result;

    finalResult.x() = m_left + (1.f + finalResult.x()) * Width()/2;
    finalResult.y() = m_top + (1.f - finalResult.y()) * Height()/2;
    finalResult.z() = finalResult.z() + m_minDepth;

    return finalResult;
}
```

3.4 Unproject (Screen to World)

While *project* is a function to bring a world space coordinate into screen space, *unproject* is the opposite operation, given a screen space position, we want to calculate a corresponding world space position. The use of *unproject* seems less intuitive at first glance, as you can imagine there may be infinite coordinates in world space under any given point on the screen, however, rather than passing a 2D vector of screen coordinates, we can pass a 3D vector, using the *z* component as a ratio into the depth of the view frustum.

A common use for this is for picking or determining whether your input cursor, whether a mouse click, or a finger tap on the display intersects with any objects in the 3D world.

The idea behind it is, begin by unprojecting a screen position at depth 0.0, this represents the near clipping plane of the view frustum; keep the world space position you retrieved, we will call this p_0. Next, *unproject* the same screen position at a depth of 1.0, this represents the far clipping plane of the view frustum, we will also keep this position, and call it p_1. Now we have two positions in 3D space from which we can construct the direction vector

$$v = |p_1 - p_0|$$

At this point you can create a ray using p_0 and v which you can use to perform intersection testing against the objects in the game's world.

The first step to *unproject* a screen space position is to frame the world space position within the viewport, in normalized coordinates from -1 to 1.

$$p'_x = \frac{2(p_x - x)}{w} - 1$$

$$p'_y = \frac{2(p_y - y)}{h} - 1$$

$$p'_z = \frac{p_z - depth_{min}}{depth_{max} - depth_{min}}$$

There is a special case to be aware of when calculating p', it is possible for $depth_{max} - depth_{max}$ to yield 0.0, which would result in a division by zero, if this is the case, we set p'_z to 0.0.

As with project, we want to compute the world/view/projection matrix, however, because our goal is to bring a world space coordinate into screen space, we need the inverse matrix.

$$M = (WVP)^{-1}$$

We then transform our point p' by this matrix.

$$r = p'M$$

Finally we need to convert our vector into non-homogeneous coordinates, dividing by the homogenizing factor r_w.

$$r = \frac{r}{r_w}$$

r now holds the position in world space we were looking for.

```cpp
vector3 Unproject(vector3 screenPos, matrix world, matrix view, matrix projection)
{
    vector4 result;
    result.x() = (2.f * (screenPos.x() - m_left) / Width()) - 1.f;
    result.y() = 1.f - (2.f * (screenPos.y() - m_top) / Height());
    result.z() = screenPos.z() - m_minDepth;

    if ( IsEqual(m_maxDepth - m_minDepth, 0.f ) )
        result.z() = 0.f;
    else
        result.z() = result.z() / (m_maxDepth - m_minDepth);

    result.w() = 1.f;

    matrix iwvp = matrix::Invert(world) * matrix::Invert(view) *
matrix::Invert(projection);

    vector4 finalResult = vector4::Transform(result, iwvp);
    finalResult /= finalResult.w();
    return finalResult;
}
```

3.5 Picking

As we saw earlier, *unprojecting* is commonly used to determine if the player may be trying to interact with a game object in 3D space.

Given an input position $i = \{i_x, i_y, i_z\}$ we will calculate a ray that we can use within our game's world to determine if there are any objects that intersects it.

First for $i_z = 0$, which scales the unprojected point towards the near clipping plane

$$p_0 = \text{unproject}(\{i_x, i_y, 0\}, W, V, P)$$

Then, for $i_z = 1$, which scales the unprojected point towards the far clipping plane

$$p_1 = \text{unproject}(\{i_x, i_y, 1\}, W, V, P)$$

Having two points in world space we can now calculate a normalized direction vector

$$\hat{v} = |p_1 - p_0|$$

We can now create a ray such that its position is p_0 and it points in the direction $\hat{v}$, we send this ray to our world database or physics system and we can perform intersection testing to find what objects lie behind the input position $i = \{i_x, i_y, i_z\}$.

```
ray GetRayFromMouseClick(const vector2& screenPosition, const matrix& world, const
matrix& view, const matrix& projection, const viewport& viewport)
{
    vector3 p0 = screenPosition;
    p0.z() = 0.f;
    vector3 p1 = screenPosition;
    p1.z() = 1.f;

    p0 = viewport.Unproject(p0, world, view, projection);
    p1 = viewport.Unproject(p1, world, view, projection);

    vector3 direction = vector3::Normalize(p1 - p0);
    return ray(p0, direction);
}
```

Now that we have a ray we will need to use it to query the game world or physics system to find if there are any collisions, this will depend largely on how each game organizes its data, but typically you will have an engine function we can call that will return a list of contacts that intersect with the ray.

3.6 VERTEX BUFFERS

Vertex data is stored in memory buffers, that contain the representation of a vertex as it will be used by the graphics driver (position, color, normal vector, etc.) these memory buffers reside in memory directly on the GPU, often referred to as video memory. Vertex buffers provide an efficient way of reusing geometry, it is possible to create a vertex buffer and draw the geometry within it multiple times without needing to perform additional transformations or lighting calculations. It is possible to render portions of a vertex buffer, this gives us flexibility of storing a model's data but applying different texture settings to different parts of the model.

The creation of vertex buffers is dependent on the platform, but conceptually similar. Vertex data needs to be come from a source, this could be an array of vertices or streamed from an external source, a file on disc for example.

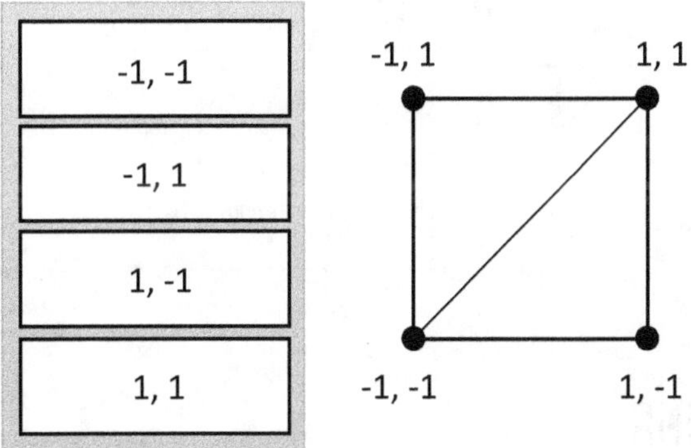

Figure *33* - Vertex buffer representation.

Vertex buffers can be used by themselves to render geometry, or they can be used in conjunction with index buffers to render indexed primitives.

3.7 Index Buffers

Index buffers are memory buffers that hold integer offsets into vertex buffers. An index buffer allows us to reduce the amount of memory needed by vertex data, a quad consists of four vertices and two triangles, to represent the quad using vertex data alone we need to store six vertices, two of them duplicated. Using index buffers we can avoid this vertex duplication.

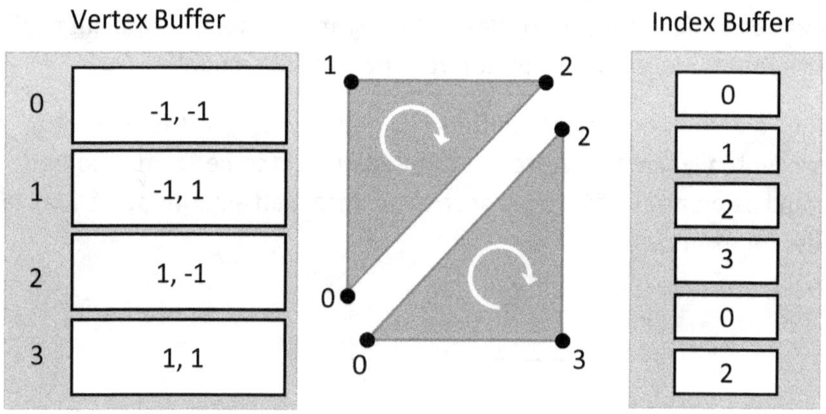

Figure *34* - Index buffer representation.

3.8 Culling

Culling refers to the culling of faces that may not be visible to the player, any triangles that are facing away from the player's camera are called back facing triangles and as an optimization the video hardware is able to skip drawing it, culling it before it reaches the rasterizer stage. There are three options available to enable culling and they require some knowledge about how the geometry was built.

None

No culling, this means no triangles will be culled, even if they're facing away from the camera, sometimes this is necessary, an example is when rendering primitives in wireframe, if we want to be able to see the full shape of the primitive, we can disable culling.

Clockwise

The name clockwise refers to the order in which a face is created, if the order of the vertices to draw was defined in clockwise order, any back facing vertices will be culled.

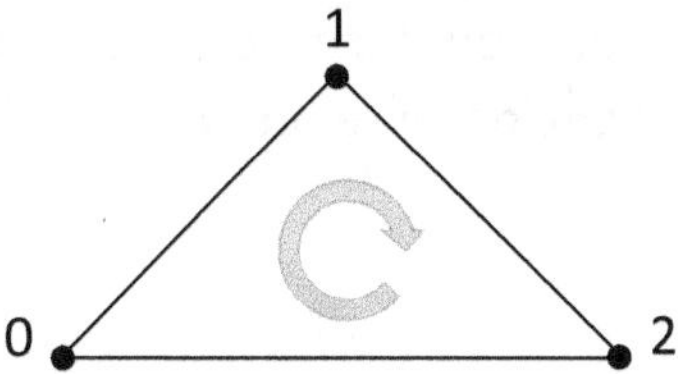

Figure 35 - Clockwise winding order of a triangle's vertices.

The ordering of the vertices is determined either by the order they appear in the vertex buffer, or the order of the indices in the index buffer, of if drawing in immediate mode, the order of function calls.

Using a vertex buffer:

```
vertex_type vertices[] = {
{0,0,0},
{0,1,0},
{1,0,0} }; // clockwise winding order
```

Using indices:

```
// clockwise winding order
unsigned short cw_indices[] = { 0, 1, 2 };

// counter clockwise winding order
```

```
unsigned short ccw_indices[] = { 0, 2, 1 };
```

Immediate mode:

```
glBegin(GL_TRIANGLES);
   glVertex3f(0.f, 0.f, 0.f);
   glVertex3f(0.f, 1.f, 0.f);
   glVertex3f(1.f, 0.f, 0.f);
glEnd();
```

Counter-Clockwise

As with clockwise culling, counter-clockwise will cull any back facing vertices defined in counter clockwise order.

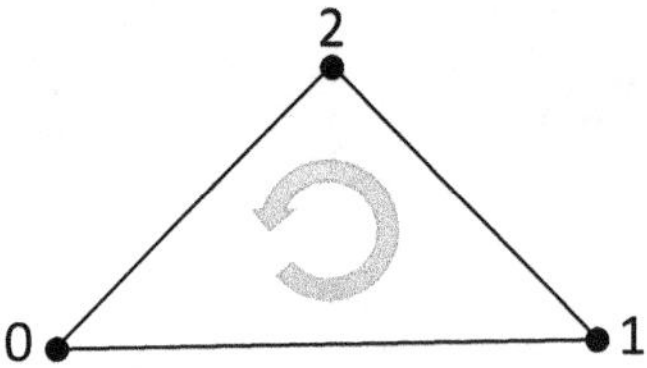

Figure *36* - Counter-clockwise winding order of a triangle's vertices.

Using a vertex buffer:

```
vertex_type vertices[] = {
{0,0,0},
{1,0,0},
{0,1,0} }; // clockwise winding order
```

Using indices:

```
// clockwise winding order
unsigned short cw_indices[] = { 0, 2, 1 };

// counter clockwise winding order
```

```
unsigned short ccw_indices[] = { 0, 1, 2 };
```

Immediate mode:

```
glBegin(GL_TRIANGLES);
   glVertex3f(0.f, 0.f, 0.f);
   glVertex3f(1.f, 0.f, 0.f);
   glVertex3f(0.f, 1.f, 0.f);
glEnd();
```

We need to be aware of the culling mode enabled when rendering geometrical data that we generated or imported, if the primitive or model is not showing up, or it looks inside out, it is possible the winding order or the culling mode is not set to the correct value.

3.9 Color

Color can be represented using different data types, depending on the target platform some color formats may be more appropriate. For simplicity and compatibility, we will describe and operate on colors internally using floating point values in the {0..1} range that represent the contribution of each color channel towards the final color, this makes the different mathematical operations more intuitive to work with. We will then provide the means to convert this representation into an integer format that is useable by the graphics device. It is important to understand the color format our target platform requires to make sure we provide the corresponding conversion facilities.

The example code is built on Direct3D, so we will focus primarily on using colors in an ARGB 8-bit format (and in some situations in ABGR), this means that for each color channel we will use 8 bits of data, this will allow us to represent a color in an unsigned 32-bit type.

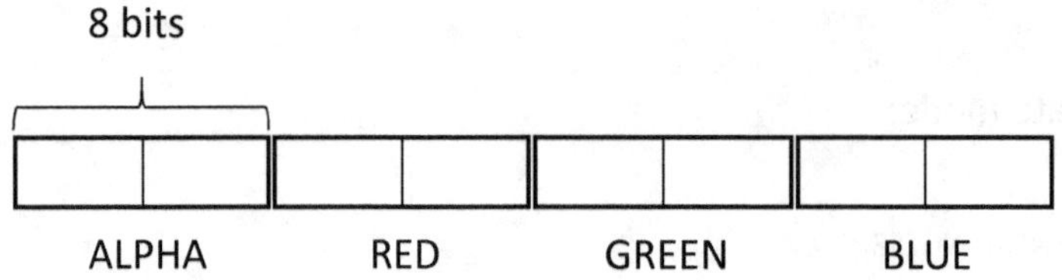

Figure 37 - Color represented by four 8-bit channels.

An unsigned 8 bit value has a range from {0..255} if we represent an unsigned 8 bit value in hexadecimal, the value ranges from {0..FF} which allows us to represent colors in the familiar hexadecimal notation used across the web.

It's useful to understand how to convert from one color format to another, particularly when working in multiple platforms, if our yellows have become cyan, and our red have become blue, then we may need to be certain we are sending the colors in the right format to the graphics hardware.

The first thing we need to do is bring the floating point representation of a color into the 8 bit range, we do this by multiplying it by 255. Once we have the 8 bit value for each color channel, we will need to combine them into a single 32-bit type, an unsigned int. We do this with bit manipulation, we have 4 8-bit values that we need to bit shift into place into the destination type. We are using ARGB as out format, this means that the alpha channel is the first value we need to place at the leftmost position of our 32-bit value. We will look at the bit manipulation operations we need to perform in order to combine all the color channels into a single color, this is a very brief introduction to a very small part of bit manipulation, if you are already comfortable manipulating bits, feel free to skip ahead.

If we display the alpha channel (FF) as a 32bit value, we would see it preceded by six zeros.

```
000000FF
```

If we go further, in binary, this is

```
0000 0000 0000 0000 0000 0000 1111 1111
```

We count the number of 0's that would place our alpha value at the leftmost position, starting from the leftmost 1, this means we need to shift our value 24 positions to the left.

```
1111 1111 0000 0000 0000 0000 0000 0000
```

Which back in hexadecimal notation puts the alpha at the leftmost position of the 32-bit value.

```
(000000FF << 24) = FF000000
```

Next up is the red channel, similarly we find that we need to shift the red color into position, doing the same procedure we find we need to shift by 16,

```
(000000FF << 16) = 00FF0000
```

Then we shift the green channel by 8 bits.

```
(000000FF << 8) = 0000FF00
```

And finally, the blue channel is already at the rightmost position so there is no need to shift it. The final step in the process is to combine the channels into a single 32-bit value at their respective positions. With the bitwise OR operator we compare two bits, if either bit is 1, the resulting bit will be 1, for example:

```
10110010 |
00100101 =
--------
10110111
```

In our case we need to do a bitwise OR operation on all the shifted channels, to store the final result in a single 32bit value.

```cpp
unsigned int color = (alpha << 24) | (red << 16) | (green << 8) | blue;
```

To make our color class intuitive to use, we will provide a type operator that will perform the conversion from floating point representation to a 32-bit value.

```cpp
class color
{
public:

    color::operator const unsigned int() const;

    enum { R, G, B, A };

private:
    float m_color[4];
};

inline color::operator const unsigned int() const
{
    auto red   = static_cast<unsigned char>(m_color[R] * 255.f);
    auto green = static_cast<unsigned char>(m_color[G] * 255.f);
    auto blue  = static_cast<unsigned char>(m_color[B] * 255.f);
    auto alpha = static_cast<unsigned char>(m_color[A] * 255.f);

    return (a << 24) | (r << 16) | (g << 8) | b;
}
```

3.10 Blend Modes

Blend states are rendering controls that allow us to specify how we need color and alpha values to be blended into a render target. When we render we are taking some source data and converting it into a set of pixels that we will store in a render target, this render target may be empty or may already contain some pixels set in previous rendering operations, blending takes place when we combine the source pixels with the existing pixels in the render target.

Each pixel has a numerical representation, blending is done by applying different mathematical operations on the pixels to calculate the resulting pixel. A blend can be seen as a function $f(a, b)$ where a is the source pixel color and b is the pixel color in the render target, f then will be the final color that will be stored.

Blend states are configured by sending different flags to the rendering device, these flags represent blend factors that specify how the value of the source pixel and the destination pixel will be applied such that the final color is determined by to formula:

$$f(a, b) = (a * bf_a) + (b * bf_b)$$

Where bf_a , bf_b are the blend factors for a and b respectively, and they consist of four elements, such that

$$bf \rightarrow \{R, G, B, A\}.$$

Depending on the platform it is possible to configure colors blending, and also how the alpha is blended by setting different blend factors for the source color, destination color, source alpha and destination alpha. Not every blend mode can be achieved using the device's blend factors, some blend modes need to be implemented through pixel shaders in the programmable rendering pipeline.

Direct3D (prefix D3DBLEND_)	OpenGL® (prefix GL_)	$bf_x \rightarrow \{ R_x, G_x, B_x, A_x\}$ $x = s$, is the source pixel. $x = d$, is the destination pixel
ZERO	ZERO	$\{0,0,0,0\}$
ONE	ONE	$\{1,1,1,1\}$
SRCCOLOR	SRC_COLOR	$\{ R_s, G_s, B_s, A_s\}$
INVSRCCOLOR	ONE_MINUS_SRC_COLOR	$\begin{Bmatrix} 1 - R_s, \\ 1 - G_s, \\ 1 - B_s, \\ 1 - A_s \end{Bmatrix}$
SRCALPHA	SRC_ALPHA	$\{ A_s, A_s, A_s, A_s\}$
INVSRCALPHA	ONE_MINUS_SRC_ALPHA	$\begin{Bmatrix} 1 - A_s, \\ 1 - A_s, \\ 1 - A_s, \\ 1 - A_s \end{Bmatrix}$
DESTALPHA	DST_ALPHA	$\{ A_d, A_d, A_d, A_d\}$
INVDESTALPHA	ONE_MINUS_DST_ALPHA	$\begin{Bmatrix} 1 - A_d, \\ 1 - A_d, \\ 1 - A_d, \\ 1 - A_d \end{Bmatrix}$
DESTCOLOR	CONSTANT_COLOR	$\{ R_d, G_d, B_d, A_d\}$
INVDESTCOLOR	ONE_MINUS_CONSTANT_COLOR	$\begin{Bmatrix} 1 - R_d, \\ 1 - G_d, \\ 1 - B_d \\ , 1 - A_d \end{Bmatrix}$
SRCALPHASAT	SRC_ALPHA_SATURATE	$\{x, x, x, 1\} \rightarrow$ $x = \min(A_s, 1 - A_d)$

× Unity has nearly the same set of blend factors within ShaderLab.

3.10.1 Opaque

The standard blending mode is called opaque as it does not apply any transparency values, it will replace the target pixels with those from the source.

$$f(a, b) = a$$

It is defined by applying the blend factors:

ONE, ZERO

This generates the following formula:

$$f(a, b) = (a * \{1,1,1,1\}) + (b * \{0,0,0,0\}) = a$$

This means that no amount of the destination color, the color in the render target will be applied towards the final pixel color.

3.10.2 Alpha

There are several ways in which translucency and transparency are implemented. The alpha value of a color is used to modulate how much of the color is blended with the colors underneath it, and the modulation function may vary depending on the effect that we are trying to achieve.

3.10.2.1 Non-Premultiplied Alpha (or Conventional Alpha)

Transparency is achieved with a blend mode with which we apply the alpha value to the source color and the inverse of the source alpha to the destination color, with primitives sorted farthest to nearest.

SRC_ALPHA, INVSRCALPHA

This generates the formula:

$$f(a, b) = (a * \{A_s, A_s, A_s, A_s\}) + (b * \{1 - A_s, 1 - A_s, 1 - A_s, 1 - A_s\})$$

In this case it is easier to see the result with some sample values, if we consider that the alpha value A_a is 0.25, the blend will be the result of 25% of the source color plus the destination color at the 75% value of the source alpha.

$$f(a, b) = (a * 0.25) + (b * 0.75)$$

We can substitute a, b by some color values, $a = \{0.37, 0.37, 0.37, 0.25\}$ and $b = \{1,1,1,1\}$ this will blend a dark gray color onto a white render target.

$$f(a, b) = \{0.09, 0.09, 0.09, 0.0625\} + \{0.75, 0.75, 0.75, 0.75\}$$
$$= \{0.84, 0.84, 0.84, 0.8125\}$$

The result is a light gray color.

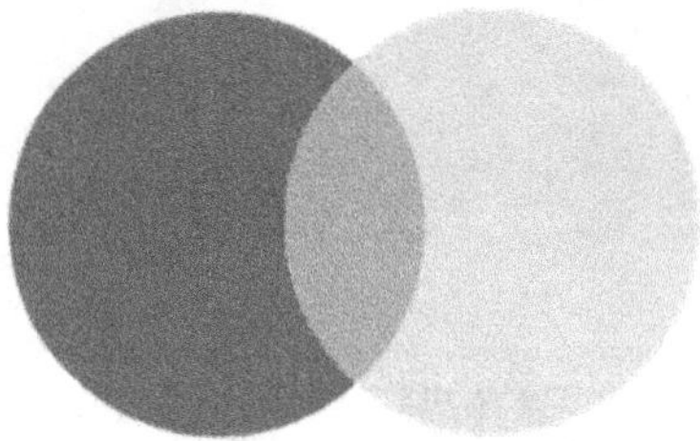

Figure 38 – Alpha blending.

Note that the calculations are done in normalized values [0..1], however the final pixel value is represented in 8 bits (assuming we are using an 8-bit per channel format); a value from [0..255] often represented in hex as [0x00..0xff], in this example the final color value is 0xd7 or 215.

3.10.2.2 Premultiplied Alpha

In some cases, the source alpha can be premultiplied to the color of the image, it avoids performing these multiplications during the blend. If our source color is $\{1,0,0,0.5\}$, we would premultiply it by 0.5 such that the final color would be red at 50% intensity $\{0.5,0,0\}$. Usually the premultiplication is done as part of a pre-process on the source image.

Why is it different than conventional non-premultiplied alpha blending? At a glance it would appear as if there is no significant difference except of when the multiplication takes place, however there are a few things to consider, the first one being filtering. Filters are applied when some amount of scaling occurs; when scaling up we need to fill in some pixels in the space in between source pixels and when scaling down we want to blend pixels together to ensure the destination image retains enough information and quality. The problem becomes particularly noticeable when there is a sharp discontinuity between an opaque pixel (alpha = 1.0) and a transparent pixel (alpha = 0.0), a linear interpolation filter will take the two pixels and average them together, resulting in an alpha value of 0.5, this is the alpha value that the conventional alpha blend will use.

Consider the following example:

The source pixel color is red $p_s = \{1,0,0,1\}$ and its neighbor is a border pixel $p_b = \{0,0,0,0\}$. In this situation if a filter is applied, the filtered color will be

$$p_f = \frac{p_s + p_b}{2} = \{0.5, 0, 0, 0.5\}$$

Now, this will be the source pixel used by the color blend operation, consider that we blend this pixel onto a green pixel on the render target $p_{rt} = \{0,1,0,1\}$.

Using conventional alpha blending:

$$f(p_f, p_{rt}) = (p_f * 0.5) + (p_{rt} * (1 - 0.5)) = \{0.25, 0.5, 0, 0.5\}$$

The red component of the final color is actually darker than we expected. Given an alpha value of 0.5, we expected the resulting color after the blend to be $\{0.5, 0.5, 0, 0.5\}$.

Premultiplied alpha uses the blend factors:

ONE, INVSRCALPHA

This yields the formula:

$$f(a, b) = (a * \{\, 1,1,1,1\, \}) + (b * \{1 - A_s, 1 - A_s, 1 - A_s, 1 - A_s\})$$

Continuing the previous example, we can see that with premultiplied alpha we do not have the same problem:

$$f(p_f, p_{rt}) = (p_f * 1) + (p_{rt} * (1 - 0.5)) = \{0.5, 0.5, 0, 0.5\}$$

Which is the result we expected.

Premultiplied alpha also has a performance advantage as we avoid performing the multiplications during the blend. In extreme cases, such as in conjunction with some compression algorithms premultiplication may produce a significant loss of quality.

3.10.3 Additive

An additive blend state is very useful when we want colors to blend such that they grow in intensity as they are blended, often you see particle effects using an additive blend mode to simulate heat as each particle's pixels are blended additively with the pixels underneath they will approach white.

Additive blending is done by setting the source blending factors to SRC_ALPHA and the destination factors to ONE.

SRC_ALPHA, ONE

This results in a formula that states that the source color, scaled by its alpha value will be added directly to the pixel color on the render target.

$$f(a, b) = (a * \{A_s, A_s, A_s, A_s\}) + (b * \{1,1,1,1\})$$

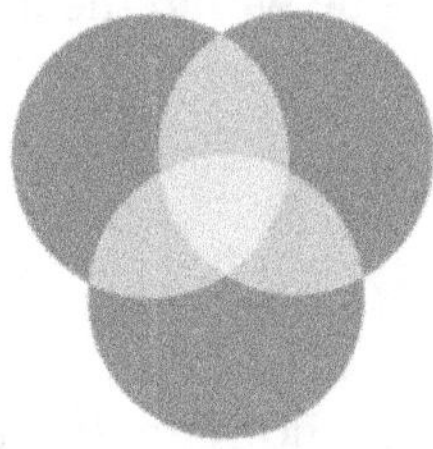

Figure 39 - Additive blend mode.

3.10.4 Multiplicative

Multiplicative blending is a mode that behaves as light passing through a color filter, the destination pixel becomes darkened with the color of the source pixel. The only exceptions are when one of the pixels is white, in which case the color remains unchanged or one of the pixels is black, in which case the result will be black.

ZERO,   SRC_COLOR

Because of the darkening effect it produces, multiplication can be used to create shadow effects.

$$f(a, b) = (a * \{0,0,0,0\}) + (b * \{R_s, G_s, B_s, A_s\})$$

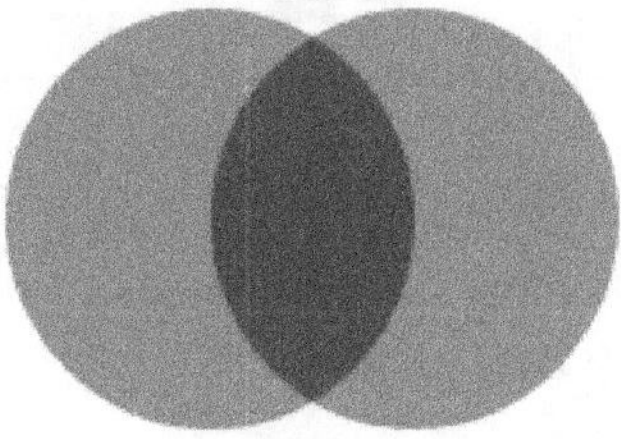

Figure 40 - Multiplicative blend mode.

Each circle has a value of {0.5, 0.5, 0.5}, the intersection portion of the circles is blended multiplicatively and the result is:

$$f(a, b) = (a * \{0,0,0,0\}) + (\{0.5,0.5,0.5,1\} * \{0.5,0.5,0.5,1\})$$
$$= \{0.25,0.25,0.25,1\}$$

Which is precisely the color value within the intersection.

3.10.5 Screen

To apply the screen blend mode, both the source and destination pixels are inverted then multiplied and inverted again.

$$f(a, b) = 1 - (1 - a)(1 - b)$$

The formula can be further simplified to the form.

$$f(a, b) = (1 - a)b + a$$

In this form we can see that the blend state can be set with the blend factors.

ONE, INVSRCCOLOR

Screen lightens the underlying pixels without lightening the darkest areas excessively, it's similar to an additive blend mode; not as extreme, so it will not produce over lightening that can occur in additive blend.

3.11 Programmable Rendering Pipeline

The programmable rendering pipeline is a part of the overall rendering pipeline in which graphics programmers have the ability to manipulate vertex and pixel data before they are rasterized.

Data sent to the graphics device will pass through different programmable stages, these stages are programmed in a language that depends on the target platform in which the game is running. Commonly, Direct3D uses the High Level Shading Language, HLSL and OpenGL® uses the OpenGL® Shading Language, GLSL. The languages share similarities and it is often not difficult to port features from one to another. That said, there is often significant overhead in maintaining shaders when working on multiple platforms concurrently.

To abstract the platform-specific language details away from programmers and to provide special effect, or shader artists with user-friendly environments to develop effects, teams usually acquire or develop visual graph-based tools that allow for quick development and iteration on shaders, without writing any code.

3.11.1 Vertex Shaders

We can think of a vertex shader as a small executable program that is run on every vertex in a set prior to rendering. This program may apply different properties to vertices as they are processed, color, lighting, deformations, the job of the vertex shader is to transform vertices and prepare them for the next stage in the pipeline. The programming languages used by vertex shaders vary slightly depending on the hardware vendor, API or platform. At the core, shaders are a form of assembly language, which tends to frighten many programmers, however, for a few years vertex and other hardware shaders have evolved to use a high level languages that greatly simplifies programming the GPU.

A vertex shader receives vertex data as input, at the least this means a position, but often it may include texture coordinates, blend indices or custom data for special effects.

A straightforward vertex shader that transforms geometry from world space into screen space may be implemented as follows:

```
float4x4    view;
float4x4    projection;
float4x4    world;

struct SInputData
{
    float4 position  : POSITION;
    float4 color     : COLOR0;
    float2 texCoord : TEXCOORD0;
};

struct SVertexData
{
    float4 position   : SV_Position;
    float4 color      : COLOR0;
    float2 texCoord : TEXCOORD0;
};

SVertexData vs_default( SInputData input )
{
    SVertexData output;
    output.position = mul(projection, mul(view, mul(world, input.position)));
    output.texCoord = input.texCoord;
    output.color = input.color;
    return output;
};
```

The first part defines the values that we will expect to be set into the constant registers of the graphics hardware, this is done on the CPU side just prior to rendering, in this case we expect that a valid view, projection and world matrix will be provided, each as a block of 4x4 float matrices. Different hardware and different hardware versions will have varying limitations on the number of constant registers available.

The next part defines a structure, *SInputData*, this structure holds the layout of the geometry's data as it will be sent from the CPU to the graphics device, this structure must match the structure of the vertex data used to create the geometry.

The next structure that we define *SVertexData* is the output data sent from the vertex shader to the pixel shader, whatever operations the vertex shader performs, the results will be stored in this structure and later on it will be used as the input parameter for the pixel shader.

Finally, the vertex shader program itself, this simple shader computes the projection/view/world transform and then transforms the input world-space position into screen space.

```
float4x4 wvp = mul(projection, mul(view, world));
output.position = mul(wvp, input.position);
```

The operation being done is the following, given the vertex's position p.

$$M = World \cdot View \cdot Projection$$

The screen-space position will be given by:

$$p' = pM$$

The texture coordinates and color are left unmodified and will be pass down to the pixel shader.

3.11.2 Pixel Shaders

The pixel shader is small executable program that calculates the color of a pixel on a render target. Pixel shaders receive the data it needs to compute the final color value from the vertex shader and from user defined custom parameters that are stored in constant register space on the graphics hardware.

Pixel shaders are used to output a calculated color that may be sent down by the vertex, compute the color and apply lighting properties, translucency, normal mapping, shadows, and any number of per pixel effects.

A simple pixel shader that outputs per-vertex color information may look like the following:

```
struct SVertexData
{
   float4 position : SV_Position;
   float4 color   : COLOR0;
   float2 texCoord : TEXCOORD0;
};


float4 ps_vertexcolor(SVertexData input) : SV_Target0
{
    return input.color;
};
```

The input parameter is sent by the vertex shader and contains the screen space position of the pixel, its interpolated texture coordinate and a vertex color that was set during the creation or last update of the vertex buffer.

In order to apply a texture in a pixel shader, a texture and its respective sampler must be provided so that it can be sampled at the interpolated texture coordinate sent by the vertex shader.

```
Texture2D texture0 : register(t0);
SamplerState sampler0 : register(s0);


float4 ps_texture(SVertexData input) : SV_Target0
{
    return texture0.Sample(sampler0, input.texCoord);
};
```

3.12 Rendering Primitives

During the development of a game there is often need for tools and features that only serve as a way to provide visual feedback about the game's world that is not visible to players. One common example is the visual representation of the physical properties of game entities, gameplay, AI and physics programmers often need to see the game as it is simulated to understand how different systems are behaving. But beyond development tools, understanding how to generate primitives is a useful tool for user interface programmers as it may lead to new ideas and new ways of presenting information to players, the concepts behind the geometry generation of a sphere for example could be used to create a 3D dynamic menu in which menu options are presented as quads oriented along a sphere.

In this section we will see how to generate the geometry for different primitives, the focus of this section is on the algorithms necessary to generate the geometry, however it is important to go further and create a batching system that stores all primitives of the same type within the same buffers or an instancing system that given one primitive it will create multiple instances of itself transformed differently. Otherwise, large-scale use of these systems is likely to cause performance problems.

The primitives we create will be unit primitives, meaning they will have a radius or width of exactly one unit and they will be centered about the origin, this allows us to reuse the geometry data with different transforms to translate, position or scale the primitives as needed.

All primitives will share the same vertex type, this will make it easier and consistent when it's time to batch all primitives.

```
struct vertex_default
{
    vector3 position;
    color diffuse;
    float u, v;
};
```

3.12.1 Quads

A quad is one of the most straightforward primitives to draw, it consists of two triangles and four vertices, there are a few ways to draw a quad however, we could use four vertices in a vertex buffer and six indices in an index buffer to map both triangles in the quad, then draw it as a triangle list. We could use four vertices in a vertex buffer and draw it as a triangle strip, or we could use six vertices, duplicating two of them to draw two separate triangles again using a triangle list.

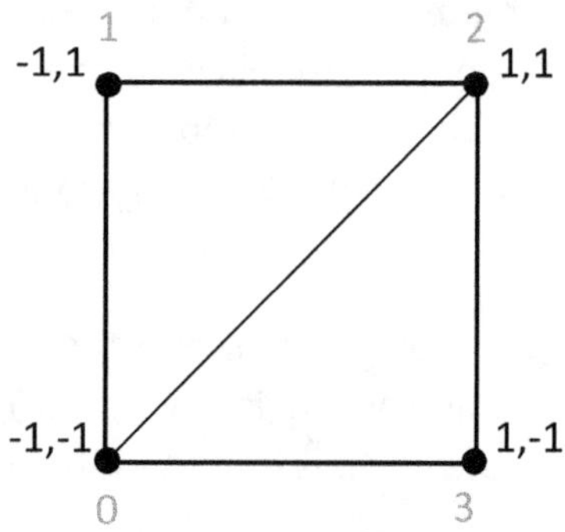

Figure *41* - A quad consists of four vertices and two triangles.

```
const vertex_default vertices_indexed[] =
{
    vertex_default(math::vector3(-1, -1, 0), color::WHITE, 1.f, 1.f),
    vertex_default(math::vector3(-1,  1, 0), color::WHITE, 1.f, 0.f),
    vertex_default(math::vector3( 1,  1, 0), color::WHITE, 0.f, 0.f),
    vertex_default(math::vector3( 1, -1, 0), color::WHITE, 0.f, 1.f),
};

const unsigned short indices[] = { 0, 1, 2, 3, 0, 2 };
```

If we use this data to create a vertex and index buffer, we would draw a proper texture mapped quad on screen, this works well, but it is very verbose, and we start running into some difficulties later when we want to generate other primitives that have more faces. We can produce a more general way of creating a quad.

```
math::vector3 normal(0, 0, 1);
math::vector3 right = normal.Cross( math::vector3::UnitY ) / 2.f;
math::vector3 up = right.Cross( normal );

const vertex_default vertices_gen[] =
{
    vertex_default( right + up, color::WHITE, 1.f, 0.f),
    vertex_default( right - up, color::WHITE, 1.f, 1.f),
    vertex_default(-right - up, color::WHITE, 0.f, 1.f),
    vertex_default(-right + up, color::WHITE, 0.f, 0.f),
};
```

We will start with the z unit vector, which represents the quad's face normal. We will build the quad around this direction. First we calculate the basis vector *right* by taking the cross product of the normal and the world's *y* axis. Because we are interested in creating a *unit square*, we will divide this vector by 2, this will ensure that the width and height of the quad will be one.

To guarantee that the basis is orthonormal, we will recalculate the *up* vector (the *y* axis) by computing the cross product of the *right* and the *normal*. The resulting vectors will be perpendicular to the right and the normal and can now be used to position the vertices by adding and/or subtracting them to the origin.

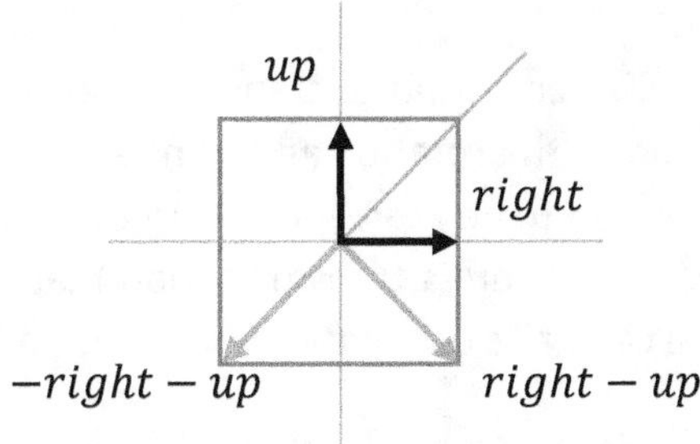

Figure *42* - Generation of a quad using basis vectors.

Now we will have generated the geometry for a unit quad, the next step will be to render it. Before we render it we will need to know what the behavior we expect for this quad, if the quad is a world-space object, we can use a world space transformation that will orient it and place it at the desired location, however, there are more ways in which we can transform quads that are useful, particularly in the context of user interface development.

The default case will be to transform the quad with a user provided transformation matrix. The quad's world transformation matrix is passed through the *quad::Draw* function and then sent to the vertex buffer.

3.12.1.1 Screen Aligned Quad

Often we need to display information within the game universe, but we need to make sure it is always visible to the player, this is usually the case for user interface elements that highlight game objects, such as loot or parts of the universe that are interactive.

The quad generation is no different from a standard quad, in fact, we can reuse the same code and add a flag to the quad object that will make the quad screen aligned. We will perform the alignment of the quad at the moment we draw it, it is at this point in which we will have the most up to date view matrix, which we need to compute the direction vector to the camera.

The camera's view matrix is used to transform vertices from world-space into view-space, it holds the rotation and translation magnitudes by which vertices are transformed to be represented in view space. The inverse view matrix represents the camera's transformation matrix, this is the world-space matrix of the camera's orientation and position in the world.

Given the view matrix:

$$M_v$$

We will need to calculate the inverse view matrix, which we will use to extract the camera's world space position p from.

$$M_v^{-1}$$

$$p = \begin{bmatrix} {M_v^{-1}}_{3,0} \\ {M_v^{-1}}_{3,1} \\ {M_v^{-1}}_{3,2} \end{bmatrix}$$

With the camera's world space position we can now calculate the direction vector from the quad's world space position q to the camera's p.

$$\hat{v} = |q - p|$$

The direction vector $\hat{v}$ is also the quad's normal vector, given the normal vector $\hat{v}$ we can construct the orthonormal basis by computing the cross product of the normal vector with the camera view's up vector, this will give us a perpendicular vector we will call the right vector.

$$\hat{u} = \begin{bmatrix} M_{v1,0} \\ M_{v1,1} \\ M_{v1,2} \end{bmatrix}$$

We then use the *up* vector to compute the *right*.

$$\hat{r} = \hat{v} \times \hat{u}$$

Now we have the basis vectors complete and with the position of the quad, we can construct the screen aligned transform.

$$S = \begin{bmatrix} \hat{r}_x & \hat{u}_x & \hat{v}_x & 0 \\ \hat{r}_y & \hat{u}_y & \hat{v}_y & 0 \\ \hat{r}_z & \hat{u}_z & \hat{v}_z & 0 \\ p_x & p_y & p_z & 1 \end{bmatrix}$$

This will be the quad's world transformation we will pass to the graphics device when we want to render.

```
matrix inverseView = matrix::Invert(view);
vector3 v = world.Translation() - inverseView.Translation();
v.Normalize();
vector3 right = v.Cross(view.Up());

transform = matrix::Create(right, view.Up(), v, world.Translation());
```

3.12.1.2 World Oriented Quad

At times we want to render quads oriented to the world itself, unlike a screen aligned quad, the world oriented quad's transformation does not need to be updated to maintain it facing the camera, instead, any world space direction vector may be used as the quad's normal which we will use to build the basis around this axis.

In this case since the position and orientation of the camera is irrelevant, we do not need to calculate the inverse view matrix, rather, any direction vector $\hat{v}$ can be provided.

Given the quad's normal vector $\hat{v}$ we will compute the orthonormal basis against the world's up default direction.

$$\hat{u} = \begin{bmatrix} 0 \\ 1 \\ 0 \end{bmatrix}$$

Computing the cross product of the quad's normal with the world's up direction we will compute the right vector $\hat{r}$.

$$\hat{r} = \hat{v} \times \hat{u}$$

And finally we will use both the quad's normal and the newly computed right vector to recalculate the up vector to ensure it is orthonormal.

$$\hat{u}' = \hat{r} \times \hat{v}$$

The procedure is illustrated in Figure 43.

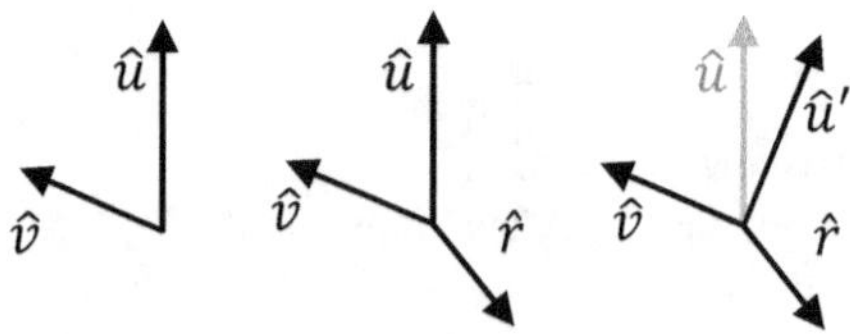

Figure *43* - Creating a world oriented orthonormal basis.

The final transformation matrix will be given by the orthonormal basis we just calculated with the translation given by the quad's world space position.

$$S = \begin{bmatrix} \hat{r}_x & \hat{u}'_x & \hat{v}_x & 0 \\ \hat{r}_y & \hat{u}'_y & \hat{v}_y & 0 \\ \hat{r}_z & \hat{u}'_z & \hat{v}_z & 0 \\ p_x & p_y & p_z & 1 \end{bmatrix}$$

This will be the transformation that we will pass down to the graphics device as the quad's world space transformation.

```
// forward is the unit vector that holds the quad's world orientation.

vector3 right = forward.Cross(vector3::UnitY);
vector3 up = right.Cross(forward);
up.Normalize();
matrix transform = matrix::Create(right, up, forward, m_position);
```

3.12.2 Cube

To generate a cube we will build upon the previous method of generating quads. A cube has six faces, each in the direction of a basis vector. We will use this fact to build one quad per direction or face normal.

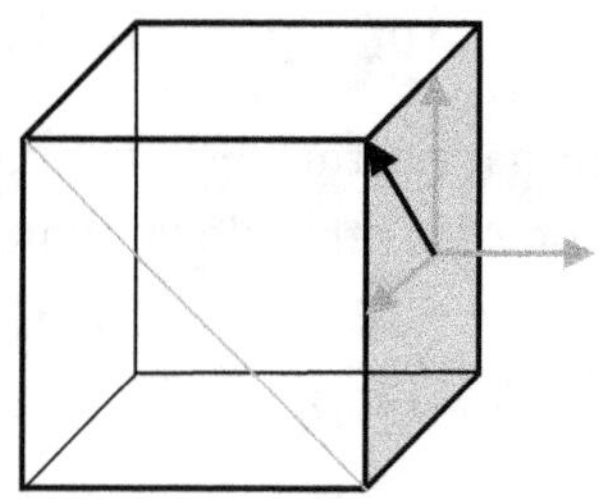

Figure *44* - For each face we use the face normal to create the basis, we then calculate the position of each vertex.

As before, we will store four vertices per quad in the vertex buffer, indexed by six indices representing two triangles.

```cpp
const math::vector3 normals[] = {
    math::vector3(0, 0, 1),
    math::vector3(0, 0, -1),
    math::vector3(1, 0, 0),
    math::vector3(-1, 0, 0),
    math::vector3(0, 1, 0),
    math::vector3(0, -1, 0),
};

const math::vector2 texcoords[] = {
    math::vector2(1, 0),
    math::vector2(1, 1),
    math::vector2(0, 1),
    math::vector2(0, 0)
};

vertex_default vertices[6 * 4];
unsigned short indices[6 * 6];

for (int i = 0; i < 6; ++i )
{
```

```cpp
    math::vector3 normal = normals[i];
    math::vector3 basis = (i >= 4) ? math::vector3::UnitZ : math::vector3::UnitY;

    math::vector3 side1 = normal.Cross( basis );
    math::vector3 side2 = normal.Cross( side1);

    const int vertexIndex0 = i * 4 + 0;
    const int vertexIndex1 = i * 4 + 1;
    const int vertexIndex2 = i * 4 + 2;
    const int vertexIndex3 = i * 4 + 3;

    vertices[vertexIndex0] = vertex_default( normal - side1 - side2, color::WHITE,
texcoords[0]);
    vertices[vertexIndex1] = vertex_default( normal - side1 + side2, color::WHITE,
texcoords[1]);
    vertices[vertexIndex2] = vertex_default( normal + side1 + side2, color::WHITE,
texcoords[2]);
    vertices[vertexIndex3] = vertex_default( normal + side1 - side2, color::WHITE,
texcoords[3]);

    indices[i* 6 + 0] = vertexIndex0;
    indices[i* 6 + 1] = vertexIndex1;
    indices[i* 6 + 2] = vertexIndex2;
    indices[i* 6 + 3] = vertexIndex0;
    indices[i* 6 + 4] = vertexIndex2;
    indices[i* 6 + 5] = vertexIndex3;
}
```

First we will define an array of face normals, these are unit vectors in each of the possible directions each of the cube's faces can be in. Next, we keep an array with the possible texture coordinates for each quad, this allow us to index the vertex coordinates as we build the cube.

We will need 24 vertices, this is 6 faces times 4 vertices per face and we will need 36 indices, this is 6 faces times 6 indices per face, we create two arrays that will hold this data. We iterate over the number of faces, taking each of the face normals as our direction vector to calculate the quad, the next line may seem a little confusing:

```cpp
math::vector3 basis = (i >= 4) ? math::vector3::UnitZ : math::vector3::UnitY;
```

We cannot use *UnitY* as the basis when using the face normals: normals[4] and normals[5] because the cross product of a vector against itself would be a zero vector, which would fail to create the basis we are looking for, so for these two face normals we replace the basis vector by *UnitZ*, this will ensure we will get a perpendicular vector as the result of the cross product against the face normal.

Having determined the basis, we can calculate the sides for the face, this is done by computing the cross product between the face normal and the basis, and then the cross product of the face normal against the recently computed side.

```
math::vector3 side1 = normal.Cross( basis );
math::vector3 side2 = normal.Cross( side1 );
```

Having the sides we can now calculate the vertices in the same way as we calculate the geometry for a quad, with one extra step, we need to add in the normal vertex to be certain that the vertex is offset in the direction of the face we are computing.

```
const int vertexIndex0 = i * 4 + 0;
vertices[vertexIndex0] = vertex_default( normal - side1 - side2, color::WHITE,
texcoords[0]);
```

We precompute each of the vertex indices because we will use them later, it is always important to avoid performing the same calculation multiple times, in particular within a loop. Finally since we have already calculated the vertex indices for each of the face vertices, we just need to map them into the proper position within the index buffer.

```
indices[i* 6 + 0] = vertexIndex0;
indices[i* 6 + 1] = vertexIndex1;
indices[i* 6 + 2] = vertexIndex2;
indices[i* 6 + 3] = vertexIndex0;
indices[i* 6 + 4] = vertexIndex2;
indices[i* 6 + 5] = vertexIndex3;
```

3.12.3 Pyramid / Cone

A cone is made up by creating a circle with a vertex in the middle then extruding that middle vertex by some distance, if we lower the resolution enough on a cone we end up with a cone with four sides, or a pyramid.

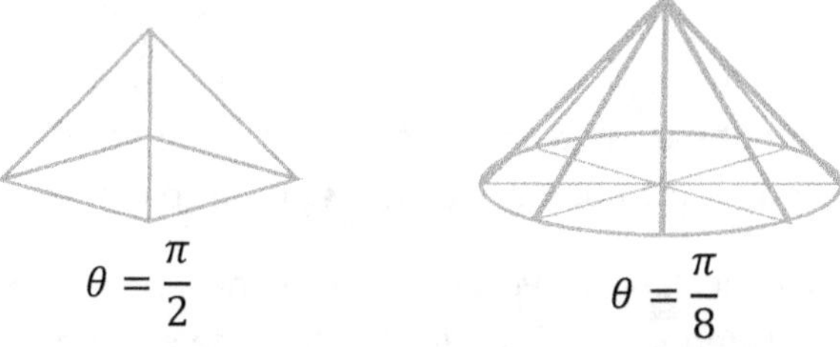

Figure 45 - A pyramid and a cone can be generated with the same algorithm.

The first piece of information we will need to create a cone is the angle.

$$\{\theta \in \mathbb{R} \mid 0 < \theta \leq \pi\}$$

The smaller the angle, the smoother the cone; as the angle becomes larger the cone will lose resolution, so that if we need to produce a pyramid we would choose $\frac{\pi}{2}$ as the angle. An angle of π will produce a flat triangle.

The first step will be to calculate the number of vertices we will need, for the base of the cone we use a circle cut up into pieces by the angle θ, from this we can determine that the number of vertices x will be:

$$x = \frac{\theta}{2\pi} + 3$$

We need three additional vertices, one will be the origin, set at the center of the circle which we will use to cap the cone, the other one is the top vertex, and the last one is used to duplicate the closing vertex. Without this duplicated vertex the texture coordinates would not be correct and the texture mapping would have artifacts.

Setting the origin and top vertices is trivial and we can do it right away.

```cpp
const int numVertices = (360 / degrees) + 3;
vertex_default vertices[numVertices];

vertices[0] = vertex_default(math::vector3::UnitY, color::WHITE, math::vector2(0.5f, 1.f));
vertices[numVertices - 1] = vertex_default(-math::vector3::UnitY, color::WHITE,
math::vector2(0.5f, 0.f));
```

Notice in this case we opt for working in degrees, it provides a more straightforward input parameter for users and it also simplifies using loops as we avoid doing floating point calculations at the cost of some precision.

The next step is to calculate the vertices of the cone's circle, we iterate over a full circle in increments of θ, and we calculate the x, z coordinates, the y coordinate will remain fixed at -1, which is where we set the origin.

```cpp
for ( int i = 0, j = 1; i <= 360; i += degrees, ++j )
{
    const float theta = math::DegreesToRadians(i);
    const float x = sinf(theta);
    const float z = cosf(theta);
    vertices[j] = vertex_default(math::vector3(x, -1.f, z), color::WHITE, math::vector2((j %
2) == 0 ? 0.f : 1.f, 0.f));
}
```

We now have all the vertices that will make up the cone, the next step is to calculate the indices for the triangles that will make up the sides of the cone as well as the cap.

The number of indices will be three times the number of vertices for the sides plus the three time the number of vertices for the cap (the cap has the same amount of faces as the sides).

```cpp
unsigned short indices[2 * (numVertices * 3)];
```

The sides and the cap share the same vertices, the only thing that changes is the first vertex, we can calculate the indices all within the same loop.

```
const int offset = (numVertices - 2) * 3;
for (unsigned short i = 0, j = 0; i < (numVertices - 2) * 3; i += 3, ++j )
{
    indices[i + 0] = 0;
    indices[i + 1] = j + 1;
    indices[i + 2] = j + 2;

    indices[i + offset + 0] = (numVertices - 1);
    indices[i + offset + 1] = indices[i + 1];
    indices[i + offset + 2] = indices[i + 2];
}
```

All the sides have one vertex in common, they all reference the top vertex, and this is why the first index for all the sides is 0. We also need to make certain that if we reach the end of the cone we need to wrap around the index to make sure it is properly closed. The cap uses the same indices with the exception of the first index, which references the origin vertex we stored at vertices[numVertices-1].

A note on texture mapping, the texture mapping applied is a per-face mapping, the top of the cone maps to U:0.5, V:0 and each face's bottom vertices will range from 0 to 1. There are different ways to apply texture mapping to a cone, which one to use will depend on the feature being developed. A cylindrical texture mapping algorithm may give better results.

3.12.4 Ellipsoid / Sphere

A sphere is a very useful primitive to be render during the game's development, it can be used to display information that is not normally visible, like an object's bounding volume, a point in world space, a point light, we can even project spheres from world space onto screen space, one useful application may be to represent nodes in an object hierarchy as spheres.

The algorithm to generate a sphere's mesh works by separating a sphere into vertical segments, we can think of these as the rings that make up the sphere from top to bottom, then each ring is divided into horizontal segments, these for the connections between rings to form the triangles around the sphere, the vertical segments, represent the latitude while the horizontal segments the longitude.

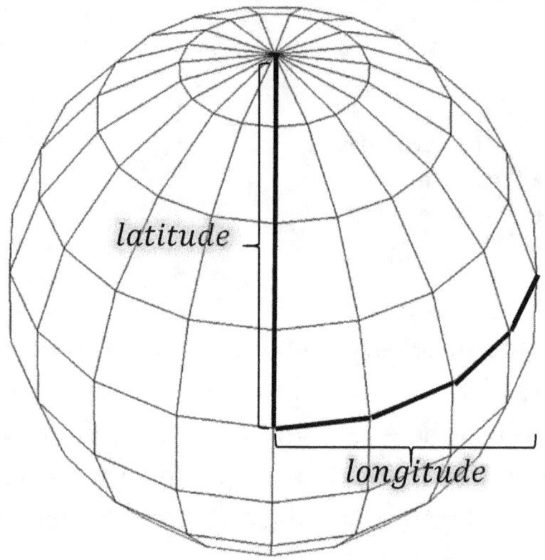

The user can control the smoothness of the sphere by providing the number of latitudinal segments, and we will set twice as many longitudinal segments as there are latitudinal.

We will begin by generating the vertex data for the sphere, this involves iterating over the latitude where we calculate the polar coordinates for the latitudinal ring. Then we will iterate over the longitudinal segments generating all the vertices along the ring.

Given the number of latitudinal segments n the latitude φ of each segment i will be given by:

$$\varphi_i = i * \frac{\pi}{n} - \left(\frac{\pi}{2}\right)$$

We then calculate the polar coordinates for the latitude,

$$\Delta\varphi_y = \sin \varphi_i$$

$$\Delta\varphi_{xz} = \cos \varphi_i$$

The $\Delta\varphi_y$ coordinate will give us the coordinate in the **y** axis for all the vertices in the current ring, the $\Delta\varphi_{xz}$ represents the distance from the center of the sphere to the current ring, a ratio of the radius for the current ring.

Then we will iterate over the longitude segments m creating the vertices, the longitude λ of each segment j is given by:

$$\lambda_j = 2\pi \cdot j$$

We also calculate the polar coordinates for the longitude, scaling them by the radius of the current ring given by $\Delta\varphi_{xz}$.

$$\Delta\lambda_x = \sin\lambda_j \cdot \Delta\varphi_{xz}$$

$$\Delta\lambda_z = \cos\lambda_j \cdot \Delta\varphi_{xz}$$

The vertex location is then given by:

$$p = \{\Delta\lambda_x, \Delta\varphi_y, \Delta\lambda_z\}$$

During the geometry generation we can also calculate the texture coordinates, the vertical texture coordinate **v** can be calculated during the latitude iteration and is given by the inverse factor of the latitude and the number or latitudinal segments.

$$v = 1 - \frac{i}{n}$$

The **u** coordinate is given by the ratio of the current longitudinal segment to the number of segments.

$$u = \frac{j}{m}$$

For convenience we can use an STL vector to store the generated vertices and use it to create the vertex buffer.

```cpp
const float radius = 0.5f; // We are creating a unit sphere

const unsigned short verticalSegments = 20;
const unsigned short horizontalSegments = verticalSegments * 2;
for (size_t i = 0; i <= verticalSegments; ++i)
{
    const float v = 1.f - static_cast<float>(i) / verticalSegments;
```

```cpp
const float latitude = (i * math::Pi / verticalSegments) - math::HalfPi;

const float dy = sinf(latitude);
const float dxz = cosf(latitude);

for (size_t j = 0; j <= horizontalSegments; ++j)
{
    const float u = static_cast<float>(j) / horizontalSegments;
    const float longitude = j * math::TwoPi / horizontalSegments;

    const float dx = sinf(longitude) * dxz;
    const float dz = cosf(longitude) * dxz;

    math::vector3 p = math::vector3(dx, dy, dz);
    math::vector2 textureCoord = math::vector2(u, v);

    vertex_default v(p, color::WHITE, textureCoord, p * radius);
    vertices.push_back(v);
}
}
```

The next part of the sphere generation is to calculate the connectivity information, the indices. The connectivity is done by joining two latitudinal rings by triangles.

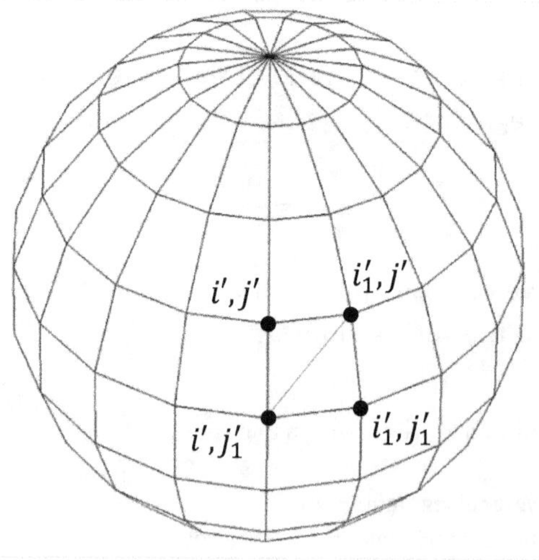

Figure 46 - Indexing of a sphere's vertices.

We iterate over each of the latitudinal segments and for each of them we will iterate over all the longitudinal segments, generating two triangles each time, the triangles will be given by the six indices:

$$i' = i \cdot m$$

$$i'_1 = (i + 1) \cdot m$$

$$j'_1 = (j + 1) \bmod (m + 1)$$

When calculating the vertices along the longitude we will at some point reach the end, when this happens we will wrap around and grab the first vertex to close the ring. The indices to the two triangles are given by:

$$t_0 = i' + j \qquad\qquad t_3 = i' + j'_1$$

$$t_1 = i'_1 + j \qquad\qquad t_4 = i'_1 + j$$

$$t_2 = i' + j'_1 \qquad\qquad t_5 = i'_1 + j'_1$$

As a convenience we can use an STL vector to store the indices that we can later use to build the index buffer.

```cpp
unsigned short stride = horizontalSegments + 1;
for (unsigned short i = 0; i < verticalSegments; ++i)
{
    for (unsigned short j = 0; j <= horizontalSegments; ++j)
    {
        const unsigned short i1 = i + 1;
        const unsigned short j1 = (j + 1) % stride;

        const unsigned short ip = i * stride;
        const unsigned short np = i1 * stride;

        indices.push_back(ip + j);
        indices.push_back(np + j);
        indices.push_back(ip + j1);

        indices.push_back(ip + j1);
        indices.push_back(np + j);
        indices.push_back(np + j1);
    }
}
```

3.12.5 Matrix Axes

During development it is often very useful to render the transformation matrix for any object in the game world. Typically the axes are drawn using the same convention used for colors, RGB, for R we render the x axis red, for G we render the y axis green and for B we render the z axis blue. We render the matrix axes using line primitives, and because we want to put our newfound knowledge to good use, we will cap each axis' with a cone to make an arrow.

The goal is that given a transformation matrix, we will draw its basis vectors.

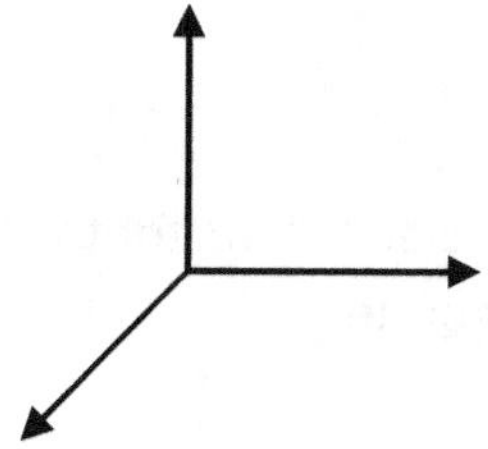

Figure *47* - A visual representation of a transformation matrix.

The first part is generating the geometry for the axis lines, we need 3 lines, consisting of two vertices each, this is to allow us to color each line independently, as we saw before, we will represent the axes X,Y,Z by the colors R,G,B respectively.

```
vertex_default vertices[6];
// x-axis
vertices[0] = vertex_default(math::vector3::Zero, color::RED);
vertices[1] = vertex_default(math::vector3::UnitX, color::RED);

// y-axis
vertices[2] = vertex_default(math::vector3::Zero, color::GREEN);
vertices[3] = vertex_default(math::vector3::UnitY, color::GREEN);
```

```
// z-axis
vertices[4] = vertex_default(math::vector3::Zero, color::BLUE);
vertices[5] = vertex_default(math::vector3::UnitZ, color::BLUE);
```

We will create a vertex buffer with these vertices and this will be used to render the axis lines. If we wanted, we could stop here and only display the axes as three color-coded lines, but we can use our newfound knowledge and cap each line with a pyramid, or a cone (though, a pyramid has fewer faces).

Since our cone object is by default a unit cone, we only need to create one instance of it that we will render three times, one per axis. We will need to transform the cone three times to set it at the correct position on the axis and we will rotate it so it points outwards, like an arrow, we will start by declaring the cone's transformation.

```
math::matrix coneTransform = math::matrix::Identity;
```

For the x-axis, we will want to roll the cone so its tip points outwards from the x-axis, given that the cone initially points up in the y-axis, we need to roll it by $\pi/2$ and then translate it by one in the x-axis direction. We will fix the scale of the cone to 10% of its initial value, this is purely cosmetic and could be exposed as a configurable value.

```
coneTransform = math::matrix::CreateRotationZ(math::Pi/2);
coneTransform.Scale(0.1f);
coneTransform.Translate( math::vector3::UnitX );
```

Now that the cone is rotated and translated into position, still within local space, we will draw the cone, but we also must make sure we transform the cone into world space, this is done by multiplying the *coneTransform* matrix we just created by the world transform passed into the Draw function.

```
m_cone.Draw( coneTransform * world , view, projection, nullptr, render::color::RED);
```

We then do the same operation for each of the cones, except for the z-axis cone that needs to be rotated to point down the negative z-axis, for this we rotate it by $-\frac{\pi}{2}$ in x, and $-\frac{\pi}{2}$ in z.

```
coneTransform = math::matrix::Identity;
coneTransform.Scale(0.1f);
coneTransform.Translate(math::vector3::UnitY );
m_cone.Draw( coneTransform * world, view, projection, nullptr, render::color::GREEN);

coneTransform = math::matrix::CreateRotationX(-math::Pi/2) *
math::matrix::CreateRotationZ(-math::Pi/2);
coneTransform.Scale(0.1f);
coneTransform.Translate(math::vector3::UnitZ);
m_cone.Draw( coneTransform * world, view, projection, nullptr, render::color::BLUE);
```

To a programmer developing transformation hierarchies as we will do in a later chapter, this can be a very useful development and debugging tool, allowing us to see where our transformations are and how they are oriented.

3.12.6 World Space Text

One feature that is very useful as a development aid during a game's production but that is often a game feature is the ability to render text in world space. Some features require text to be rendered screen aligned which is useful to display information that is visible to the players regardless of their view direction, for example items that can be picked up are often labeled with screen aligned text that shows the name, type and quantity of an item, it is also useful for game developers during production to label areas of interest or states, modern augmented reality displays are done using view aligned text.

Another option is to display text oriented in the game world, this option can be used to label the physical world without regard to the player's view direction.

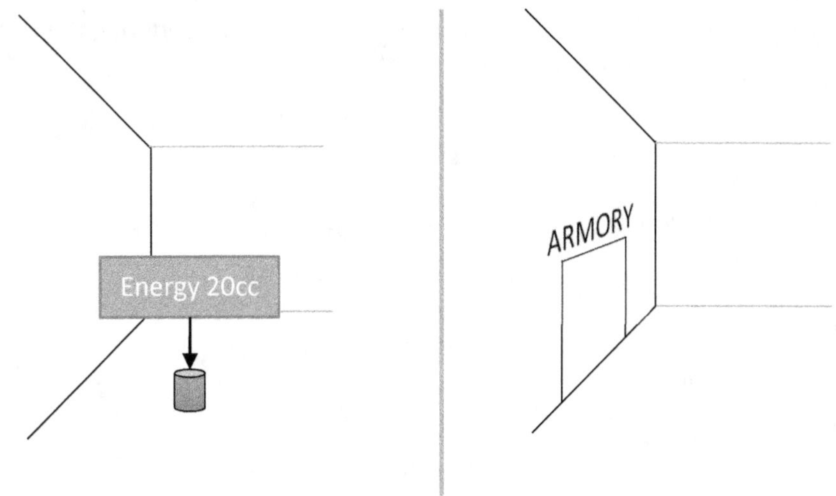

Figure *48* - On the left, a screen aligned text label, on the right a world oriented text label.

Whichever way we choose to display the text, the first step is to bring the text into a format that can be mapped onto 3D geometry. One way to do this is to render the text into a texture, then create and transform a quad into the position and orientation desired and apply the render target that contains the text as the quad's texture.

We will construct an object called text which we will use to render text in world space, the first step will be to create a render target large enough to hold the text required. If the text is static, meaning it will not change after construction, then the process is straightforward, measure the size of the text to render and use its dimensions to create the render target. If the text can change however, we cannot use the measured size as the size of the render target, it would need to be created to a specified maximum size, and any text that overflows the render target would get clipped.

It is important to query the graphics device for the capability of creating non-power of two textures, if the hardware does not support them, we will need to calculate the minimum power of two size that will fit the text, this may lead to wasted texture space, we will see a strategy for reusing texture space for text a bit later.

Rendering the text happens in two parts, the first part is rendering the text itself onto the render target.

```
m_device->SetRenderTarget(m_renderTarget);

m_spriteBatch->Begin(DirectX::SpriteSortMode_Deferred);
{
    m_font->DrawString(m_spriteBatch.get(), m_text.c_str(), math::vector2::Zero,
m_color, 0);
}
m_spriteBatch->End();

m_device->ResetRenderTarget();
```

We set the device's active render target to the one we created and we then render the text into it, we render it to the position 0,0 which means it will be rendered onto the renter target's top left corner. After we have finished drawing, we reset the device's render target to its default, the frame buffer.

At this point, we have a texture in memory that contains the text we rendered in it, so we can render a quad and apply this render target as its texture. We can now decide how we want to draw the quad, whether it will be world oriented or screen aligned.

For a world oriented quad, in addition to the world space position of the text, we can provide a direction vector, a normal. Given a normal, we will call it the forward vector, we can create the world oriented transformation matrix to apply to the quad as described in **World Oriented Quad.**

```
forward = m_normal;
forward.Normalize();
right = forward.Cross(vector3::UnitY);
up = right.Cross(forward);
transform = matrix::Create(right, up, forward, m_position);
```

If we wish the text to be screen aligned, we can toggle the *ViewAlign* flag on the quad object (see **Screen Aligned Quad**) and we then only need to provide a matrix with the translation.

```
if ( m_viewAlign )
{
    m_quad->ViewAlign() = true;
    transform = math::matrix::CreateTranslation(position);
}
```

Finally we call the Draw function for the quad and we pass the desired transform and we use the render target that we created.

```
m_quad->Draw(transform, view, projection, m_renderTarget);
```

One thing to consider when rendering in-world geometry, is whether we want it to write its depth data or not, for screen-aligned text, we don't want to write into the depth buffer, this would cause text to get depth sorted, possibly intersecting with the world's geometry as its alignment changes to face the camera. For world-oriented text, we can use the default behavior of the depth buffer. At the start of the depth test the value of the depth buffer is set to the largest possible value, as each polygon is rendered, it is tested against the corresponding value for each pixel in the depth buffer, if the depth value of our text quad is smaller than the value stored in the depth buffer, then this depth value is stored in the depth buffer, this will treat our world-oriented text as part of the scene and it will become occluded by geometry (such as players, and other game objects) as they are drawn.

As it is this method is likely to have some performance implications. Every time some text is rendered we are switching render targets, drawing, resetting the render target then drawing again. While it doesn't sound like much, these context changes may have a significant performance cost depending on the platform.

It would be best to batch all the text that is to be drawn in-world, render it all into a single texture and then use this texture to render the world-space quads, which we can also batch into a single vertex/index buffer. This gives us the ability to render some or all of the in-world text in a single draw call.

3.13 Binary Space Packing

Binary space packing is the action of taking some area of space and subdividing it with the goal of finding the best organization of data within the available space. This is an optimization intended to reduce the number of context switching in the graphics device, changing rendering states, render targets, and issuing multiple draw calls all add up to the overall time cost of the game's frame. For world space text rendering, we can take advantage of this binary space packing algorithm that will allow us to batch as much as text as we can into a single render target in order to render some or all of it in a single draw call.

We will proceed by analyzing the use of this binary space packing algorithm as applied to texture packing. In this case, we have a finite amount of 2D space in the form of a texture, and we wish to store rectangles of arbitrary widths and heights into it.

The first step in creating the binary space partition is when we insert some amount of data in the shape of a rectangle. We will divide, or partition the free texture space by two as many times as needed until we can fit the rectangle, or until we find that it is impossible to fit it. If we are unable to fit the rectangle into the available space, we would have to incur the cost of creating additional render targets, or perform individual draw calls for any items that did not fit. Given a large enough render target, this situation should not occur frequently.

Figure 49 illustrates the way the algorithm will behave when we add a smaller texture into the larger texture space.

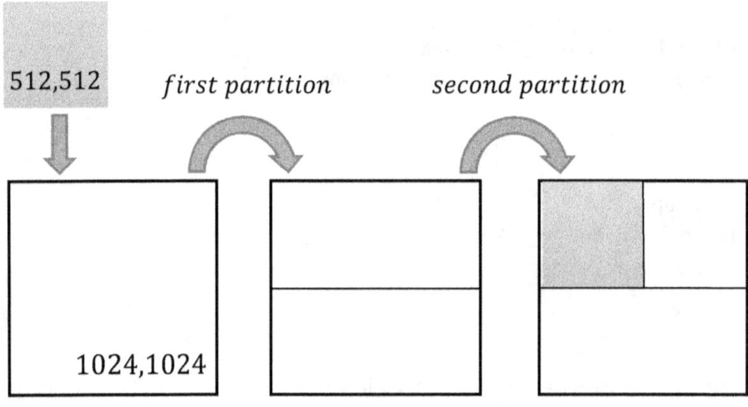

Figure *49* - Inserting a 512x512 texture into a larger texture by using binary space partition.

First, we will determine that there is no exact fit within the texture, so we will split the texture vertically using the items' height and trying to fit it again into the first child in the new partition, if it fits vertically, the next step is to try and fit it horizontally, the process is the same, it will continue partitioning the space horizontally until the object fits, or until it determines that it cannot fit.

We will start by defining the node, a node will represent an area of space, it may be empty, in which case it may be partitioned if necessary, or it may be in use, which means there is a texture in it. A node may also be a leaf, this means it is un-partitioned space (it has no children nodes).

```cpp
class node
{
public:

    node() : m_isEmpty(true) { }

    std::shared_ptr<node>& Child(int i) { return m_children[i]; }

    const bool IsLeaf() const
    {
        return m_children[0] == nullptr &&
                m_children[0] == m_children[1];
    }
```

```
    bool& IsEmpty() { return m_isEmpty; }
    math::rectangle& Rectangle() { return m_rectangle; }

private:

    bool m_isEmpty;
    std::shared_ptr<node> m_children[2];
    math::rectangle m_rectangle;
};
```

The entry point for the algorithm is inserting a new rectangle into the texture, it is a recursive process that begins by creating the root partition if one does not yet exist.

```
std::shared_ptr<node> Insert(const math::rectangle& rectangle)
{
    if ( m_root == nullptr )
    {
        m_root = std::shared_ptr<node>(new node() );
        m_root->Rectangle() = rectangle;
        return m_root;
    }

    return Insert(m_root, rectangle);
}
```

The algorithm lives within the private Insert function which takes two parameters, a node and the area that is being added, if successful, the algorithm will return the node in which the rectangle was added, if it fails it will return *nullptr* and it will be up to the caller to handle the error case.

```
std::shared_ptr<node> Insert(std::shared_ptr<node>& n, const math::rectangle&
rectangle)
{
    if ( !n->IsLeaf() ) {
        auto newNode = Insert( n->Child(0), rectangle );
        if ( newNode != nullptr )
            return newNode;

        return Insert(n->Child(1), rectangle);
```

```cpp
    }
    else
    {
        if ( !n->IsEmpty() )
            return nullptr;

        auto& parentRect = n->Rectangle();

        if ( rectangle.Width() > parentRect.Width() || rectangle.Height() >
parentRect.Height() )
            return nullptr;

        // If it fits perfectly, we found our node
        if ( math::IsEqual(parentRect.Width(), rectangle.Width() ) &&
math::IsEqual(parentRect.Height(), rectangle.Height() ) )   {
            n->IsEmpty() = false;
            return n;
        }

        n->Child(0) = std::shared_ptr<node>(new node());
        n->Child(1) = std::shared_ptr<node>(new node());

        auto w = parentRect.Width() - rectangle.Width();
        auto h = parentRect.Height() - rectangle.Height();

        if ( w > h )
        {
            n->Child(0)->Rectangle() = math::rectangle::MakeRectangle(parentRect.Left(),
parentRect.Top(), parentRect.Left() + w, parentRect.Bottom());

            n->Child(1)->Rectangle() = math::rectangle::MakeRectangle(parentRect.Left() +
w, parentRect.Top(), parentRect.Right(), parentRect.Bottom());
        }
        else
        {
            n->Child(0)->Rectangle() = math::rectangle::MakeRectangle(parentRect.Left(),
parentRect.Top(), parentRect.Right(), parentRect.Top() + h);

            n->Child(1)->Rectangle() = math::rectangle::MakeRectangle(parentRect.Left(),
parentRect.Top() + h, parentRect.Right(), parentRect.Bottom());
        }
        return Insert(n->Child(0), rectangle);
    }
}
```

At the beginning we check if the node is not a leaf, if it is not, it means it has children, so we will recursively call Insert with the first child node and attempt to fit the rectangle there, if it fails, we will call Insert with the second child and we will return whether successful or not.

If the node is a leaf, then we can begin to check if our rectangle can fit in it, or if we need to partition the area. The first thing we check is if this node is already in use, meaning it's not empty, if so, there's nothing to do and we return *nullptr*. The next checks are for fit, if the rectangle we are inserting is larger than the area available to us, we cannot continue, but if the space is precisely the size that we are trying to insert, then we have found our node, we will mark it as no longer empty and return it.

If none of the first conditions were met, it means we are in a larger area than can fit the item we are trying to add, so we will partition the space. We create the two child nodes, and we compute the difference in size between them, this allows us to determine which way we will create the partition. If the rectangle is wider than it is tall, we will partition the space horizontally, if the rectangle is taller than it is wide, we will partition the space vertically.

Once partitioned, we will recursively call Insert again using the first child we just created.

After each insertion into the binary space partition tree, we get a pointer to the node in which our texture was stored, only we haven't stored anything, and the best part is that we really don't need to. Once we insert a node into the bsp tree, we can query the tree for the texture coordinates of this node.

```cpp
const math::vector4 TextureCoordinates(const std::shared_ptr<node>& node) const
{
    auto width = m_root->Rectangle().Width();
    auto height = m_root->Rectangle().Height();
    const auto& rectangle = node->Rectangle();

    return math::vector4(rectangle.Left() / width, rectangle.Top() / height,
rectangle.Right() / width, rectangle.Bottom() / height );
}
```

These will be the normalized UV coordinates we will need to use to render the text into the render target.

The following pseudocode shows how the bsp tree information would need to be used anytime a world space text is added (it will not be rendered right away).

```
bsp_packer bsp;
auto rtWidth = m_renderTarget->Width();
auto rtHeight = m_renderTarget->Height();

// Insert the root node into the BSP tree
bsp.Insert(math::rectangle(0,0,rtWidth,rtHeight));
```

The first part is creating the BSP tree somewhere, its root node's size must match the render target's size. The next part would be to set the render target active on the graphics device and proceed to add all the world space text that we wish to draw in this frame.

```
m_device->SetRenderTarget(m_renderTarget);
for ( auto& txt : worldSpaceTextList )
{
    textBatch.Add(txt, rtWidth, rtHeight);
}
```

The Add function will measure the screen space extents of the text and insert a rectangle of that size into the BSP, if successful, we will calculate the UV coordinates for that node and use them to calculate the x,y position into the render target into which we will render the text.

```
void text::Add(const std::wstring& txt, size_t rtWidth, size_t rtHeight)
{
    auto size = m_font->MeasureString(txt.c_str());
    auto& node = bsp.Insert(rectangle(0, 0, size.x, size.y));

    if ( node != nullptr )
    {
        auto uv = bsp.TextureCoordinates(node);
```

```
        float x = uv.x() * rtWidth;
        float y = uv.y() * rtHeight;

        m_font->DrawString(m_spriteBatch.get(), txt.c_str(), math::vector2(x,y),
render::color::WHITE, 0);
    }
}
```

At this point there is only one thing missing, we still need to render the actual world space text, and we need to do so using the same UV coordinates that we have just used to store our text into the render target. In order to do this, we will need to extend the quad primitive to support UVs to be provided at render time, this can be done by modifying the vertex shader to receive scaling and bias parameters to remap the existing UVs.

3.14 DirectXTK

The DirectX ToolKit is a useful collection of classes that provide efficient and straightforward interfaces for writing Direct3D 11 applications in C++. To people with experience developing with XNA in C# these classes will be familiar.

This section will provide a light reference to the DirectX Toolkit to introduce the two most used objects in the example code, the *SpriteBatch* and the *SpriteFont*, these are two very useful classes that provide an efficient interface for rendering 2D elements and text.

3.14.1 SpriteBatch

A sprite batch as the name suggests allows us to batch 2D elements to be drawn at a time, it does a great job at abstracting a lot of the Direct3D low level code that can be daunting to manage. Roughly speaking a SpriteBatch allows us to draw a texture at some position on the screen by calling one of its Draw functions.

We start by calling Begin, where we can specify how we want our batch to be drawn, we can provide a sort mode, blend, sampler, depth/stencil states and rasterizer states as well as provide a custom set of shaders to use and a transformation matrix to be applied on the batch. This will save the state of the device and change it to the states we pass it, or use the defaults if no states are given.

We then can issue any number of Draw calls, there are different function overloads depending on what we need to draw. For a sprite sheet for example, we would use the overload that would allow us to specify a source rectangle, which would define the coordinates of a single sprite frame within the larger sprite sheet texture.

Once all the necessary draw calls have been issued we need to call End to close the rendering of the SpriteBatch, this will restore the device's state to the way it was before the call to Begin.

3.14.1.1 Device States

Calling Begin on a SpriteBatch allows us to set the device states we need when the batch is drawn, first we must specify when the device states need to be applied, this is done by specifying the SpriteSortMode.

Deferred (default)	Sprites will be drawn in the order the Draw calls were made when End is called, the devices states are applied just before drawing. This mode allows multiple SpriteBatch instances to issue Draw calls without the possibility of conflicting device states.
FrontToBack	Same as Deferred, except sprites are sorted by depth in front to back order before drawing, use this mode when drawing opaque sprites at varying depths.

BackToFront	Same as BackToFront, except sprites are sorted by depth in back to front order. Use this mode when rendering transparent sprites at varying depths.
Immediate	Graphics device settings are applied in the Begin call and sprites are drawn within each Draw call. To avoid the possibility of introducing conflicting device states, there can only be one active SpriteBatch instance.
Texture	Same as Deferred, except sprites are sorted by texture before drawing, this may improve performance when drawing non-overlapping sprites of uniform depth.

DirectXTK provides a group of preset states that we may use in the majority of situations, we access these through the CommonStates class.

```
DirectX::CommonStates states(device);
m_spriteBatch->Begin(DirectX::SpriteSortMode_Deferred, states.NonPremultiplied());
```

BlendState

The first parameter we need to provide to the Begin function is the BlendState. CommonStates gives us the following preset blend states:

Opaque	No alpha blending
AlphaBlend (default)	Premultiplied alpha blending, recall for premultiplied alpha blending, textures need to be preprocessed to multiply the alpha value with the respective pixel color.
Additive	Pixels colors are added, growing in intensity when pixels overlap.
NonPremultiplied	Conventional alpha blending, the alpha value is multiplied with the pixel's color at runtime, use this

	mode when textures have not been preprocessed to premultiply their alpha.

DepthStencilState

The next parameter controls how the sprite will interact with the depth stencil buffer.

DepthNone (default)	Do not use the depth stencil buffer. The rendered sprite data will not be applied into the depth stencil buffer.
DepthDefault	Enables using the depth stencil buffer, the sprite rendered will be written into the depth stencil buffer. Use this when rendering opaque
DepthRead	Enables using the depth stencil buffer in a read only way, the sprite will compare its depth value against the depth stencil buffer, but will not write into it.

SamplerState

The next parameter specifies the texture sampler's state, this defines which filtering option to use and the wrapping behavior of the sampler.

PointWrap	Point sampling with texture wrapping, texture wrapping controls the behavior of the texture mapping when it goes beyond the [0..1] range in texture space, causing the texture to be repeated.
PointClamp	Point sampling with texture clamping, when the values go beyond the [0..1] range in texture space it will use the nearest edge pixel.
LinearWrap	Linear filtering and texture wrapping.
LinearClamp (default)	Linear filtering and clamping.
AnisotropicWrap	Anisotropic filtering, good quality filtering with a performance cost and texture wrapping.

AnisotropicClamp	Anisotropic filtering with texture clamping.

RasterizerState

The final state parameter is the RasterizerState, this parameters specifies how the actual drawing, producing the final images in pixels will behave.

CullNone	No primitives will be culled, this means even back-facing primitives will be rendered.
CullClockwise	Any primitives with clockwise winding order will not be rendered.
CullCounterClockwise	Any primitives with counter-clockwise winding order will not be rendered.
Wireframe	Primitives will be rendered in wireframe.

Custom Shaders

It's possible to override the default shaders used by a sprite batch by providing a function that sets the new shaders to use on the device,

```cpp
spriteBatch->Begin(SpriteSortMode_Deferred, nullptr, nullptr, nullptr, nullptr, [&]
{
  deviceContext->PSSetShader(...);
  deviceContext->PSSetConstantBuffers(...);
  deviceContext->PSSetShaderResources(...);
});
```

Transform

The final parameter for Begin is a transform matrix that can be used to apply a global scale or translation, or depending on the way sprite batches are setup could allow for hierarchical transformations.

3.14.2 SpriteFont

This is a very useful class that wraps the necessary functionality to render text using different fonts. It's best to use the tool MakeSpriteFont included as part of DirectXTK to convert any font into the format needed by SpriteFont, on XNA this is done automatically during the building of a SpriteFont XML source, however, MakeSpriteFont is a console application that needs to be run manually to generate the desired font's data.

Once a font is provided, we use it to construct a SpriteFont object which has facilities for drawing strings and calculating the extents for text using the SpriteFont's font using the function MeasureString. Another useful function is GetLineSpacing, it allows us to know how much space the font requires vertically, it's useful when displaying rows of text.

A SpriteFont is used in conjunction with a SpriteBatch, when we wish to render a string of text onto the screen, we need to provide the sprite batch that will hold the sprites for each of the font's glyphs.

```cpp
std::unique_ptr<SpriteBatch> spriteBatch(new SpriteBatch(deviceContext));

std::unique_ptr<SpriteFont> spriteFont(new SpriteFont(device, L"font.spritefont"));

spriteBatch->Begin();

spriteFont->DrawString(spriteBatch.get(), L"Hello, world!", XMFLOAT2(x, y));

spriteBatch->End();
```

The DirectX toolkit is continually being developed and has support for rendering geometry, including 3D models. DirectXTK supports all the modern *Microsoft*® platforms.

You can read more about it at: directxtk.codeplex.com

3.15 Cinder

Cinder is a free, open source, multi-platform, C++ library for programming graphics, audio, networking and more. It's very easy to learn and very quick to begin developing on.

It is well designed and allows us to get up and running quickly by automating the project creation process.

The project code generated by *Cinder* shares many similarities with the way different examples in this book are presented. This makes it possible to use *Cinder* as a way to quickly work on user interface concepts without the steep learning curve and setup process required by other toolkits.

The generated project will use the OpenGL® API, this means some of the syntax or the process to prepare the geometry will be slightly different from the example code, however, *Cinder* provides a very rich library that already gives us many of the functions we have discussed. Armed with the knowledge of what these functions do and how they do it, we can focus on the implementation of user interface concepts.

```cpp
#include "cinder/app/AppNative.h"
#include "cinder/gl/gl.h"

using namespace ci;
using namespace ci::app;
using namespace std;

class UIPGApp : public AppNative {
  public:
    void setup();
    void update();
    void draw();

  private:

    CameraPersp m_camera;
};
```

```
void UIPGApp::setup()
{
    m_camera.setPerspective(60.0f, getWindowAspectRatio(), 5.0f, 3000.0f );
    m_camera.lookAt(Vec3f(0.f, 0.f, 10.f), Vec3f(0.f, 0.f, 0.f));
}

void UIPGApp::update() { }

void UIPGApp::draw()
{
    // clear out the window with black
    gl::clear( Color( 0, 0, 0 ) );

    // apply the camera's transformation matrices
    gl::setMatrices(m_camera);

    // render a unit sphere at the origin
    gl::drawSphere(Vec3f(0.f,0.f,0.f), 1.f, 24);
}

CINDER_APP_NATIVE(UIPGApp, RendererGl )
```

This is a complete, albeit simple example of a *Cinder* project that places a perspective camera at the 0,0,10 world space position, looking towards the origin. At the origin it renders a white sphere. While this is a very simple example, it does show how little code is required to begin implementing concepts or prototyping new ideas.

The *Cinder* library is far too extensive to present it in its entirety here, but it's definitely worth checking it out. As a beginner it will give you a great head start by providing a less intimidating experience, you can skip the complexity of configuring third party libraries and get right down to coding.

Read more about it here: http://libcinder.org/

4 User Interface Essentials

There are many technologies at our disposal when developing user interfaces, our choice of technology will depend on many factors. If we are working on a licensed game engine, there may already be some user interfaces technologies available to us, which may include user interface development middleware based on popular web authoring tools.

In this book we aim to present the core technologies we need to develop user interfaces when no existing user interface technology is available. And use this technology we develop as the framework upon which user interface features will be built.

4.1 Sprites

A sprite is a 2D image used to represent entities in games, typically animated to simulate some form of motion, like a character walking or to achieve certain special effects, like water or fire. Sprites can be used to create user interfaces as well, we can create sprites for buttons, knobs, elements of a radar, input cursor, and many other user interface elements that we may want to make dynamic and visually pleasing.

Sprites as a construct for user interfaces has the advantage that it gives artists a great deal of control over the look and feel of the UI, it is also painless to get a placeholder control in place that meets all the requirements, but may lack detailed animation frames. The disadvantages are that the overall video memory cost is higher, and that it may represent a significant amount of work for artists if the user interface is extensive or highly detailed.

While a sprite based approach may not yield the best results in terms of production performance, it serves as an introduction to a more advanced system of animation using timelines, key frames, transformations and interpolation curves to create complex animations, such a system is truly powerful as long as it has an authoring tool to go along with it. For the scope of this book and the example code, we will use sprites to create visually pleasing controls.

In the system we will implement a sprite is the entity that is animated and drawn on-screen. Each sprite is an instance, this means each sprite will keep its own animation state, two instances may be playing two different animations at the same time, yet the underlying data is the same. This avoid duplication of assets in memory, as long as the same sprite sheet is not loaded more than once.

4.1.1 Animation

A sprite's animation will be defined by specifying regions of a sprite sheet, each region we specify will be an animation frame and will be visible on-screen for some specified amount of time. This gives us the flexibility of creating sprites of varying sizes.

```cpp
class animation
{
public:
    animation()
        : m_time(0.f)
        , m_currentFrame(0)
    {}

    explicit animation(const std::wstring& name)
        : m_name(name)
        , m_time(0.f)
        , m_currentFrame(0)
    {   }

    frame& AddFrame(const math::rectangle& region, float duration)
    {
```

```cpp
        frame f(region, duration);
        m_frames.push_back(f);
        return m_frames.back();
    }

    bool& Loop() { return m_loop; }
    const frame& Frame(int index) const { return m_frames[index]; }
    const std::wstring& Name() const { return m_name; }
    size_t FrameCount() const { return m_frames.size(); }

private:

    std::wstring m_name;
    float m_time;
    bool m_loop;
    std::vector<frame> m_frames;
    size_t m_currentFrame;
    event_handler<animation&> m_onAnimationFinished;

};
```

The *animation* class will hold the information required to perform a sprite's animation. In order to support sprite instancing, the animation behavior will not be implemented as part of this class. Instead, we will have a specialized object whose responsibility will be to keep the animation state for a sprite.

4.1.1.1   Animation Track

In order to support sprite instancing, we introduce a class that will perform the animation based on the sprite's animation data, we can think of the sprite's animation data as read-only, while the animation track object is a live object that will advance a sprite instance's animation frames.

```cpp
class animation_track
{
public:
    explicit animation_track(const animation& anim)
```

```cpp
        : m_animation(anim)
        , m_currentFrame(0)
        , m_time(0.f)
    {}

    void Start(unsigned int frame=0)
    {
        if ( frame >= m_animation.FrameCount() )
            return;

        m_currentFrame = frame;
        auto& currentFrame = m_animation.Frame(m_currentFrame);
        m_time = currentFrame.Duration();
    }

    void Update(float deltaTime);

    const animation::frame& CurrentFrame() const { return
m_animation.Frame(m_currentFrame); }

private:

    float m_time;
    unsigned int m_currentFrame;
    const animation& m_animation;
};
```

The animation track is constructed with a given animation's data, we must call Start to specify the frame from which we want to begin animating, usually this will be the first frame.

The Update function is responsible for advancing the animation track each game frame.

```cpp
void animation_track::Update(float deltaTime)
{
    if ( m_animation.FrameCount() == 0 || (!m_animation.Loop() && m_currentFrame >
m_animation.FrameCount() ) )
    {
        return;
    }

    m_time -= deltaTime;
```

```cpp
if ( m_time <= 0.f )
{
    ++m_currentFrame;
    if ( m_currentFrame >= m_animation.FrameCount() )
    {
        if ( m_animation.Loop() )
        {
            m_currentFrame = 0;
        }
        else
        {
            m_onAnimationFinished.Invoke(this, *this);
        }
    }

    auto& currentFrame = m_animation.Frame(m_currentFrame);
    m_time = currentFrame.Duration();
}
}
```

The *m_time* variable is set to the current frame's duration, each game frame we decrement it, once it reaches zero or less we advance to the next frame. By default the sprite will loop back, however in some cases we may want to perform some "single shot" animations, so if we don't need to loop, we will fire an event to notify the user that the animation track has completed.

4.1.1.2   Animation Frame

An animation frame is defined by a region and a time. The region is a rectangle that defines some area within the sprite sheet, the time is the duration that this particular frame will be visible on-screen.

```cpp
class frame
{
public:

    frame(const math::rectangle& region, float duration)
        : m_region(region)
        , m_duration(duration)
    {}

    float Duration() const { return m_duration; }
    const math::rectangle& Region() const { return m_region; }

private:

    math::rectangle m_region;
    float m_duration;
};
```

The frame data will be configured after loading the sprite sheet and will be considered read-only at runtime.

4.1.2 Sprite Sheets

A sprite sheet is a single image that contains many frames for a given sprite, each collection of frames can be thought of as an 'animation', so a sprite sheet may contain different animations, for example a character sprite would likely contain animations for walking up/left/right/down, running, jumping, etc. In the case of user interface controls, such as a button, a spritesheet could contain animations that show when the button is in-focus, pressed or released.

The sprite sheet will contain the texture and the animation data required for drawing sprites on screen, it will also own the sprite batch object for the sprite to ensure that all instances of a given sprite will be batched together.

The sprite sheet will then serve as a factory of sprites, allowing to create as many instances of a given sprite sheet as we need.

```cpp
std::shared_ptr<sprite> Create()
{
    std::shared_ptr<sprite> newSprite = std::shared_ptr<sprite>(new sprite(*this));
    m_sprites.push_back(newSprite);
    return newSprite;
}
```

Given that the sprite sheet is responsible for holding a sprite's data, we will need a way to create animations.

```cpp
animation& CreateAnimation(std::wstring name, size_t& animationID)
{
    if ( GetAnimationID(name, animationID) )
    {
        return m_animations[animationID];
    }

    animation anim(name);
    m_animations.push_back(anim);
    animationID = m_animations.size()-1;
    m_animationIDMap[name] = animationID;

    return m_animations[animationID];
}
```

It is useful to give animations a name, as it makes them easier to refer to them, however, working with directly with strings, especially in situations that would demand a string comparison is not a good practice. So while we provide each animation with a name, this is mostly for information and debugging purposes (such as displaying the name of the animation a given sprite is playing at runtime), rather once we create an animation, we create an identifier and we store the animation's name in a map.

```cpp
bool GetAnimationID(const std::wstring& name, size_t& id)
{
    id = SIZE_MAX;

    if ( m_animationIDMap.find(name) == m_animationIDMap.end() )
    {
        // The animation does not exist in the map.
```

```
        return false;
    }

    id = m_animationIDMap[name];

    return true;
}
```

In retrieving the animation ID we will incur the cost of string comparisons, these will be done during the animation construction which should happen during the loading stage of the game. During runtime, when performance is critical, we will refer to the animation by its non-string ID.

The following code provides an example on how sprite sheets are loaded and animations can be created. This is a code driven example for simplicity, ideally this sort of construction could be done using data driven mechanisms, such as parsing an XML file.

```
auto spriteSheet = std::unique_ptr<render::spritesheet>(new render::spritesheet(m_core->GetDevice(), spritePath));

size_t defaultAnimID = SIZE_MAX;
auto& defaultAnim = m_spriteSheet->CreateAnimation(L"default", defaultAnimID);
defaultAnim.AddFrame(math::rectangle(0,0,200,200), 0.33f);
defaultAnim.AddFrame(math::rectangle(200,0,200,200), 0.33f);
defaultAnim.AddFrame(math::rectangle(400,0,200,200), 0.33f);

size_t pressedAnimID = SIZE_MAX;
auto& pressedAnim = m_spriteSheet->CreateAnimation(L"pressed", pressedAnimID);
pressedAnim.AddFrame(math::rectangle(0,200,200,200), 0.33f);
pressedAnim.AddFrame(math::rectangle(200,200,200,200), 0.33f);

auto sprite = m_spriteSheet->Create();
sprite->Play(defaultAnimID);
```

This would load a sprite sheet, which is a texture at the location specified by *spritePath*. It will then create two animations, default and pressed, the first one consists of three frames, each frame lasting one third of a second and bound by the region specified in the rectangle we pass in. Once the sprite sheet is created and its animations configured, we can create one or more sprites from it, each of which will be an instance capable of playing its own animations.

4.1.2.1 Animation Events

It is not always enough to play sprite animations, in the context of a game, we often want animations to cause damage to other entities at a precise point in the animation, for user interfaces we may want to play a sound, an animation or invoke a function.

To support this, we can provide events on the animation track which are invoked when a frame starts, another when the frame ends and for non-looping animations we can provide one when the animation is finished. This allows us to introduce custom functionality at precise moments during a sprite's animation.

```
sprite = m_spriteSheet->Create();

sprite->OnEnterFrame() += [&](void*, const animation_track & track)
{
    if ( track.FrameNumber() == 3 )
    { PlaySound(SOUND_SLIDE); }
};

sprite->OnExitFrame() += [&](void*, const animation_track& track)
{
    if ( track.IsLastFrame() )
    { PlaySound(SOUND_CLICK); }
};
```

In this example when the animation enters its third frame, it will play a "sliding" sound that may last the duration of a few of the sprite frames, when the animation reaches the last frame it will play a "clicking" sound.

4.2 CAMERAS

A camera in games is a useful device by which we can navigate the world and change the parameters by which we draw it. It is useful to think of cameras as entities that exist and can be moved and aimed throughout the game world, and for that we strive to create interfaces that are intuitive and straightforward to use.

Internally, a camera consists of not much more than two transformations, a projection transformation, which defines how geometry will be projected from 3D space onto the 2D screen, and the view matrix, this is a matrix that transforms geometry from world space into view space, we will see exactly what this means a bit further down.

A good camera implementation will provide users with enough features to allow them to place a camera and aim it in a variety of ways, in some situations it is useful to aim a camera by providing two locations, the camera's location and some target location to look at. In other cases the user may need to explicitly provide a world transform for the camera, another approach is to provide a location for the camera and a direction vector, more specialized cameras may provide even more useful ways to place, aim and even animate cameras.

4.2.1 Projection

A perspective projection matrix converts the viewing frustum into a cuboid shape in which the nearest plane is the plane that would appear closest to the screen and the farthest plane is larger, this is what gives the appearance of perspective as objects expand as they get closer to the near plane.

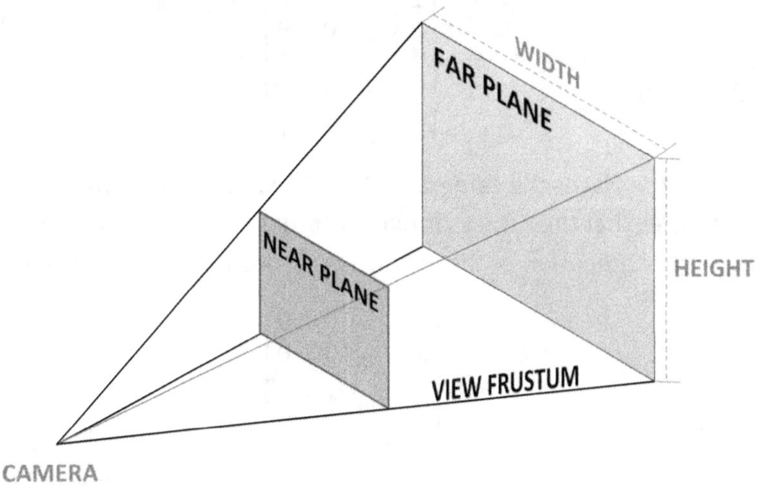

Figure 50 - Perspective projection frustum.

Any object that lies before the near plane, or beyond the far plane will not be considered for rendering. Objects that do not intersect the view frustum may also be ignored during rendering as they will not be visible.

In addition to culling objects from rendering, the view frustum also serves to transform the object's geometry to give the impression of perspective.

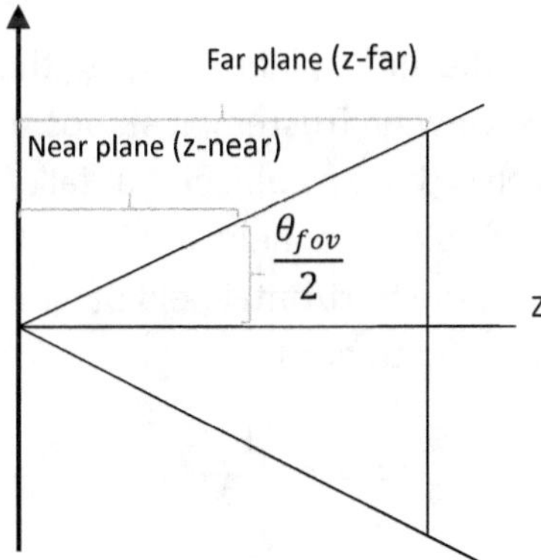

Figure 51 - Top down view of the perspective projection frustum.

At its most basic the projection matrix will be given using *D* as the distance from the camera to the origin of the space defined by the view transform.

$$M = \begin{bmatrix} 1 & 0 & 0 & 0 \\ 0 & 1 & 0 & 0 \\ 0 & 0 & 1 & \dfrac{1}{D} \\ 0 & 0 & 0 & 1 \end{bmatrix}$$

The view matrix places the camera at the origin of the scene, the projection matrix requires that the camera is placed at (0,0,-D), translated in the z-axis by −D, the concatenation of these matrices yields the composite matrix:

$$N = \begin{bmatrix} 1 & 0 & 0 & 0 \\ 0 & 1 & 0 & 0 \\ 0 & 0 & 1 & \dfrac{1}{D} \\ 0 & 0 & D & 1 \end{bmatrix}$$

This matrix translates and scales objects from some distance to the camera's near plane but it does not take into account the field of view and the z values it produces at a distance may be nearly identical making depth comparisons unreliable. To address these issues the projection matrix can be adjusted to take into account the field of view.

$$M = \begin{bmatrix} w & 0 & 0 & 0 \\ 0 & h & 0 & 0 \\ 0 & 0 & Q & 1 \\ 0 & 0 & -Qz_n & 1 \end{bmatrix}$$

Where z_n is the value of the near plane, that is, the distance from the camera to the start of the viewing frustum, it stands that z_f represents the far plane, the idea of which is that any object that falls beyond this distance is not considered to be visible. The field of view of the camera can be represented by two angles, the horizontal field of view θ_w and the vertical field of view θ_h which are used to derive the values for w and h.

$$w = \cot\frac{\theta_w}{2}$$

$$h = \cot\frac{\theta_h}{2}$$

$$Q = \frac{z_f}{z_f - z_n}$$

It is more practical however to represent w and h in terms of the near and far clipping plane and the viewport's resolution (v_w, v_h).

$$w = \frac{2z_n}{v_w}$$

$$h = \frac{2z_n}{v_h}$$

4.2.2 View

Next is the view matrix, this matrix is used to transform all the geometry from world space into camera or view space. In view space, the camera is at the origin looking down the positive z axis (left handed coordinate system). The view matrix can be thought of as the concatenation of the translation and rotation matrices for each axis by which the geometry will be transformed to bring it in front of the viewer. The translation and rotation properties of the view matrix are based on the camera's position and orientation in world space, the matrix will apply rotations of opposite magnitude to the rotation of the models in world space and translate the object into view space.

Given the position of the camera, and a point in space to which we wish to look towards, we can derive vectors that describe the orientation for each of the camera's axes.

We start by creating the basis vectors for the rotation, the forward direction is the subtraction of the look at position l by the camera's world space position c, we also need to provide the world's up axis, $\hat{u}_{world}$.

$$\hat{v} = l - c$$
$$\hat{u} = \hat{u}_{world} \times \hat{v}$$
$$\hat{r} = v_z \times v_y$$

This produces the forward ($\hat{v}$), up ($\hat{u}$) and right ($\hat{r}$) vectors for the camera space in terms of world space. We can then calculate the translation factors.

$$t_x = -(v_x \cdot c)$$

$$t_y = -\left(v_y \cdot c\right)$$
$$t_z = -\left(v_z \cdot c\right)$$

The view matrix can then be represented by:

$$\begin{bmatrix} r_x & u_x & v_x & 0 \\ r_y & u_y & v_y & 0 \\ r_z & u_z & v_z & 0 \\ t_x & t_y & t_z & 1 \end{bmatrix}$$

This view matrix now contains all the elements necessary to transform vertices from world space into camera space.

```
matrix lefthanded::LookAt(const vector3& eyePosition, const vector3& targetPosition,
const vector3& up)
{
    vector3 vz = vector3::Normalize(targetPosition - eyePosition);
    vector3 vx = vector3::Normalize(vector3::Cross(up, vz));
    vector3 vy = vector3::Cross(vz, vx);

    matrix result = matrix::Identity;
    result(0,0) = vx.x();
    result(0,1) = vx.y();
    result(0,2) = vx.z();
    result(1,0) = vy.x();
    result(1,1) = vy.y();
    result(1,2) = vy.z();
    result(2,0) = vz.x();
    result(2,1) = vz.y();
    result(2,2) = vz.z();
    result(3,0) = -vector3::Dot(vx, eyePosition);
    result(3,1) = -vector3::Dot(vy, eyePosition);
    result(3,2) = -vector3::Dot(vz, eyePosition);

    return result;
}
```

One important thing to remember about the view matrix is that, its inverse, is the camera's transformation matrix, given the camera's view matrix we are able to find the position of the camera in-world by computing its inverse.

This is because the job of the camera's view matrix is to bring world space geometry and transform it so that it is in front of the camera by applying its opposite direction and orientation. In other words, the "camera" is not really an entity that moves around in space, it is actually the geometry which we transform and place in front of the camera. However, it is more intuitive to think of the camera as an object or entity that can be placed and aimed in any direction around the world, this is why usually we create a camera object that has an interface that allows us to do just that.

4.2.3 World

The world transform converts coordinates from model space to world space. Model space refers to the coordinates of a model's set of vertices relative to its own origin, think of a model exported into a file format, an artist will create the model relative to some origin that will be stored within the file. The world transform will bring those vertices and convert them to world space, relative to an origin common to all the objects in the game world.

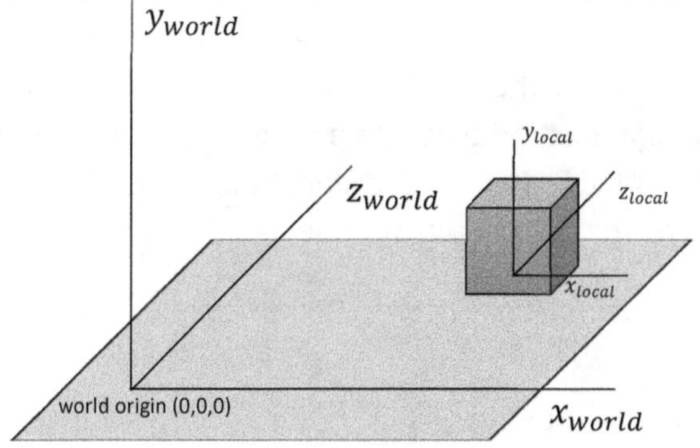

Figure 52 - World and local coordinate systems.

The world transformation may contain any combination of rotations, translations, scale and shears. In the context of cameras, the world transformation, sometimes referred to as the camera transformation represents a "physical" location and orientation for the camera, in order for the camera to transform geometry into view space, the camera's world space transform needs to be inverted.

4.2.4 Camera Interface

A camera object is a wrapper around the view and projection matrix that provides an intuitive interface for manipulating what the player can see of the game world.

These matrices are wrapped within a class that we will call *camera*, any operation we do with the camera will update these transformations. This means we can implement different cameras that exhibit different behaviors, such as first person cameras, orbiting cameras that follow objects from a certain distance, cameras that have a rigid body to allow collision with the environment, etc. by deriving from the camera class.

The first operation we want to be able to with a camera is to configure the projection settings. Projection rarely changes on a given camera during its lifetime in most games, though there is no reason why it cannot, so we will want to provide a function that sets a custom perspective projection, but we should also provide some preset functions to set different projections by just providing the parameters we need.

```cpp
void camera::SetProjection(const math::matrix& projection)
{
    m_projection = projection;
}

void camera::SetPerspectiveProjection(float yfov, float aspectRatio, float nearPlane, float farPlane)
{
    m_near = nearPlane;
    m_far = farPlane;
```

```
    m_projection = math::lefthanded::PerspectiveFOV(yfov, aspectRatio, nearPlane,
farPlane);
}
```

The next operation we want to do is tell the camera where to look.

```
void camera::LookAt(const vector3& from, const vector3& to, const vector3& up)
{
    m_view = lefthanded::LookAt(from, to, up);
}
```

It's a fairly straightforward function because the actual math to create the view matrix is implemented within the matrix class itself, this is because it's a useful function whose domain is not strictly tied to cameras. And we create the camera's world transformation by translating the camera into the "from" position in world space.

4.3 Controls

There are many well-known user interface elements that perform very precise functions, labels, buttons, lists, these are all examples of controls that we are familiar with and use frequently, the goal is to develop a working library of controls that are general enough to cover many situations, and to make them scalable to allow us to easily develop complex or game-specific controls.

The base control will provide the interface that any derived controls may implement to offer their own behavior. They may also implement how they *Update* each frame and how they respond to user input through the *HandleInput* function. Some amount of functionality is also shared among the majority of controls such as hit testing, so it is done at the base class level and derived controls can override it when necessary.

4.3.1 Properties

Most controls will share the same core set of features, placement, transparency, colors and states are all properties of controls regardless of what the control's intended purpose is. We will analyze the control class' properties and later we will do the same for its interface.

```
class control
{
public:

...

protected:

    math::rectangle m_rectangle;

    float m_alpha;

    render::color m_foregroundColor;
    render::color m_backgroundColor;

    bool m_visible;
    bool m_enabled;
    bool m_focused;
    bool m_mouseOver;

    render::viewport m_viewport;

...
};
```

All controls will use a rectangle to define their bounds on screen, these bounds are useful for calculating placement and performing hit testing to determine if the control needs to perform some action due to input. There are two ways to specify the bounds for a control, we can specify the position and size in pixels or we can use normalized coordinates [0.0,1.0] that represent the size of the viewport.

```
void control::SetPosition(const vector2& position, eUnit unit /*=Percent*/)
```

```cpp
{
    auto viewport = m_core->GetDevice()->GetViewport();
    switch ( unit )
    {
    case Percent:
        m_rectangle.SetPosition(vector2(position.x() * viewport.Width(), position.y() *
viewport.Height()) );
        break;
    default:
    case Pixels:
        m_rectangle.SetPosition(position);
        break;
    }

    Refresh();
}
```

When working in environments that may support multiple resolutions, or in order to port the game onto different platforms, including mobile platforms, we may need to change the screen resolution to conform to the hardware the game is running on. For this reason it is usually best to specify placement coordinates in normalized coordinates, this way, if the resolution change, you know that your control will always be placed at some percentage of the viewport. However, in some cases it is necessary to work directly in pixels , for example, labels in a list may use the list's screen position in pixels as their starting position, in this case it's easier to offset each label by the font height in pixels than it would be to convert it to normalized coordinates.

NOTE: Unity considers the bottom-most screen coordinate to be 0.0, and the top-most Y to be 1.0. To make our UI system compatible across multiple engines, we will need to provide functionality that can perform the appropriate calculations depending on what our platform requires and it should do so internally so that the user-facing side of our code API remains the same regardless of the target platform.

On construction we will set a control's viewport to match that of the graphics device. This makes the placement relative to the screen coordinates. We may override this viewport with a custom one to give us the ability to place controls relative to a different viewport than the screen's.

It is important to provide the means to *Refresh* a control. For example, it is not necessary for controls to calculate its placement coordinates every frame. It's best to defer performing these calculations until something changes that requires a recalculation. If we change the position of a text box, we would need to recalculate the position of the text to ensure it remains drawn within the extents of the box, we also would need to adjust the caret's position to be at the proper place, we can do this calculation by implementing it in the virtual function *Refresh*.

Next, we have chosen to provide a background and foreground color for all controls, many controls we use will contain text, the foreground color can be used when we render the text. Color configurations may vary depending on the desired feature set and controls, some controls may need more color settings, for simplicity we will stick with these two and if more are necessary they can be added to the relevant control's code.

Another important property is the alpha value, this controls the overall transparency of the object and is applied to both the foreground and background color to guarantee that the entire control can fade away and become invisible if necessary.

Finally, we have some state flags, these are used to determine the behavior of the control, some are user-set, such as visible and enabled, others are automatically set as a response to some form of input, focused refers to an object being the most recent recipient of some form of input, and *mouseOver* is used to know if the input cursor is presently within this control's bounds.

One important way to allow users to implement behaviors based on the control's behavior is to expose some events.

```
event_handler<const control&> m_onFocusReceived;
event_handler<const control&> m_onFocusLost;
event_handler<const control&> m_onMouseEnter;
event_handler<const control&> m_onMouseLeave;
```

These events allow users to respond to events and even make custom changes to the control itself.

```
progressbar->OnMouseEnter() += [&](void*, const control&)
{ progressbar->SetForegroundColor(render::color::YELLOW); };

progressbar->OnMouseLeave() += [&](void*, const control&)
{ progressbar->SetForegroundColor(render::color::CYAN); };
```

This example changes some progress bar's foreground color to yellow when the mouse first goes within its bounds, and then sets it to cyan once it leaves the bounds. This example is trivial, but it illustrates how easily we can add behaviors that respond to user input, sounds can be played when the mouse cursor enters or leaves a control, animations could be triggered on the control itself, even gameplay systems could listen for this events and cause elements in the game world to react to the player's input.

4.3.2 Interface

Some controls may require calculations to be performed each frame, we can implement this in the Update function and it can be different for each deriving control. One common behavior in the base Update function is to set the alpha of both foreground and background colors to that of the *m_alpha* property to make sure the control always has the same transparency.

```
void control::Update(float deltaTime)
{
    m_backgroundColor.A() = m_foregroundColor.A() = m_alpha;
}
```

Each control will need to be able to draw itself, for this we can implement a virtual draw function. As it happens often in games, in some situations users may want to alter the way an instance of a control looks, without changing all the existing controls or using a custom object for one place.

We can provide a way for the drawing of a control to be provided by an external source by adding a custom draw function.

```cpp
void control::Draw()
{
    if ( m_customDrawFunction != nullptr )
    {
        m_customDrawFunction(*this);
    }
    else
    {
        InternalDraw();
    }
}
```

Drawing a control then means, checking if a custom draw function is available, if it is, we will use it and we will pass the control itself as reference to this function. Otherwise we will call the interface's virtual *InternalDraw* function, which is where the default appearance of a control will be drawn.

For example, we could provide a custom draw function using a lambda that overrides the background color of a progress bar and pads its size a little bit.

```cpp
m_progressbar->SetCustomDrawFunction(
    [=](const control& c)
{
    const progress_bar& progressbar = static_cast<const progress_bar&>(c);
    rectangle r = progressbar.GetRectangle() + rectangle(5.f,0,0.f, 0.f);
    rectangle rc = progressbar.GetRectangle();
    rc.Left() -= 10.f;
    rc.Width() += 20.f;
    auto whiteTexture = *m_element.GetCore()->GetWhiteTexture()->GetView();
    m_spriteBatch->Draw(whiteTexture, r, nullptr, render::color::DARKCYAN);
    m_spriteBatch->Draw(whiteTexture, r, nullptr, progressbar.GetForegroundColor());
});
```

This can be a useful feature not only to change the drawing of a given control's instance, but for quickly prototyping visual changes. That said, most of the time it is best to derive from the control we want to change and override the virtual function *InternalDraw*.

All controls may potentially handle some user input, the virtual function *HandleInput* will be called each frame for all visible controls, the base implementation will detect if controls should come into focus or if the mouse may be hovering over the control, when any of these actions occur we will send out an event allowing other systems to register their own event handlers.

```cpp
bool control::HandleInput(float deltaTime, const input::input_state& inputState)
{
    UNREFERENCED(deltaTime);

    auto mouse = inputState.GetMouse();
    if ( mouse != nullptr )
    {
        if ( m_rectangle.Contains( mouse->GetPosition() ) )
        {
            if ( !m_mouseOver )
            {
                m_onMouseEnter.Invoke(this, *this);
                m_mouseOver = true;
            }

            if ( !m_focused && mouse->ButtonPressed(input::mouse::eButton::Left) )
            {
                m_onFocusReceived.Invoke(this, *this);
                m_focused = true;
                return true;
            }
        }
        else
        {
            if ( m_mouseOver )
            {
                m_onMouseLeave.Invoke(this, *this);
                m_mouseOver = false;
            }

            if ( m_focused && mouse->ButtonPressed(input::mouse::eButton::Left) )
            {
                m_onFocusLost.Invoke(this, *this);
```

```cpp
                m_focused = false;
            }
        }
    }

    return false;
}
```

There are two distinct cases we are testing for, the first one is if the mouse is within the control or not, we are only interested in knowing when the mouse went in and when it went out, it's not necessary to send an event every frame while the mouse is hovering over a control.

The second case is when the control comes into focus, this is done by some interaction from the user. If the user presses within the control's rectangle the control will come into focus and we will invoke the *OnFocusReceived* event, otherwise if the button press happened outside the control (or on another control) we will invoke *OnFocusLost*.

The default hit testing is done using the control's rectangle boundary, if some controls need more precise hit testing, they can override the *HandleInput* function and perform the calculations there, always making sure to invoke the events to maintain the expected functionality of controls.

If the input was handled we return true, otherwise we return false; this allows us to chain input handling calls and stop when someone has successfully handled the input.

The remaining interface provides the access functions to the properties.

```cpp
float& Alpha() { return m_alpha; }

const math::vector2 Position() const
{ return m_rectangle.Position(); }

const math::vector2 Size() const
{ return m_rectangle.Size(); }

void SetPosition(const math::vector2& position, eUnit unit=Percent);
void SetSize(const math::vector2& size, eUnit unit=Pixels);
```

```cpp
void SetExtents(const math::vector4& extents, eUnit unit=Percent);

const render::color& ForegroundColor() const
{ return m_foregroundColor; }

const render::color& BackgroundColor() const
{ return m_backgroundColor; }

void SetForegroundColor(const render::color& color)
{ m_foregroundColor = color; Refresh(); }

void SetBackgroundColor(const render::color& color)
{ m_backgroundColor = color; Refresh(); }

const math::rectangle& Rectangle() const { return m_rectangle; }

typedef std::function<void(const control&)> custom_draw_function;

void SetCustomDrawFunction(custom_draw_function customDrawFunction)
{
    m_customDrawFunction = customDrawFunction;
}
```

We will also need to manage the visibility of controls. There are mixed opinions on what is more intuitive, calling separate functions that represent the action, *Show* and *Hide* or calling a single function that uses a parameter to set the state, *SetVisibility*. The fact is, it is useful to provide both. While it is true that it seemingly exposes two ways of applying the same behavior, there will be situations in which the visibility may be given by a parameter, in which case *SetVisibility* is less verbose than an if/else to call *Show/Hide*.

```cpp
void Show() { SetVisibility(true); }
void Hide() { SetVisibility(false); }
virtual void SetVisibility(bool show) { m_visible = show; }
```

The important thing is that the behavior should be exactly the same in both cases. In other words, *Show* should internally call *SetVisibility(true)* and *Hide* should call *SetVisibility(false)*.

Show and *Hide* are provided as a convenience, however when there are multiple people working on the same code, it may happen that someone mistakenly (or unknowingly) modifies Show/Hide to have a different behavior than *SetVisible*, if this happens you can expect some difficulties down the line. If the risk of this situation is high, choose the function or functions that will provide you and other programmers the best development experience.

However, by making *SetVisibility* a virtual function, we allow for more complex behaviors to be applied during a visibility change, such as performing a fade out or a fade in. The important part to remember is that *Show* and *Hide* should never do anything else than call *SetVisibility* otherwise we could no longer guarantee any sort of consistency in our framework.

Before we begin discussing individual controls and their behavior, we will need a place to add controls into, we will create an object called a *container.*

4.3.3 Container

A container is a special control that is used to store other controls, it provides the entry point towards drawing a user interface and is used to call the functions responsible for updating, handling input and drawing all the controls within.

The motivation for the container object is to group controls tougher but also to make the creation of user interfaces straightforward from the user perspective, a container may also work as a viewport enabling any controls within it to be drawn relative to its position and size.

```cpp
class container : public control
{
public:

    container(std::shared_ptr<core_ui> core, const
std::shared_ptr<render::platform::font>& font)
        : control(core, font, nullptr)
```

```cpp
    {}

    template <typename T>
    std::shared_ptr<T> Add()
    {
        auto ctrl = factory::Create<T>(m_core, m_font, m_spriteBatch);

        ctrl->SetViewport(m_viewport);
        ctrl->SetPosition(math::vector2::Zero);

        m_controls.push_back(ctrl);

        return ctrl;
    }
```

A container is a control as any other, with the exception that it does not allow an external sprite batch object to be passed in, all controls in a container will use the same sprite batch. This restriction is in place to reduce the possibility of certain types of bugs to be introduced.

Adding a control to a container is done using templates, this allows us to specify the type of the control we wish to add, we then use a factory to create the instance of the control of that type.

```cpp
class factory
{
public:
    template <class T>
    static std::shared_ptr<T> Create(std::shared_ptr<core_ui> core, const
std::shared_ptr<render::platform::font>& font, const
std::shared_ptr<render::platform::sprite_batch> spriteBatch)
    {
      return std::shared_ptr<T>( new T(core, font, spriteBatch) );
    }
};
```

The use of the factory within the Add function of the containers allows us to write very clean, straightforward code to create user interface controls.

```cpp
auto uiContainer = std::unique_ptr<ui::container>((new ui::container(m_coreUI,
spriteFont)));
```

```
auto exampleLabel = uiContainer->Add<ui::label>();
```

By default, a container will have the dimensions of the screen resolution, setting a position or size will change the container's viewport and the placement of any controls within the container will be relative to the new viewport. We can do this by overriding the *Refresh* function.

```
virtual void Refresh()
{
    m_viewport = render::viewport(m_rectangle.Left(), m_rectangle.Top(),
m_rectangle.Right(), m_rectangle.Bottom(), 0.f, 1.f);
}
```

This way, if the size or position of the container changes, the container's viewport will be placed or resized accordingly.

4.3.4 Labels

A label is used as a way to display text, it cannot be interacted with and has no actual functionality except to convey information. Labels provide us with a text field on which to display information to users, the information can be static, meaning the label does not change; for example when displaying titles or captions. Or, it can be dynamic, the content of the label may be a game variable, scores, player names or an active game state, a dynamic label's value will be provided by some external source and may change every frame.

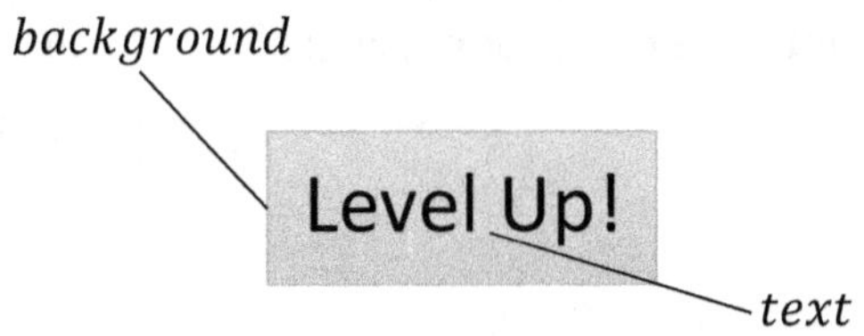

Figure 53 - A label's two main parts, the background and the text field.

A label has very few parts, it can be done with a background and the text. The background may be as simple as a color rectangle, it is best when the background is set to automatically resize based on the content of the label. This is especially important when doing localization for a game, as it will guarantee that regardless of the length of the text, it will always have a background. One useful feature to implement in labels is the ability to specify the text alignment within a label's bounds.

```cpp
void label::Refresh()
{
    math::vector2 textSize = GetTextSize();
    m_textRectangle = math::rectangle::MakeRectangle(
            m_rectangle.Left(),
            m_rectangle.Top(),
            m_rectangle.Left() + textSize.x(),
            m_rectangle.Top() + textSize.y() );

    align a(m_textRectangle, m_rectangle, m_alignment);
    a.Apply();
}

math::vector2 GetTextSize() const
{
    return math::vector2(m_font->MeasureString(m_text.c_str()));
}
```

We measure the size of the text, then place it at the origin of the viewport, then we run it through the alignment helper to finalize the text positioning.

Drawing the label means drawing two things, the background and the text, we may optionally not use a background, which is useful in many situations.

```cpp
void label::InternalDraw()
{
    m_backgroundColor.A() = m_alpha;
    m_foregroundColor.A() = m_alpha;

    if ( m_showBackground )
    {
        m_spriteBatch->Draw(*m_core->GetBlackTexture()->GetView(),m_autoSize ?
m_textRectangle : m_rectangle, nullptr, m_backgroundColor);
    }

    m_font->DrawString(m_spriteBatch.get(), m_text.c_str(), m_textRectangle.Position(),
m_foregroundColor, 0.f, math::vector4::Zero, math::vector4::One,
DirectX::SpriteEffects_None, 0.f);

}
```

Notice that depending on whether we have specified if the label should *AutoSize* we render the background differently. When we *AutoSize* a label we draw the minimal encompassing extents around the text, otherwise we will use the size as it was specified with *SetSize*.

To validate that labels are drawing and aligning properly, we can draw lines around the different parts of a label. First we should draw an outline over the label's maximum size, this is the label's *m_rectangle* field. Next we should draw two lines that run across the center horizontally and vertically of the label, this will aid a lot when we verify alignment. Finally we can draw lines around the text extents themselves, with these lines enabled we can validate or debug the labels' positioning and alignment.

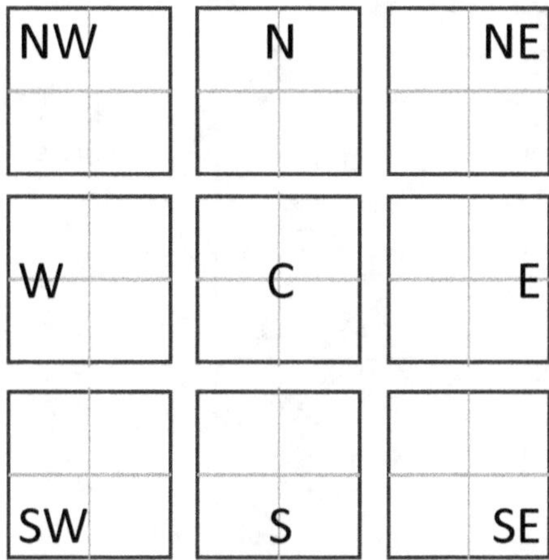

Figure 54 - Using debug lines we can validate or debug any label's position and alignment.

4.3.5 Buttons

A button is one of the most common devices for the player to interact with the game. There are many different types of buttons, but the majority share a common set of features. We will start by focusing on the core functionality that most buttons should have. A button is a user interface element that has a state, its default state is when the button is not pressed and ready for input. It can be active, or selected, which could mean the presence of some input device is over it, like a mouse cursor. When input is received, the button is pressed and at some point it will be released. Some buttons may also have some additional properties, such as being checked or disabled to prevent any input from the player.

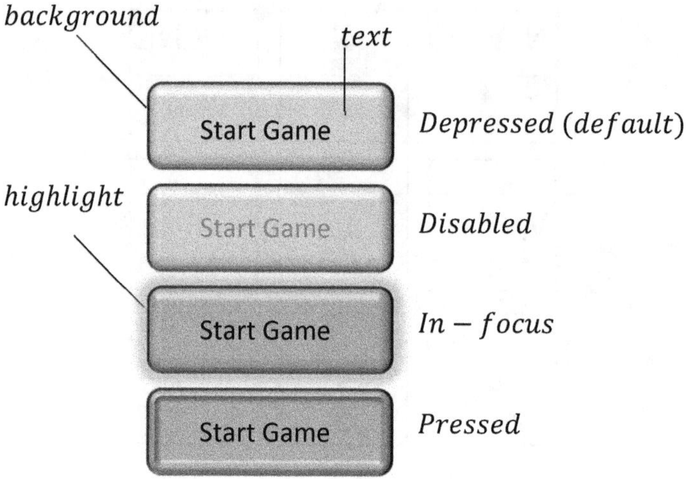

To implement a functional, working button we do not need to worry too much about what a button will look like. We will begin by writing the inner workings of a functional button and towards the end, to make buttons more visually interesting we will make use of the sprite class (see **Sprites**). Using sprites we can use different animations depending on the state of a button.

The button class will derive from the control class, inheriting a good amount of functionality in terms of determining if the button is in focus or if the mouse is hovering over it.

```cpp
class button : public control
{
public:

    enum eState
    {
        Default,
        Pressed,
        Disabled,
        StateCount
    };

    event_handler<const button&>& OnPressed()
    { return m_onPressed; }
```

```
    event_handler<const button&>& OnReleased()
    { return m_onReleased; }

    button(std::shared_ptr<core_ui> core, const std::shared_ptr<render::platform::font>&
font, const std::shared_ptr<render::platform::sprite_batch> spriteBatch)
        : control(core, font, spriteBatch)
        , m_state(Default)
        , m_alignment(ui::align::Center | ui::align::Middle)
    {}

protected:

    virtual void InternalDraw();
    virtual bool HandleInput(float deltaTime, const input::input_state& inputState);

    eState m_state;

    event_handler<const button&> m_onPressed;
    event_handler<const button&> m_onReleased;

    align::eAlignmentFlags m_alignment;
};
```

Buttons need to have a way to allow users to implement behaviors as a result of input. We can do this by providing event handlers when the users press and releases a button. Typically a button will perform its intended function upon its release. Knowing that a button has been pressed may be useful to provide feedback to the player, for example, by playing a sound.

```
void InternalDraw()
{
    if ( m_spriteSheet != nullptr )
    {
        m_sprite->Draw(m_rectangle.Position());
    }
    else
    {
        render::color color = m_colors[m_state];
        m_spriteBatch->Draw(*m_core->GetWhiteTexture()->GetView(), m_rectangle,
nullptr, color);
    }
```

```cpp
    if ( m_showText )
    {
        math::vector2 size = static_cast<math::vector2>( m_font-
>MeasureString(m_text.c_str()) );

        math::rectangle textRectangle = m_rectangle;
        textRectangle.SetSize(size);

        align a(textRectangle, m_rectangle);
        a.Apply(m_alignment);

        m_font->DrawString(m_spriteBatch.get(), m_text.c_str(),
textRectangle.Position(), m_foregroundColor);
    }
}
```

To draw our button we will support two cases, the first one is if we are using a sprite. In this case drawing is fairly straightforward, we call the sprite's own draw function, to which we provide the coordinate at which to draw the button. The next case does not use a sprite but rather just a colored rectangle, this is useful primarily for development or debugging, or perhaps in extremely low memory situations.

The next part is to draw any text associated with the button, in order to draw the text, we need to determine the text's position in a way that it will fit within the button. By default, the text is aligned to the center of the button, and then it is drawn using the color specified in the *m_foregroundColor* variable.

In addition to the input handling done by the base control class, a button has its own input handling to do. The two situations we are interested in handling are a button *press* and a *release*. The base control already gives us information when the mouse cursor is over its bounds, we can take advantage of this information to avoid duplicating the boundary checking and just check the value of *m_mouseOver*.

To determine if a button has been pressed we need to pass three tests, first is the mouse over the button, second is the button not already pressed and finally is the mouse button pressed, this will avoid notifying the button press while the mouse button is held down. In some cases we may want to know if the button is held down on a button, if so, we should add a separate event and leave *OnPress* to only mean a single press.

To determine if the button has been released we first check if the button is in the *Pressed* state, if it is and the mouse button is not pressed, then we can revert the button's state back to *Default.* There is an edge case that we need to consider. What should the behavior be if the mouse button is released while the mouse cursor is no longer within the button's boundaries? This situation unfortunately removes some of the uniformity of the code as we need to add a variation to the code such that, if the button is released while the cursor is beyond the button's bounds, then we reset the state of the button but we do not invoke the *OnRelease* event.

```cpp
bool button::HandleInput(float deltaTime, const input::input_state& inputState)
{
    auto mouse = inputState.GetMouse();
    if ( mouse != nullptr )
    {
        const bool leftMouseButtonPressed = mouse-
>ButtonPressed(input::mouse::eButton::Left);

        if( m_state == Pressed )
        {
            if ( !leftMouseButtonPressed )
            {
                ChangeStateTo(Default, m_mouseOver);
            }
        }
        else
        {
            if ( m_mouseOver && leftMouseButtonPressed )
            {
                ChangeStateTo(Pressed, true);
            }


        }
    }
    return control::HandleInput(deltaTime, inputState);
}

void button::ChangeStateTo(eState state, bool invokeEvent)
{
```

```
        m_state = state;

        if ( invokeEvent )
        {
            switch (state)
            {
            case Default:
                m_onReleased.Invoke(this, *this);
            break;
            case Pressed:
                m_onPressed.Invoke(this, *this);
            break;
            }
        }

        if ( m_sprite != nullptr )
        {
            m_sprite->Play(state);
        }
}
```

Using *Sprite* animations we can display the different states of a button, this allows us to create a single *spritesheet* for a given button that contains animated version of each of the button's state. When we call *ChangeStateTo* we play the animation for that particular state, whether it's the *Default*, *Pressed*, *Disabled* or any other custom state your buttons may have.

```
m_button = std::unique_ptr<ui::button>(new ui::button(m_element.GetCore(),
m_spriteFont, m_spriteBatch));
m_button->SetSize(math::vector2(160.f, 160.f));
m_button->SetPosition(math::vector2(10.f, 10.f), control::Pixels);
m_button->SetText(L"Start Game!");
m_button->OnReleased() += [&](const ui::button&) { StartGame(); };
```

Creating a button is fairly straightforward, initialize it to the desired position, size and provide the desired behaviors on pressed or on released.

4.3.6 Text Boxes

Text boxes are the way to allow data entry through a keyboard, and their behavior is well understood at this point, so when they are poorly implemented they can be a source of annoyance and frustration.

A text box must first, allow text entry of course, this means that when you type on a physical keyboard or a virtual one on a portable device, the key you tapped must immediately display the corresponding character within it. Next, typing must be instantaneous, some people can type very fast, any artificial delay in the text boxes input is going to severely hinder the user's experience and will give the impression that the software is running slowly; it must not, however, be so fast that holding a key for a fraction of a second would display the character multiple times. This means we need to detect a long key press and in this case, provide a small delay and then accelerate the rate of character entry, this is especially true for backspace, delete and the space bar.

Another thing that is expected during text entry is a caret, typically the caret is a thin pipe that blinks to represent the location at which the next character will be displayed, in some cases it may be a small square or some other shape that may depend on the art direction.

4.3.6.1 Caret

The caret as we discussed is a thin pipe that blinks to represents the position at which characters will be displayed anytime we do any kind of text entry, as such it benefits of being implemented as a reusable object.

Fortunately, it takes very little code to implement a nice looking caret that gently fades rather than an abrupt blink in/out.

The main part of the caret's behavior takes place in the Update function, every frame we decrease *m_blinkTimer* by the frame's *deltaTime*, when it reaches zero, we flip the toggle and reset the timer. The alpha component of the caret's color is determined as the ratio of how much time has elapsed and a target duration.

```cpp
void Update(float deltaTime)
{
    m_blinkTimer -= deltaTime;
    if ( m_blinkTimer <= 0.f )
    {
        m_blinkTimer = m_blinkRate;
        m_visible = !m_visible;
    }

    m_color.A() = m_toggle ?  1.f - (m_blinkTimer / m_blinkDuration) :  (m_blinkTimer / m_blinkDuration);
}
```

Rendering the caret is a straightforward quad render that uses a texture or solid color with the position and size defined in *m_rectangle*.

```cpp
void Draw(std::shared_ptr<render::texture> texture,
std::shared_ptr<DirectX::SpriteBatch> spriteBatch)
{
    spriteBatch->Draw(*texture->GetView(), m_rectangle, nullptr, m_color);
}
```

The size of the caret is often one or two pixels wide, and the height is font-dependent; 80% of the font's line spacing as height, with a padding of 10% from the top will generate a pleasing result.

Alternatively, as we will see later in **Animation with Interpolation Curves**, we could replace the code that handles the blink timer/duration with an animation.

```cpp
void caret::Update(float deltaTime)
{
    m_interpolator.Update(deltaTime);

    animation caretAnimation(m_color.A(),
                m_toggle ? 1.f : 0.f,
                0.25f,
```

```
                    curves::ease_in_out<curves::linear>,
                    [&] { m_toggle = !m_toggle; } );

        if ( m_interpolator.ActiveAnimationCount() == 0 )
        {
            m_interpolator.Add(caretAnimation);
        }
```

These few lines of code replace the timer and duration variables we were keeping around only for the blinking of the caret. Instead, what we do is through an interpolator, we create an animation that when *m_toggle* is true it will animate *m_color's* alpha value towards 1.0 at the rate of 4 times per second. Once the animation is complete, we flip *m_toggle* through a lambda function, the next animation we create will animate the alpha value of *m_color* back towards 0.

4.3.6.2 Auto Completion

It's a good idea to implement auto completion for text boxes that expect user input, it simplifies text entry and nowadays from the behavior of web browsers and other software we have become used to it, there is no reason not to provide the same functionality within our games when appropriate.

Trie

A common data structure used for storing predictive text is a trie is a type of tree (term appears to come from the word re**trie**val), it's not the most compact way to store autocomplete data, but it has good performance and it is not difficult to implement.

Every node in a trie may have up to n nodes under it, where n is the number of characters that may succeed any given node, for example, in some limited implementations it could be up to twenty six, the number of characters in the English alphabet, however, no limitation should be enforced, after all, we may want to support alphanumeric characters, symbols, or other alphabets.

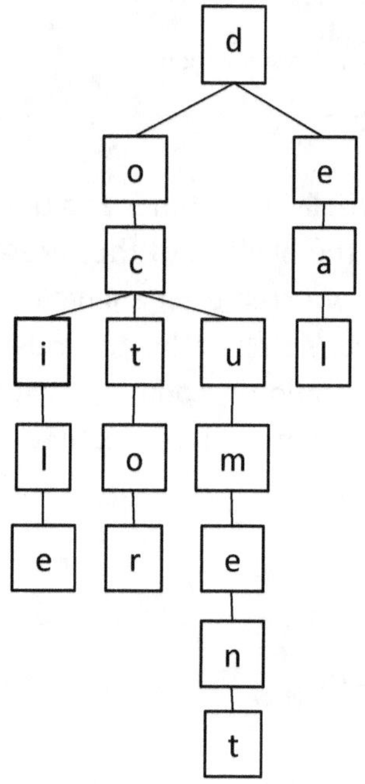

Figure *55* - A visual representation of a trie.

The trie holds a root node, an insertion function and some query functions. Nodes hold four members, first the character they represent, next a flag that identifies as a node as a word, children nodes and an index that we will use while iterating through the different children.

This description of a trie's node can be defined by the following code.

```
class node
{
private:
    wchar_t m_character;
    bool m_isWord;
    size_t m_index;
    std::vector<std::shared_ptr<node>> m_children;
};
```

The node is keyed with the character it represents, this is not strictly necessary and may be adapted to serve more general purposes. The children are stored in a vector of nodes, this will make iterating over them straightforward using the m_index member. Finally, m_isWord is a flag that we will set when a node may be considered a full word, this is useful to know when we can stop iterating through children nodes and return what we've found.

Before we look further inside the node, let's take a moment to analyze the algorithm used to add a word into our trie.

```cpp
void trie::add(const std::wstring word)
{
    if ( word.size() == 0 )
    {
        return;
    }

    std::shared_ptr<node> current = m_root;

    for ( size_t i = 0; i < word.size(); ++i )
    {
        wchar_t character = word.c_str()[i];
        auto child = current->find(character);
        if ( child != nullptr )
        {
            current = child;
        }
        else
        {
            auto tmp = std::shared_ptr<node>(new node(character));
            current->push_back(tmp);
            current = tmp;
        }

        if ( i == word.size() -1 )
        {
            current->MarkWord();
        }
    }
}
```

The main part of the algorithm iterates over every character in the word we wish to insert into the trie; during the iteration we search the current node to see if the character is already a child within it, if it is, we set the node we found as our current node and we continue iterating until we reach a point in which we don't find a node. If the character does not exist, we then create a new node and initialize it to the character and we push this new node into the current node's children vector, finally if we are at the final character of the word, we will flag the node to reflect this fact.

The find function in nodes is a straightforward iteration and compare, if we find a match, we return a pointer to the node, and otherwise we return null, to indicate no match was found.

```cpp
std::shared_ptr<node> node::find(wchar_t character)
{
    for ( auto& n : m_children )
    {
        if ( n->GetCharacter() == character )
        {
            return n;
        }
    }
    return nullptr;
}
```

Now we can build up a trie out of a set of words, for example, we could parse an entire dictionary file and send the words into the trie, once constructed we will want to retrieve information from it.

While there are a few useful functions to implement in a trie, such as functions to verify if the trie contains a given word, or a given prefix. For text entry we are interested in retrieving the information required to build an auto completion system that is smart enough so that, as we type, the system automatically inserts the closest match it finds.

Figure *56* - Auto completion is done as the user is writing.

The first function that will help us achieve this we will call it *find_prefix* it will receive some text as input, in the example above it would receive the word "play" and it will return the node at which the letter y is found. Then we will call a second function called *get_from_prefix*, this function will receive a node and a reference to a string, it will then iterate down the children of the node we provided and build a string for the remainder of the word. The reason we return the node in which the letter y is found is that, this node will contain all the children that share the same prefix up to the letter y, allowing us to call the node's next function to iterate over its children, this allows us to implement a method to cycle through auto complete suggestions by binding the call to next to a key press, typically using the TAB key.

```cpp
std::shared_ptr<node> trie::find_prefix(const std::wstring& prefix) const
{
    if ( prefix.size() == 0 )
    {
        return nullptr;
    }

    std::shared_ptr<node> current = m_root;
    std::shared_ptr<node> last = nullptr;

    while ( current != nullptr )
    {
        for (size_t i = 0; i < prefix.size(); ++i )
        {
            auto tmp = current->find(prefix.c_str()[i]);
            if ( tmp == nullptr )
            {
```

```
                return nullptr;
            }

        current = tmp;

        if ( !current->IsWord() )
        {
            last = current;
        }
      }
    break;
  }

  if ( !current->IsWord() )
  {
      return last;
  }

  return nullptr;
}
```

The goal of *find_prefix* is to traverse the tree, searching for each of the characters in the prefix, once we have finished iterating over the prefix, we will return the last node that was not flagged as a word, this will allow us to cycle over the results with ease. If at any moment during the iteration we do not find a match from the prefix, we return *nullptr* to indicate that no match was found or if we have found a full word, we also return nullptr, no need to return the prefix if it is the full word.

The next important function is the one that will build a string by traversing down a branch of the trie, *get_from_prefix*.

```
bool trie::get_from_prefix(std::shared_ptr<node> from, std::wstring& s)
{
    if ( from == nullptr )
        return false;

    std::shared_ptr<node> current = from;

    wchar_t c = current->GetCharacter();
    if ( c != 0 )
    {
```

```cpp
        s.push_back( c );
    }

    if ( current->IsWord() )
    {
        return true;
    }

    std::shared_ptr<node> n = current->next();
    while ( n != nullptr )
    {
        if ( get_from_prefix(n, s) )
        {
            return true;
        }

        n = n->next();
    }

    return false;
}
```

This is a recursive implementation that begins by getting the character from the current node and pushing it back into the output string *s*, if the current node defines a word, we can return true, this means we have reached the end of the branch and we have a complete word in the output string reference s; otherwise, for each child of the current node, we will recursively call *get_from_prefix*, if ever this returns true then we have found a complete word and we can return. If we run out of children, then there are no words with this prefix and the function will return false.

The last function left to discuss is the next function in the node class, this function will advance an index and return the child node at that position, and it's the important function that will allow us to implement cycling through auto complete possibilities.

```cpp
std::shared_ptr<node> node::next()
{
    if (  m_children.size() == 0 )
    {
        return nullptr;
```

```cpp
    }

    if ( m_index >= m_children.size() )
    {
        m_index = 0;
    }

    auto& next = m_children.at(m_index);
    ++m_index;
    return next;
}
```

The first part will return *nullptr* if this node has no children, the second part will wrap the index around to prevent accessing the vector out of bounds, and finally we will retrieve the node at the index, increment the index and return.

The best part of using such a self-contained solution is that using this feature becomes trivial and can be reused by different systems.

Finally we will need to apply the auto completion, we store the portion of auto completion text as a separate member variable, this way we can append this variable to the user's input using a different font style or color to indicate that it's a suggestion and only if the player commits the auto completion by pressing TAB or ENTER then it becomes the contents of the text box and we clear the stored auto complete text.

```cpp
void textbox::AutoComplete(bool reset = false)
{
    if ( reset || m_currentResult == nullptr ) {
        m_currentResult = m_trie->find_prefix(m_text);
    }

    if ( m_currentResult != nullptr ) {
        m_autocompleteText.clear();
        m_trie->get_from_prefix(m_currentResult->next(), m_autocompleteText);
    }
    else {
        m_autocompleteText.clear();
    }
}
```

The parameter reset is used when the auto complete text may have changed enough that the prefix is no longer valid, this can happen when the user presses backspace and erases a part of the prefix.

4.3.7 Message Box

It's useful to have a way to communicate with the user, whether it's the player or the developer that something has happened. One example of a situation in which a message box comes in handy is in console games when the controller becomes disconnected. Other uses could be to notify that a game was successfully saved, to confirm some action, such as deleting a saved game, etc.

The goal of the message box code is to be straightforward to use, a reasonable approach is to construct the message box by passing in the configuration settings and calling a Show function that waits for the message box to return with some result value from the user, unfortunately, it is rarely this simple. Usually in games we can't simply stop the execution of the game code and wait in some loop for some action to occur, the situation is more delicate if the game update loop is running in a different thread than the rendering loop.

The message box that we will design is modal, meaning that the user is required to interact with it before the game can return to its previous state. This means that when we open a message box, we will have to pause the game. The pausing mechanic is specific to each game, though usually, it involves a function we can call to request the game to pause, or in some cases it is a message we broadcast or in more frightening cases, it's a global boolean variable we toggle.

```cpp
void save_system::DeleteSavedGame(const std::wstring& saveGameURI)
{
  game::RequestGamePause();

  ui::MessageBox msg(L"Are you sure you wish to delete this saved game?",
ui::MessageBox::YesNo, saveGameURI, &save_system::OnConfirmDelete);
  msg.Show();
```

```cpp
}
...

void save_system::OnComfirmDelete(const MessageBox<const std::wstring&>& msgBox)
{
    if ( msgBox.Result() == ui::MessageBox::Yes )
    {
        const std::wstring& saveGameURI = msgBox.Data();
        Delete(saveGameURI);
    }

  game::RequestResume();

}
```

From a usability perspective, message boxes should not spawn new message boxes, however should that be necessary, it's important to keep a stack of any modal message boxes opened.

Remember that a stack is a last-in, first-out operation. This means that as each modal message box is opened it will be pushed to the stack when the user closest the top-most message box, it will be popped from the stack until there are no more open message boxes.

4.3.8 List Box

A list box is a container that may hold many items, all or some may be visible at a time and the user can choose one or many items to make a selection.

The simplest case to illustrate a list box's functionality is using text strings as the items in the list, this will be the focus of this example. However, to give list boxes more flexibility, we can implement it so that each item in the listbox is a user interface *control,* by doing this we can create list boxes of more complex items, such as game elements represented by an image and text, even include the item's description directly in the list box.

The first part of the list box we will look into is the list item. A list item will be an object that implements the minimum functionality for a working listbox. A listbox item must have some value, typically a text string. We will need to control the visibility of each item so that items that go beyond the bounds of the listbox control will not be visible. Another important aspect of a listbox item is to notify the user when it has been selected or clicked by the player.

In order to allow for future specialization of list items, we will create a base class from which we will later implement the actual working item. This base class will contain the fundamental information to ensure the list box functions, then we will create a specialized listbox item that draws a string of text.

```cpp
class listboxitem
{
public:

    listboxitem(listbox* owner)
        : m_owner(owner)
        , m_selected(false)
        , m_visible(false)
    {}

    virtual void Draw(const math::vector2& position, std::shared_ptr<DirectX::SpriteFont>
font, std::shared_ptr<DirectX::SpriteBatch> spriteBatch)
    {
    }

    virtual bool HandleInput(float deltaTime, const input::input_state& inputState)
    {
        return false;
    }

    virtual bool Selected() const { return m_selected; }
    virtual bool& Visible() { return m_visible; }

    virtual const math::rectangle& Rectangle() const
    { return m_rectangle; }

    event_handler<listboxitem*>& OnSelected()
    { return m_onSelected; }
```

```cpp
protected:

    virtual void SetPosition(const math::vector2& position)
    { m_rectangle.SetPosition(position); }

    virtual void SetSize(const math::vector2& size)
    { m_rectangle.SetSize(size); }

    bool m_visible;
    bool m_selected;
    math::rectangle m_rectangle;
    event_handler<listboxitem*> m_onSelected;
    listbox* m_owner;
};
```

With this listbox item base class we can implement all of the listbox's behavior and defer the actual responsibility of handling input and drawing to a specialized class, this gives the ability to create any number of items, whether text, image or more complex items that use containers of UI controls.

To keep things simple we will implement a text based item that handles the basic set of features we would expect from a list box.

```cpp
class listboxitemtext : public listboxitem
{
public:

    listboxitemtext(listbox* owner, const math::vector2& size, const std::wstring& text,
const render::color& color = render::color::WHITE)
        : listboxitem(owner)
        , m_size(size)
        , m_text(text)
        , m_color(color)
        , m_inputDelay(0.1f)
    {
    }

    virtual void Draw(const math::vector2& position, std::shared_ptr<DirectX::SpriteFont>
font, std::shared_ptr<DirectX::SpriteBatch> spriteBatch);

    virtual bool HandleInput(float deltaTime, const input::input_state& inputState);
```

```
protected:

    math::vector2 m_size;
    render::color m_color;
    std::wstring m_text;
    bool m_mouseOver;

    countdown m_inputDelay;

};
```

Let's begin by looking at how we will handle input. An item is a part of the listbox control and will receive a *HandleInput* function call from the listbox's own *HandleInput*. What we are looking to detect here is whether the mouse is presently hovering over the item, and whether the item has been clicked, or selected.

```
void listboxitemtext::Update(float deltaTime)
{
    if ( !m_visible ) return;

    listboxitem::Update(deltaTime);
    m_inputDelay.Update(deltaTime);
}

bool listboxitemtext::HandleInput(float deltaTime, const input::input_state& inputState)
{
    if ( !m_visible )
        return false;

    auto mouse = inputState.GetMouse();
    if ( mouse != nullptr )
    {
        math::rectangle rectangle = m_owner->Rectangle();
        rectangle.Top() = m_rectangle.Top();
        rectangle.Height() = m_size.y();
        m_mouseOver = rectangle.Contains(mouse->GetPosition());
        if ( m_mouseOver )
        {
            if ( m_inputDelay.IsDone() && mouse-
>ButtonPressed(input::mouse::eButton::Left) )
            {
```

```
                m_inputDelay.Start();
                m_selected = !m_selected;
                m_onSelected.Invoke(this, this);
                return true;
            }
        }
    }
    return false;
}
```

As you probably noticed, we have a small helper countdown object *m_inputDelay*. When we click the mouse, the actual duration of the click may last one or several game frames no matter how quick our mouse clicking might have been. To avoid multiple clicks from being handled each frame, whenever we detect a mouse click we will trigger this countdown object, while the object is active no further mouse clicks will be handled.

The rest of the function consists of building the rectangular area that is covered by the item, and testing if the mouse coordinates are within this rectangle. If they are, we may set the *m_mouseOver* flag to true, this will allow us to highlight items that we are currently hovering over. Furthermore, if *m_mouseOver* is true, and we detect a left mouse button click, we will toggle the *m_selected* flag, and we will notify the user that a selection has occurred. Admittedly, we could provide a different notification event if the selection was true or false (if the item was already selected we actually unselected by this action), however, when we broadcast the selection event, we are providing the item as the event's parameter, so the client can test if the item is selected or not using the *Selected()* function. This is one of many small, but important design choices we must make when creating systems that will be used by other programmers, keeping in mind that the design decision must be consistent across the rest of the controls.

The next function that we need to implement is the ability to draw the item, this will ultimately depend on the type of game or system that is being developed.

```cpp
void listboxitemtext::Draw(const math::vector2& position,
std::shared_ptr<DirectX::SpriteFont> font, std::shared_ptr<DirectX::SpriteBatch>
spriteBatch)
{
    if ( m_visible )
    {
        SetPosition(position);

        render::color color = m_color;
        if ( m_mouseOver )
        {
            color = render::color::RED;
        }

        if ( m_selected )
        {
            color = render::color::GREEN;
        }

        m_owner->Font()->DrawString(spriteBatch.get(), m_text.c_str(), position, color );
    }
}
```

For this simple example we'll take the liberty of hardcoding the colors of the item. It is the listbox control that will calculate the position for each item as it iterates over the list of visible items, this is why the position is passed in and we forward it to the item itself using *SetPosition*. Finally, in our overly simplistic example, if we have set the *m_mouseOver* flag, we will draw the item in red, if the item is selected, we will draw it in green, otherwise it will draw in its default white.

Now that we the workings of the listbox item defined, we will need to focus on the listbox itself. The listbox will be a list of items, of which we will potentially draw a subset of.

```cpp
class listbox : public control
{

public:

    enum eSorting
```

```cpp
    {
        Ascending,
        Descending
    };

    listbox(std::shared_ptr<core> core, const std::shared_ptr<DirectX::SpriteFont>& font,
const std::shared_ptr<DirectX::SpriteBatch> spriteBatch)
        : control(core, font, spriteBatch)
        , m_scrollBar(core, font, spriteBatch)
        , m_lastMouseWheelValue(0)
        , m_sorting(Descending)
    {}

    virtual ~listbox();

    virtual void Refresh();
    virtual bool HandleInput(float deltaTime, const input::input_state& inputState);
    virtual void InternalDraw();

protected:

    eSorting m_sorting;

    scrollbar m_scrollBar;

    std::list<listboxitem*> m_items;
    std::list<listboxitem*> m_selectedItems;

    int m_lastMouseWheelValue;

};
```

A listbox is a control, a control that will host several items and will allow us
to view a subset of these items at a time. In addition to the list of items, we
also keep a list of those items that have been selected.

```cpp
void listbox::Refresh()
{
    auto backRect = m_rectangle;

    m_scrollBar.SetBackgroundColor( render::color::LIGHTGRAY );
    m_scrollBar.SetForegroundColor( render::color::GREEN );
```

```cpp
    if ( m_items.size() > 1 )
    {
        backRect.Top() = m_rectangle.Top();
        backRect.Height() = m_font->GetLineSpacing() * ((m_items.size()/2) );

        m_scrollBar.Visible() = true;
    }
    else
    {
        m_scrollBar.Visible() = false;
    }

    m_scrollBar.SetSize( math::vector2(m_rectangle.Width() * 0.1f, backRect.Height() ) );
    m_scrollBar.SetPosition( math::vector2(m_rectangle.Right() - m_scrollBar.Size().x(),
m_rectangle.Top() ) );

}
```

One important component of a listbox is the scrollbar which we discuss in detail below. The important thing is that if the number of items in a listbox changes so that there are more items in the list than the size of the list, then we need to display the scrollbar. We also need to configure the position and size of the scrollbar. For this example the scrollbar is fixed at 10% of the width of the listbox control, however in production code this value should be exposed so that it becomes configurable by users.

Next we will need to handle input on the listbox, most of the input is actually deferred to either the listbox items or the scrollbar, and in fact, the only input we manage directly in the listbox is that of the mouse wheel. Even then, if we detect any mouse wheel movement, we forward it to the scrollbar which will then control the actual position of the listbox's visible items.

```cpp
bool listbox::HandleInput(float deltaTime, const input::input_state& inputState)
{
    UNREFERENCED(deltaTime);

    if ( inputState.GetMouse() != nullptr )
```

```cpp
    {
        auto mouse = inputState.GetMouse();
        if ( m_rectangle.Contains(mouse->GetPosition()) )
        {
            if (mouse->GetMouseWheelValue() != m_lastMouseWheelValue)
            {
                float delta = static_cast<float>( m_lastMouseWheelValue - mouse->GetMouseWheelValue() );

                m_scrollBar.ApplyMovement(delta);
                m_lastMouseWheelValue = mouse->GetMouseWheelValue();
                return true;
            }
        }
    }

    if ( m_scrollBar.HandleInput(deltaTime, inputState) )
    {
        return true;
    }

    for ( auto it : m_items )
    {
        if (it->Visible() && it->HandleInput(deltaTime, inputState))
            return true;
    }
    return false;
}
```

Drawing is relatively straightforward, we start by drawing the background of the listbox, next we begin drawing the items, starting at the top of the listbox.

We use the scrollbar to calculate the ratio, a percentage of how far down the list we are currently looking at. As we iterate over the list, we test if the item's index is below the visible index, if so we flag the item as invisible and we keep iterating, otherwise we mark the item visible and we draw it. If we draw an item we update the vertical position.

If we have more items than the size the listbox control can draw, then we will draw the scrollbar.

```cpp
void listbox::InternalDraw()
{
    auto& textureView = *m_core->GetWhiteTexture()->GetView();

    auto backRect = m_rectangle;
    backRect.Top() = m_rectangle.Top();
    backRect.Height() = m_font->GetLineSpacing()  * (m_items.size()/2);

    m_spriteBatch->Draw(textureView, backRect, nullptr, m_backgroundColor);

    math::vector2 itemsPosition = m_rectangle.Position();

    const float ratio = m_scrollBar.Ratio();
    size_t cursor = ratio * (m_items.size() - 2 );
    size_t i = 0;
    for ( auto it : m_items )
    {
        if ( i < cursor )
        {
            it->Visible() = false;
            ++i;
            continue;
        }

        it->Visible() = true;

        it->Draw(itemsPosition, m_font, m_spriteBatch);

        itemsPosition.y() += m_font->GetLineSpacing();
        if ( itemsPosition.y() >= backRect.Bottom() )
            break;

        ++i;
    }

    if ( m_items.size() * m_font->GetLineSpacing() > m_rectangle.Height() )
    {
        m_scrollBar.Draw();
    }
}
```

The next part is important, we need to add and update items as they are selected.

```cpp
void listbox::Add(const std::wstring text)
{
    listboxitemtext* item = new listboxitemtext(this, math::vector2(m_rectangle.Width(),
m_font->GetLineSpacing()), text, render::color::WHITE);

    item->OnSelected() += [=] (void*, listboxitem* item) { UpdateList(item); };

    if ( m_sorting == Descending )
    {
        m_items.push_back(item);
    }
    else
    {
        m_items.push_front(item);
    }

    Refresh();
}
```

Adding an item means creating a new item, and providing an event handler used when an item becomes selected. Once constructed, depending on the selected sorting type for the list box the item is either pushed to the back of the list or to the front. Finally we refresh the control to ensure we compute the size of the control and the scrollbar.

The *OnSelected* handler is provided through a lambda function that calls *UpdateList*. This handler checks if the item was selected or not and then adds it to the *m_selectedItems* list or removes it from it. This ensures that the list of selected items is always perfectly in sync with what is actually selected.

```cpp
void listbox::UpdateList(listboxitem* item)
{
    if ( item->Selected() )
        m_selectedItems.push_back(item);
    else
    {
        auto it = std::find(m_selectedItems.begin(), m_selectedItems.end(), item);
        if ( it != m_selectedItems.end() )
```

```
        {
            m_selectedItems.erase(it);
        }
    }
}
```

Now that the inner workings of the listbox are complete, there are some usability details that we must consider. The first is, sometimes it is desirable for users to associate some kind of data to listbox items. A straightforward way to add this support is to create an empty base class, if users are interested in providing custom data to listbox items they can derive from this class and assign the data to items.

We can add the following class within the *lisboxitem* class.

```
class data
{
};

void SetData(std::shared_ptr<data> data)
{
    m_data = data;
}

std::shared_ptr<data> Data() { return m_data; }

protected:

std::shared_ptr<data> m_data;
```

We then can modify the *Add* function to receive a *shared_ptr* of an object that derives from *data*.

```
void listbox::Add(const std::wstring text, std::shared_ptr<listboxitem::data> data = nullptr)
{
    listboxitemtext* item = new listboxitemtext(this, math::vector2(m_rectangle.Width(), m_font->GetLineSpacing()), text, render::color::WHITE);
    item->SetData(data);
    item->OnSelected() += [=] (void*, listboxitem* item) { UpdateList(item); };
```

```
    if ( m_sorting == Descending )
    {
        m_items.push_back(item);
    }
    else
    {
        m_items.push_front(item);
    }

    Refresh();
}
```

This allows to create custom data objects that we can optionally use at the time of adding items into the listbox.

```
class sampledata : public listbox::listboxitem::data
{
public:
    sampledata(int value)
        : m_value(value)
    {}

    int Value() const { return m_value; }

private:

    int m_value;
};

m_listbox->Add(L"Item 1", std::shared_ptr<sampledata>( new sampledata(0) ) );
m_listbox->Add(L"Item 2", std::shared_ptr<sampledata>( new sampledata(1) ) );
m_listbox->Add(L"Item 3", std::shared_ptr<sampledata>( new sampledata(2) ) );
```

If you have worked with C# WinForms or WPF this is conceptually similar to the *Tag* object that is used to store custom information about the listbox's item.

At some point we will want to query the listbox for its selected items. We provided a list of selected items that users can retrieve. This listbox was designed using a *std::list* as the item container, while this simplifies the listbox's code, it is not the most optimal container to use. It becomes obvious when we want to query and search for a given item. Using a vector, we could maintain a list of selected indices and then use the indices to look into the items vector and fetch those selected items, using a list we have no choice but to iterate the list and compare against the item we are interested in.

Earlier when we implemented the listbox's functionality we used a scrollbar, a scroll bar is a useful control that can be reused by different controls so we will now see how to implement it as a standalone control.

4.3.9 Scroll Bar

A scroll bar is a control that is useful in conjunction with other controls, namely with controls that have so many options that cannot be visible within the designated space. The scroll bar controls the visible elements or area of some other control.

The behavior of a scroll bar can be abstracted to work as a standalone entity that other controls use. The scroll bar will be constructed with some knowledge of the control it is linked to, its size, how many options and the size of each option. The scroll bar can be manipulated by users, scrolling between a minimum point and a maximum point. To the control that owns the scroll bar, it is the ratio, the value that represents the relative position between the minimum and maximum points that will be useful.

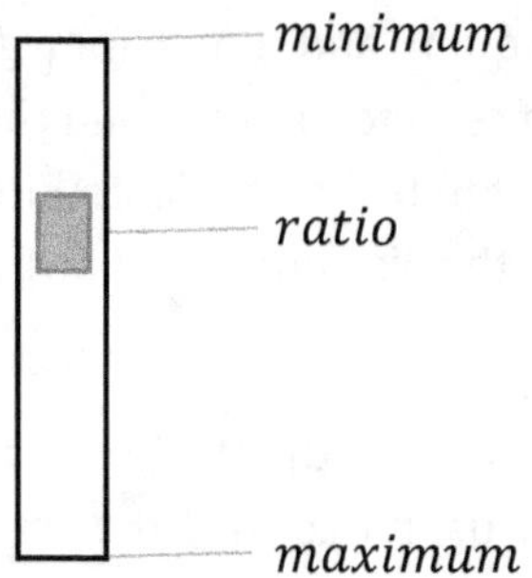

Figure 57 - A scroll bar's position represents a ratio between a minimum and a maximum value.

The scroll bar behavior can be implemented with a few parameters, for our example we will support both *vertical* and *horizontal* scroll bars. The difference in implementation between a *horizontal* scrollbar is that we need to operate on the *Left* coordinate and the *Width*, rather than the *Top* and the *Height.*

We will define the bounds of the cursor, this is the small rectangular area that represents the position or the ratio of the control being scrolled. We will need to keep track of two variables, first the state of the control, it is important to distinguish between the control being pressed, or not. Finally, at the moment of a mouse click, if the input position is within the area of the cursor's rectangle, we will record the distance from the point clicked to the top of the cursor. We need this value, we will call it Δy to make sure the cursor moves in tandem with the input cursor.

```cpp
class scrollbar : public control
{
public:
    enum eType
    {
        Horizontal,
        Vertical
    };

...
```

```
protected:

    enum eState
    {
        Default,
        Pressed
    };

    eState m_state;
    eType m_type;

    math::rectangle m_cursor;
    float m_delta;
    int m_lastMouseWheelValue;
};
```

As the scroll bar is a control, it may implement the same functions as any other controls do. The bulk of the work for a scroll bar takes place within the *HandleInput* function.

There are three distinct cases that we need to account for, the first is what happens when the user clicks within the scroll bar's cursor, the second is what happens when the user clicks within the scroll bar's boundaries, but not within the cursor. And finally, in the case that the input is coming through the mouse wheel, we will add a way to apply movement to the scroll bar from the outside, this enables the control that owns the scroll bar to change the cursor's position within its own input handler.

The first case we will handle is when the player is clicking within the scroll bar's cursor. In the event of a left mouse press, we will check the state of the scroll bar, if it's in its default state, meaning not pressed, then we will change the state into *Pressed* and we will record the distance from the point of the mouse click to the edge of the scroll bar (Δ) the edge will be the *left* of the cursor for a horizontal scroll bar or the *top* for a vertical scroll bar.

Otherwise, if the control is already in the *Pressed* state, then we will adjust the position of the cursor's top, or left coordinate to the position of the mouse input minus the recorded Δ, this will place the cursor at the precise position as the mouse is moved as long as the mouse button is held.

```cpp
bool HandleInput(float, const input::input_state& inputState)
{
    auto& edge = (m_type == Vertical) ? m_cursor.Top() : m_cursor.Left();
    auto& cursorSize = (m_type == Vertical) ? m_cursor.Height() : m_cursor.Width();
    const auto minimal = (m_type == Vertical) ? m_rectangle.Top() : m_rectangle.Left();
    const auto maximal = (m_type == Vertical)  ? m_rectangle.Bottom() -
m_cursor.Height() : m_rectangle.Right() - m_cursor.Width();

    auto mouse = inputState.GetMouse();
    if ( mouse != nullptr )
    {
        auto& input = (m_type == Vertical) ? mouse->GetPosition().y() : mouse-
>GetPosition().x();

        if ( m_cursor.Contains(mouse->GetPosition()) )
        {
            if ( mouse->ButtonPressed(input::mouse::Left) )
            {
                if ( m_state == Default )
                {
                    m_state = Pressed;
                    m_delta = input - edge;
                }
                else
                {
                    edge = input - m_delta;
                    math::Clamp(edge,  minimal, maximal);

                }

                return true;
            }
            else
            {
                if ( m_state == Pressed )
                {
                    m_state = Default;
                }
            }
        }
```

```cpp
        if ( m_rectangle.Contains( mouse->GetPosition() ) )
        {
            if ( mouse->ButtonPressed(input::mouse::Left) )
            {
                edge = input - ( cursorSize / 2 );
                return true;
            }
        }
    }

    return false;
}
```

The first part can be somewhat confusing and the syntax is less than ideal. The goal is to get a reference to the coordinate we will work on depending on whether we are using a *vertical* or *horizontal* scroll bar. We need it to be a reference to apply the movement of the cursor by actually changing its value.

If the mouse button is not pressed and our scroll bar's state is currently set to *Pressed*, then we will reset the state to indicate the scroll bar is at its *Default* state.

Next, we will handle the case in which a single mouse click is done somewhere within the scroll bar's boundaries, but outside of the mouse cursor.

```cpp
else
if ( m_rectangle.Contains( mouse->GetPosition() ) )
{
    if ( mouse->ButtonPressed(input::mouse::Left) )
    {
        m_cursor.Top() = mouse->GetPosition().y() - ( m_cursor.Height() / 2 );
        return true;
    }
}
```

In this case, we calculate the cursor's top coordinate to be at the input coordinate, but we offset vertically by half the cursor's height, this has the effect of manipulating the cursor from its middle.

Finally, we need to handle the case in which the player used the scroll wheel. For this we will introduce another variable to keep track of the value of the mouse wheel when it was last used, *m_lastMouseWheelValue*.

```cpp
if ( mouse->GetMouseWheelValue() != m_lastMouseWheelValue )
{
    int mouseWheelDelta = m_lastMouseWheelValue - mouse->GetMouseWheelValue();

    const float spacing = m_rectangle.Height() * 0.1f;
    m_cursor.Top() += (mouseWheelDelta > 0) ? spacing : -spacing;
    math::Clamp(m_cursor.Top(),  m_rectangle.Top(), m_rectangle.Bottom() -
m_cursor.Height());

    m_lastMouseWheelValue = mouse->GetMouseWheelValue();

    return true;
}
```

Using the mouse wheel consists of determining which direction the mouse wheel moved, we do this by getting the difference between the current mouse wheel value and the last value we recorded. If the mouse wheel delta is greater than zero, meaning the scroll has moved down, we will increase the cursor's top coordinate by the vertical spacing, if it's less than zero, it means the wheel was moved up and we need to decrease the cursor's top coordinate by the vertical spacing. It's important to clamp the cursor within the scroll bar's boundaries and to record the value of the mouse wheel.

Once we have handled any input by the user, we can focus on drawing the scroll bar, this is fairly straightforward, we will draw a rectangle for the scroll bar's area and a rectangle for the cursor.

```cpp
void scrollbar::Draw()
{
    auto& texture = *m_core->GetWhiteTexture()->GetView();
    m_spriteBatch->Draw(texture, m_rectangle, nullptr, m_backgroundColor);
    m_spriteBatch->Draw(texture, m_cursor, nullptr, m_foregroundColor);
}
```

Finally, the most important function to the owner of a scroll bar is the function that will return the ratio that represents the position of the cursor within the scroll bar. It's the ratio that will be used to determine which part of the owner control should be visible.

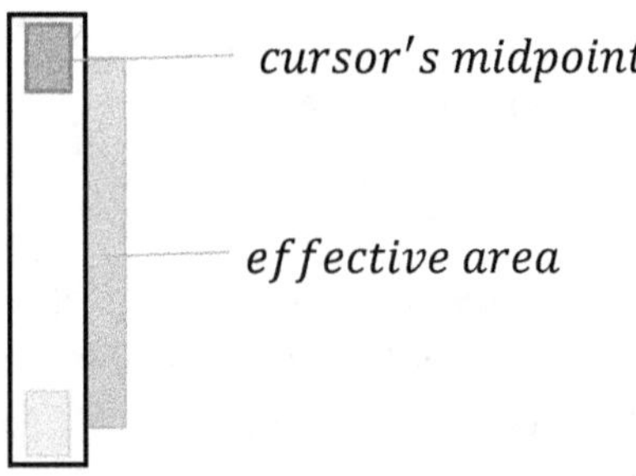

Figure 58 - Taking into account the cursor's size, the scrollbar's effective area is slightly smaller.

Since we are using the cursor's middle coordinate as the point at which we calculate the ratio, we need to subtract the cursor's half height from the scroll bar's height to make sure our ratio falls within the range of [0,1], that is, so the cursor falls within the effective area.

```cpp
float Ratio() const
{
    math::rectangle effectiveArea = m_rectangle;

    float halfSize = 0.f;
    float edge = 0.f;
    float size = 0.f;
    float coordinate = 0.f;
    if ( m_type == Vertical )
    {
        halfSize = m_cursor.Height() / 2;
        edge = effectiveArea.Top() + halfSize;
        size = effectiveArea.Height() - m_cursor.Height();
        coordinate = m_cursor.Top();
    }
```

```
    else
    {
        halfSize = m_cursor.Width() / 2;
        edge = effectiveArea.Left() + halfSize;
        size = effectiveArea.Width() - m_cursor.Width();
        coordinate = m_cursor.Left();
    }

    return ((coordinate + halfSize) - edge) / size;
}
```

The function is designed to work for either a vertical or horizontal scrollbar, the calculations are the same, what changes is the coordinates they are applied on. We calculate half the size of the cursor, half the height if it's a vertical scrollbar, half the width for a horizontal one, the beginning of the effective area will be the scrollbar's rectangle coordinates plus this half size. Conversely, we need to subtract the size of the cursor from the scrollbar's rectangle to account for the half cursor we are discarding on each edge. Finally, the ratio is given by the cursor's coordinate, either the Top or the Left, plus the *halfSize* to obtain the midpoint, to this we subtract the edge, by dividing this over the edge we will have effectively calculated a value from 0 to 1 within our effective area.

4.3.10 Dropdown Box

A drop down box is a compact container that may hold multiple options yet only one of them may be selected at a time. The selected option is visible while the remaining options are hidden and only visible when the user activates the dropdown menu.

To create a dropdown box we will take advantage of some of the other controls we have developed so far, we will use a button to open or close the dropdown list and we will use a listbox to display and select the desired item.

```
class dropdown : public control
{
```

```cpp
    dropdown(std::shared_ptr<core> core, const std::shared_ptr<DirectX::SpriteFont>&
font, const std::shared_ptr<DirectX::SpriteBatch> spriteBatch);

virtual void Refresh();
virtual bool HandleInput(float deltaTime, const input::input_state& inputState);
virtual void Update(float deltaTime);
virtual void InternalDraw();

private:

    std::shared_ptr<button> m_button;
    std::shared_ptr<listbox> m_contents;

    bool m_open;
    countdown m_inputDelay;
};
```

We will start by creating and configuring both the button and the contents
listbox in the dropdown's constructor.

```cpp
dropdown::dropdown(std::shared_ptr<core> core, const
std::shared_ptr<DirectX::SpriteFont>& font, const std::shared_ptr<DirectX::SpriteBatch>
spriteBatch)
        : control(core, font, spriteBatch)
        , m_open(false)
        , m_inputDelay(0.185f)
{
    m_button = std::shared_ptr<button>(new button(core, font, spriteBatch));
    m_button->OnReleased() += [&](void*,button&) { m_open = !m_open; Refresh(); };

    m_contents = std::shared_ptr<listbox>(new listbox(core, font, spriteBatch));
    m_contents->MultiSelection() = false;
    m_contents->OnItemSelected() += [&](void*, listbox::listboxitem&) { m_open = false;
Refresh(); };

}
```

Once we create the button, we will install an event handler on the button
release, this handler will toggle whether the dropdown is opened or not,
followed by a *Refresh* which will make sure all the elements of the control
are properly positioned.

Next we will create a *listbox*, we also will specify that the listbox will not support multiple selection, this is important given that a dropdown control can only have one active option at any given time.

Finally, we install an event handler when an item in the listbox has been selected, this will allow us to close the dropdown.

Handling the input for a dropdown means deferring input handling to each of the individual controls that make up the dropdown.

```cpp
bool dropdown::HandleInput(float deltaTime, const input::input_state& inputState)
{
    if ( !m_inputDelay.IsDone() )
        return false;

    if ( m_button->HandleInput(deltaTime, inputState) )
    {
        m_inputDelay.Start();
        return true;
    }

    if ( m_open && m_contents->HandleInput(deltaTime, inputState) )
    {
        m_inputDelay.Start();
        return true;
    }

    return false;
}
```

We use an input delay countdown to prevent multiple inputs from bombarding the input handlers of the controls. First we will handle inputs on the button, this will allow us to open or close the dropdown. If the dropdown is open we will then allow the *listbox* to handle the input. In both cases, if there is an input, we will start the input delay countdown.

Updating the dropdown is straightforward, we only need to update the controls we use and the input delay.

```cpp
void dropdown::Update(float deltaTime)
{
```

```
        m_inputDelay.Update(deltaTime);
        m_button->Update(deltaTime);
        m_contents->Update(deltaTime);
}
```

Drawing the dropdown will consist of drawing the first item in the list, alongside the button that will open the dropdown. If a selection has been made, instead of drawing the first item in the dropdown we will draw the selected item. Finally, if the dropdown box is open, we will draw the *listbox* that contains the list of items.

```
void dropdown::InternalDraw()
{
    m_button->Draw();

    auto& textureView = *m_core->GetWhiteTexture()->GetView();

    m_spriteBatch->Draw(textureView, m_rectangle, m_backgroundColor);

    listbox::listboxitemtext* selection =
static_cast<listbox::listboxitemtext*>((*m_contents->Items().begin()));
    if ( m_contents->SelectedItems().size() == 1 )
    {
        selection = static_cast<listbox::listboxitemtext*>((*m_contents-
>SelectedItems().begin()));
    }

    m_font->DrawString(m_spriteBatch.get(), selection->Text().c_str(),
m_rectangle.Position());

    if ( m_open )
    {
        m_contents->Draw();
    }
}
```

This example shows how we are able to construct a control by using a combination of controls we previously developed. The biggest advantage of reusing controls in this way is that we are using stable and tested code.

4.3.11 Slider

A slider is useful numeric input control that allows players to select between a fixed range of values. The most common place where we see slider controls is in sound configurations to control the volume of sound effects and music, but they are also used to control gamma values to calibrate displays.

Figure 59 - A slider control.

A slider's look can vary depending on the game style, but it usually will consist of a background, a cursor, a label to represent the minimum value, a label for the maximum value and a label for the current value of the slider. The position of the labels is purely cosmetic and entirely dependent on the look and feel of the game, the behavior of a slider is very similar to another control we discussed previously, the scroll bar. This is a good example of a place in which object oriented design allows us to reuse code and create new features by extending class.

```
int& Minimum() { return m_minimum; }
int& Maximum() { return m_maximum; }
int Value() const { return m_minimum + (Ratio() * m_maximum); }
```

In addition to the scrollbar's behavior, we will want to constrain the value within some limits. The cursor of the scrollbar controls the value returned by Ratio(). The only remaining thing would be to override the *InternalDraw* function to provide a custom look for a slider.

4.3.12 Menus

Menus are an important part of possibly every game that has ever been released. They provide a way for players to select certain aspects of their gaming experience, they can be as straightforward as choosing whether one or two (or more) players will play, or they can be quite complex allowing players to modify core aspects of the game.

As a user interface programmer it is important to identify the parts that all menus have in common and create a base class that handles the default behavior of any menu and also provide the means to create new menus and change their behavior based on the requirements of the game's direction.

A menu consists of items, usually labels organized in some fashion that makes them easy to select. Most menus use a top-down organization, in which the first option is used to start playing and the next options can be used to configure the game's settings. Menus must respond to different types of input, mouse input or touch input as well as keyboard or gamepad navigation.

We will create a base class that will provide the shared functionality for all menus, in most cases it should suffice, however it may happen that we want to specialize a given menu, in this case we can do so by implementing different behaviors in each of the menu's virtual interface.

In order to give menus some versatility, we will implement menus so that they support any control as a menu item. This means the code will be more complex to setup a menu than it would be for a simple menu, but we'll take some steps to try and reduce the complexity.

```
class iitem
{
public:
    virtual std::shared_ptr<control> Control() = 0;
};
```

We will start by creating an abstract interface that will allow us to retreive the control from the menu item. This will be the interface our menu items will use.

```cpp
template <typename T = control>
class item : public iitem
{
public:
    item(std::shared_ptr<T> control)
    {
        m_control = std::move(control);
    }

    virtual std::shared_ptr<control> Control() { return m_control; }

protected:

    std::shared_ptr<T> m_control;
};
```

The menu item base class will take a template which by default will be a control. We will construct a menu item by providing a control to it and the template argument will define which type of control. This means that a menu item could be a label, a button, a container of other controls, even a text box if we wanted to.

The fact that we are using template arguments, together with shared_ptr can lead to some cumbersome syntax when creating a menu item. We can simplify this somewhat by providing a typedef of some common used controls.

```cpp
typedef item<label> itemlabel;
typedef item<button> itembutton;
typedef item<container> itemcontainer;
```

Having established how menu items work, we will continue to develop the menu itself.

```cpp
class menu : public control
{
public:

    menu(std::shared_ptr<core> core, const std::shared_ptr<DirectX::SpriteFont>& font,
const std::shared_ptr<DirectX::SpriteBatch>& spriteBatch)
        : control(core, font, spriteBatch)
        , m_currentItem(nullptr)
        , m_currentItemIndex(SIZE_MAX)
    {
    }

    void AddItem(std::shared_ptr<iitem> item);
    virtual void InternalDraw();
    virtual bool HandleInput(float deltaTime, const input::input_state& inputState);

    typedef event_handler<control&> menu_event;

    menu_event& OnSelection() { return m_onSelection; }
    menu_event& OnAccept() { return m_onAccept; }
    menu_event& OnCancel() { return m_onCancel; }

protected:

    bool m_wrapAround;

    menu_event m_onSelection;
    menu_event m_onAccept;
    menu_event m_onCancel;

    std::vector<std::shared_ptr<iitem>> m_items;

    size_t m_currentItemIndex;
    std::shared_ptr<iitem> m_currentItem;

};
```

For the menu we will use a vector as the container for our items, this will allow us to work with it using an index as we cycle through menu options. What is important when working with menus is to provide a way to know when a selection has changed and when it has been accepted. Some menus may also be cancelled through an option to close the menu or by pressing a gamepad button.

The menu input will be handled to support the up and down arrows for navigation of the menu, enter for accepting a menu item and escape to exit the menu.

```cpp
bool menu::HandleInput(float deltaTime, const input::input_state& inputState)
{
    auto keyboard = inputState.GetKeyboard();
    if ( keyboard != nullptr )
    {
        if ( keyboard->KeyPressed(DIK_UP) )
        {
            if ( m_wrapAround && (m_currentItemIndex == SIZE_MAX ||
m_currentItemIndex == 0 ))
                m_currentItemIndex = m_items.size() - 1;
            else
                --m_currentItemIndex;

            auto selectedControl = m_items[m_currentItemIndex]->Control();
            m_onSelection.Invoke(this, * selectedControl);
            return true;
        }
        else
        if (keyboard->KeyPressed(DIK_DOWN) )
        {
            ++m_currentItemIndex;
            if ( m_wrapAround && m_currentItemIndex >= m_items.size() )
                m_currentItemIndex = 0 ;

            auto selectedControl = m_items[m_currentItemIndex]->Control();
            m_onSelection.Invoke(this, *selectedControl);
            return true;
        }
        else
        if ( keyboard->KeyPressed(DIK_RETURN) || keyboard-
>KeyPressed(DIK_NUMPADENTER) )
        {
            auto selectedControl = m_items[m_currentItemIndex]->Control();
            m_onAccept.Invoke(this, *selectedControl);
            return true;
```

```
        }
        else
        if ( keyboard->KeyPressed(DIK_ESCAPE) )
        {
            auto selectedControl = m_items[m_currentItemIndex]->Control();
            m_onCancel.Invoke(this, *selectedControl);
            return true;
        }
    }

    int index = 0;
    for ( auto it : m_items )
    {
        if ( it->Control()->HandleInput(deltaTime, inputState) )
        {
            m_currentItem = it;
            m_currentItemIndex = index;
            return true;
        }
        ++index;
    }

    return control::HandleInput(deltaTime, inputState);
}
```

Any time an input is handled, we trigger the appropriate event to allow us to react to the different situations. Finally since our menu items consist of controls, we give them a chance to handle any inputs themselves, this way we ensure that any inputs a control handles will get properly managed.

The next step is to draw the menu. Given that we are using controls to populate our menu, what we need to do is to iterate over the controls and allow them to draw themselves.

```
void menu::InternalDraw()
{
    auto& textureView = *m_core->GetWhiteTexture()->GetView();

    m_spriteBatch->Draw(textureView, m_rectangle, nullptr, m_backgroundColor);

    float y = m_rectangle.Top();
    for (size_t i = 0; i < m_items.size(); ++i )
    {
```

```cpp
        auto& item = m_items[i];
        auto control = item->Control();

        control->SetPosition(vector2(m_rectangle.Left(), y) );

        if ( i == m_currentItemIndex )
            control->SetForegroundColor(render::color::RED);
        else
            control->SetForegroundColor(render::color::WHITE);

        control->Draw();
        y += control->Rectangle().Height();
    }
}
```

For simplicity, as we iterate over the menu items, by default we will draw the menu options white, the selected option will be drawn in red. During the iteration we also need to set the position of each item by offsetting it vertically by the height of the control.

This type of menu has the advantage of using events to notify users of changes in menu selection, in this way there is no requirement to derive from the menu class to implement new menus. However, in some cases deriving provides us with a more specialized menu, to support this it would be worth adding virtual functions that allow derived classes to implement them.

```cpp
virtual void OnAccept(control& ctrl) {}
virtual void OnCancel(control& ctrl) {}
virtual void OnSelection(control& ctrl) {}
```

We can add then the call to these functions at their respective place alongside their event.

```cpp
if ( keyboard->KeyPressed(DIK_RETURN) || keyboard->KeyPressed(DIK_NUMPADENTER) ){
    auto selectedControl = m_items[m_currentItemIndex]->Control();
    m_onAccept.Invoke(this, *selectedControl);
    OnAccept(*selectedControl);
    return true;
}
```

The menu we have implemented is relatively straightforward, its versatility comes from the fact that menu options are themselves user interface controls. Most game menus require the use of a variety of controls to change game specific parameters such as sound and music volumes, gamma correction, brightness controls, character customization options, etc.

4.4 User Interface Elements

We will refer to user interface elements to all those features that are more complex and not entirely suitable to be developed as controls. Features like health bars, radars, counters may be created using a variety of controls, but often require more specialized code to communicate with the different game systems.

The base class for our game user interfaces will be the *element*. It will contain the main interface by which we can group and iterate over a collection of elements that make up any type of game user interface. A heads-up display (HUD) will consist of a variety of elements each of which will have a unique purpose, yet will share a common interface to take advantage of object oriented design. In particular, we will use a Model View Controller (MVC) pattern which will allow us to separate the data from the player's control and its visual representation.

```cpp
class element
{
public:

    element()
        : m_view(nullptr)
        , m_controller(nullptr)
    {
    }

    virtual ~element()
    {
        m_view = nullptr;
```

```cpp
        m_controller = nullptr;
        m_core = nullptr;
    }

    virtual void Create(std::shared_ptr<core_ui> core);
    virtual void Update(float deltaTime);
    virtual void Draw();

    std::shared_ptr<core_ui> GetCore() const { return m_core; }

protected:

    std::unique_ptr<view> m_view;
    std::unique_ptr<controller> m_controller;
    std::shared_ptr<core_ui> m_core;
};
```

It is conceivable that not every element may require a controller for example a health bar does not need any form of input or control from the player, it is optional to provide one.

```cpp
class view
{
public:

    view(element& element);
    virtual ~view();

    virtual void Create();
    virtual void Draw();

protected:

    element& m_element;

private:

    view(const view&) = delete;
    view(const view&&) = delete;
    view& operator = (const view&) = delete;

};
```

When we construct a *view* we pass the element in by reference because the view will always be a member of the element and we will need it to retrieve any sprites or controls we wish to draw, it also provides the interface to the data model. Through the *element* we can get access to the *player* whose health, ammo and other properties we can query in order to draw.

```cpp
    view(const view&) = delete;
    view(const view&&) = delete;
    view& operator = (const view&) = delete;
```

If you are wondering what the purpose of those lines is, these are a C++ feature introduced into the standard in C++11, *deleted functions*. What we are doing is explicitly telling the compiler that we do not want these functions to be a part of our class. If someone tries to copy a view or assign one view to another they will get a compilation error. In our case we are disallowing copying by constructor, copying by assignment or moving our view class because it can only belong to the *element* that created it.

The *controller* is nearly identical, the main difference is that it will only need to provide the implementation for a *HandleInput* function, within this function it can communicate any changes by the player to the *element*.

The idea is that this input function will control things relating to the element itself and not the player or the player's property directly. So for example, if we are interacting with a menu, the menus controller would be handling the input relating to cycling through menu options and accepting or changing values presented by the menu.

```cpp
class controller
{
public:
    controller(element& element);

    virtual void Create();
    virtual bool HandleInput(float deltaTime, const input::input_state& inputState);

protected:
```

```
    element& m_element;

private:

    controller(const controller&) = delete;
    controller(const controller&&) = delete;
    controller& operator = (const controller&) = delete;
};
```

This covers the base implementation for user interface elements. A user interface *element* is a complex feature that may be game-specific such as a health bar or a radar. The motivation behind having a base class for these features is to create a consistent framework that would give us the flexibility to group user interface features and perform actions on them. One common situation is that certain elements of a user interface need to be hidden depending on the state of the player, or if the player is in a combat situation his heads up display may be significantly different than when he is engaged in a conversation with another character in the game.

In the next chapter we will look at how to apply the user interface *element* model view controller design pattern by implementing a game's heads up display (HUD).

5 Heads Up Display – HUD

Very often we find ourselves having to reinvent the wheel, whether we changed project, company or technology, sometimes the mandate is to start from scratch. While sometimes it's possible to harvest code from your previous projects or technologies, in the end the new architecture may be different enough that we are better off writing our UI again.

This section aims to present many of the UI elements often used in games in a way that is game engine agnostic, easily pluggable into any game we are writing.

5.1 Health Bar

The health bar can be very straightforward to implement, it's often a progress bar on one of the corners of the screen, other times it's a numeric value that represents a percentage or an absolute number of hit points. As with all the elements we implement, we will follow an MVC pattern in which the functionality of the element is abstracted from its view, this will allow you to keep the functionality intact if you need to make changes to the way you display the data. For example, early in pre-production of your game, it may be useful to see the health as a numeric value as it helps other developers understand and tune their systems, but down the line, the art director or an artist may give you what the health bar is supposed to look like, this is when being able to change the view quickly and efficiently pays off, or when you have an art direction that changes often, which depending on the project may happen often, or not at all.

5.2 Progress Bar

In many cases the health bar is represented as a progress bar, and we may have more than one bar, we may have health and mana, or perhaps a progress bar that represents a shield's integrity. It's best to create a reusable progress bar class than to implement the progress bar behavior in each instance that uses one.

There are many ways to implement progress bars and they will vary depending on the number of features needed, the progress bar presented here will work well for deterministic progress bars, such as health bars.

Non-deterministic progress bars are not in any way useful and should be avoided. If the duration of a task is not known or is variable, it is better to replace the display to something that is not meant to convey a finite amount of time, like a circular dial used by online video streaming services. Non-deterministic progress bars do not convey useful information to the user and often are a result of confusion or frustration.

```cpp
class progress_bar : public control
{
public:
    void SetMaximum(float maximum)
    {
        if ( maximum > 0.f )
        {
            float ratio = m_value / m_maximum;
            m_maximum = maximum;
            m_value = m_maximum * ratio;
        }
        else
        {
            throw new std::exception("The maximum must be greater than zero.");
        }
    }

    void SetRatio(float ratio)
    {
        m_value = m_maximum * ratio;
        math::Clamp(m_value, 0.f, m_maximum);
```

```cpp
    }

    float GetRatio() const
    {
        return (m_maximum > 0.f) ? m_value / m_maximum : 0.f;
    }

    void SetValue(float value)
    {
        m_value = value;
        math::Clamp(m_value, 0.f, m_maximum);
    }

protected:

    float m_maximum;
    float m_value;
};
```

A progress bar works by filling an area based on a percentage of some predetermined maximum, having set the extents for the progress bar, we can draw a rectangle scaled based on the percentage.

```cpp
virtual void InternalDraw()
{
    m_spriteBatch->Draw(m_texture->GetView(), m_rectangle, nullptr,
m_backgroundColor);

    math::rectangle progressRect = m_rectangle;
    progressRect.Width() = m_progressBar.GetRatio() * m_rectangle.Width();
    m_spriteBatch->Draw(m_texture->GetView(),progressRect, nullptr,
m_foregroundColor);
}
```

The first draw call is for the background of the progress bar, this one is fixed to the extents set when the progress bar was created. For the actual progress bar, we use the same extents, however, we scale the width by the progress bar's ratio.

We need to set the ratio of the progress bar during the frame, this is given by the current health of the player divided by the maximum possible health.

```
float health = element.GetHealth();
float maxHealth = element.GetMaxHealth();
float integrity = (maxHealth > 0.f) ? health / maxHealth : 0.f;


m_progressbar->SetRatio(integrity);
```

The code for drawing does not need to be a part of the progress bar object, it is better to leave the progress bar as a purely logical object and allow our health bar class to draw based on the information therein.

5.3 Digital Displays

Often in games we want to present information to players using digital displays; that is to represent some integral value as a collection of digits. Typically this is used for ammo counters, health or energy amounts and anywhere we want to display numeric values in which an amount may change over the course of gameplay.

Using a mono-space font for numbers is a potential solution that works in some of the situations, since the size of the font glyphs are constant there is no need to do much else, as the font will behave properly with changing values. However, when using a variable-width font (the letters differ in width with one another) then we will see our numeric field growing and shrinking depending on the number being shown, this is an undesirable effect.

We can break apart the numeric value into its respective digits and extract them individually as characters. By doing this, we have complete control on how to draw the individual glyphs, we can space them apart at a fixed width, even if using a variable-width font.

The first step is to make a class that will extract the digits in a straightforward, easy to use way, the goal will be to create a class that can give us this ability.

```
digits d(4150);
d(0); // returns '4'
d(1); // returns '1'
d(2); // returns '5'
d(3); // returns '0'
d(4); // out of bounds, returns 0
```

With this available to us, we have the ability to populate the different positions of our digital display. We can construct the digits object by passing the number we need to break apart, we take the number and continuously divide it by ten while storing the remainder of the number by ten, we will then extract the digits in reverse order, what this allows us to do is retrieve the digits using indices in which zero is the most significant digit, and n-1 is the lowest significant digit; this if course could allow us to index out of bounds, in which case we will return 0.

```cpp
class digits {
public:
    digits(int number)
        : m_number(number) {
    int n = number;
    while ( n > 10 )
    {
        m_digits.push_back(n % 10);
        n /= 10;
    }
    m_digits.push_back(n);
}

wchar_t operator()(unsigned int position) {
    if ( m_number >= pow(10, position) )
    {
        return L'0' + m_digits[m_digits.size() - 1 - position];
    }
    return 0;
}
private:
    int m_number;
    std::vector<int> m_digits;
}
```

We store the number as an int to allow us to perform a validation when we try to retrieve the digit at a specified position, as long as the number is greater than or equal than $10^{position}$ then there is a digit for that position, otherwise, we return zero to indicate that there is no digit at that position.

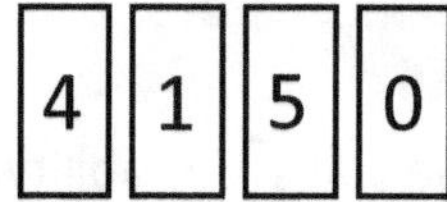

Figure *60* - Extracting single digits from a number allows us to draw them independently.

Having extracted the digits from a given number, we can use as indices to look up for the appropriate glyph in a font. Alternatively, this also opens the door to creating sprite-based numbers, we create an array of sprites from 0 to 9, then use the digit to look up the sprite we should use, giving us the ability of displaying animated digits.

5.4 Damage Indicators

Damage indicators provide a mechanism to convey to the player where damage is coming from, it's particularly useful in first person games since we are not always able to see all around us, if the player is taking damage from behind we need to bring this to his attention before it's too late. Many games display this information around the weapon's crosshair, or around the edges of the screen. The approach we will use works well in either case.

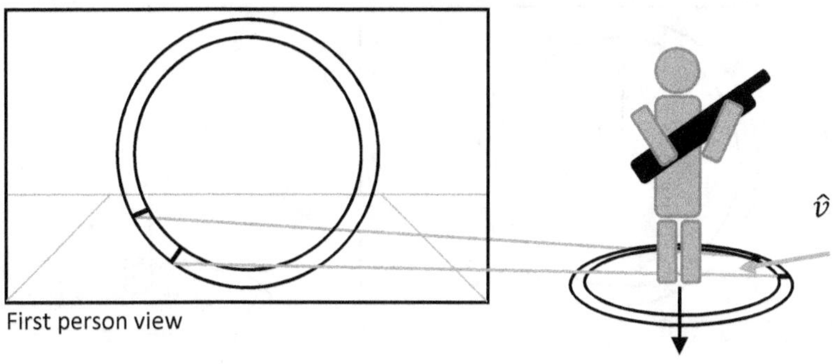

Figure *61* - Translating world space directional information to screen space.

Figure 61 illustrates the situation, on the right we have the player walking in the game, on the left is the world as seen by the player. We will represent damage using a vector $\hat{v}$ which defines the direction from where the damage is coming from, in this case it's the player's back left side. We need to bring this information and map it onto the player's view to tell him that he is incurring damage from somewhere behind and towards the left.

Let's begin by approaching this mathematically, what we are doing is moving from one coordinate system to another, from the 3D world space coordinate system where the player received damage to a screen aligned coordinate system where we will display information about the damage received. More specifically, we want to transform the direction from world space and make it relative to the center of the screen.

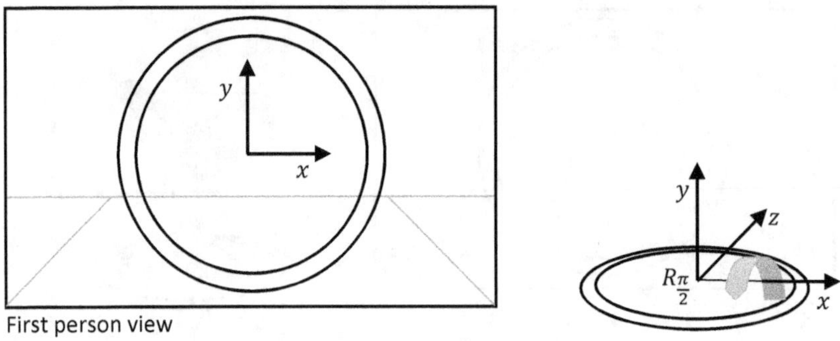

First person view

Figure *62* - Mapping the 3D coordinate space into 2D.

We will begin by defining a transformation matrix $R_{\frac{\pi}{2}}$ that we will use to rotate the damage direction vectors we receive about the x axis by 90°, this will give us a new direction vector in the screen coordinate space.

$$\hat{v}' = \hat{v}R_{\frac{\pi}{2}}$$

We can use this new direction vector to calculate the angle of rotation that represents the angle from which the damage was inflicted. The x, y axes give us the sides of a right triangle, we can then use trigonometric functions to calculate the angle of rotation.

$$\theta = \tan^{-1}\frac{y}{x}$$

This will give us the angle by which we need to rotate our sprite, however, depending on how the sprite's texture is provided, the calculation may need to be adjusted, in this example we will use the following sprite:

Figure *63* - Damage indicator texture.

The texture we will use is aligned towards the top left corner, we will have to rotate the sprite to compensate for this; we will rotate it by $3\pi/4$ to align it towards the bottom.

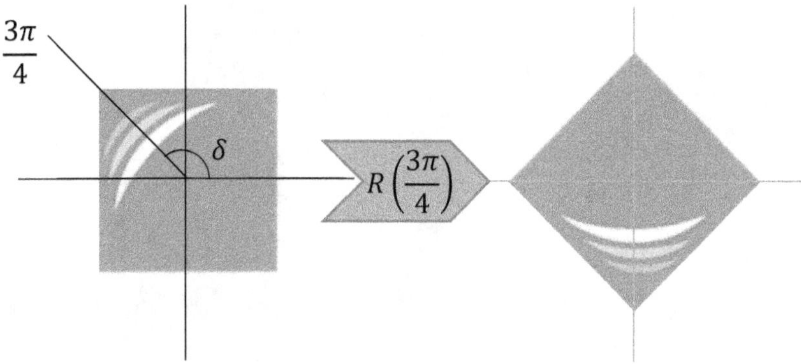

Figure *64* - Rotating the damage indicator sprite to align the arcs towards the center.

We will add the angles $\theta + \delta$ to obtain the final rotation angle for our sprite. If we were to draw the sprite on the center of the screen using the center of the sprite as its pivot, we would see it properly aligned in the direction from where damage occurred, but it would not be clear, and if we receive multiple damage events, the sprites would overlap.

To solve this problem we will use an ellipse, we will create it so that it fits nicely within the viewport, then using the direction vector $\hat{v}'$ we can calculate a point on the ellipse, we translate the sprite to this point and we will have the result we want.

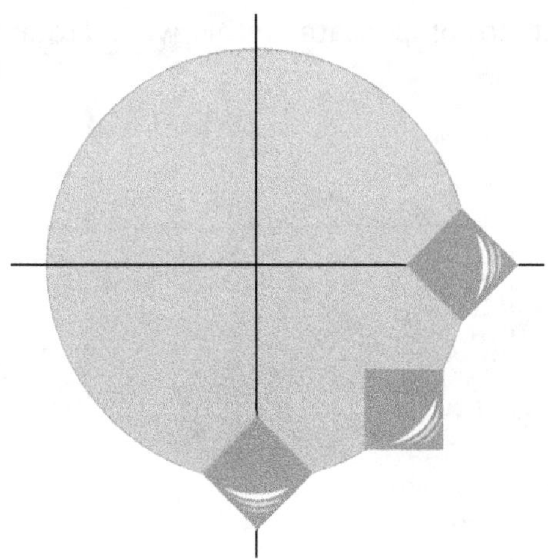

Figure *65* - Damage indicators drawn along an ellipse.

```
struct DamageIndicator
{
    math::vector3 direction;
    float duration;
    float angle;
    render::color color;
};
```

A *DamageIndicator* holds the data necessary to display an occurrence of damage on the HUD. We are interested in knowing the direction the damage came from. We can use the damage direction to calculate an angle value which we will use to rotate our sprite accordingly.

When damage occurs we will create a *DamageIndicator* instance and we will add it into our list of indicators.

```
void DamageEvent(const math::vector3& direction)
{
    DamageIndicator indicator;
    indicator.direction = direction * m_transform;
    indicator.duration = 0.5f;
    indicator.color = render::color::RED;
```

```
    indicator.angle = atan2(indicator.direction.y(), indicator.direction.x()) + 3*(math::Pi/4);
    m_indicators.push_back(indicator);
}
```

The matrix *m_transform* is a constant rotation by $R_{\frac{\pi}{2}}$ it is created using the matrix function:

```
CreateRotationX(math::HalfPi);
```

There are a few more things to consider other than just how to draw a damage indicator sprite, and they will largely depend on the game's artistic direction, for this example we use a duration field to define the lifetime of the damage indicator, each frame we will decrement this duration by *deltaTime* and when it reaches zero, we remove the indicator from the *m_indicators* list. The color of each indicator is hard coded to red, this should be configurable from some external source, and it will depend entirely on the game, damage color could be derived from the type of damage, or the damage intensity, also to keep the example simple we don't animate the color, but we could interpolate the alpha based on lifetime of the indicator to make it fade in, then out.

Now let's look at the Draw function:

```
auto device = m_core->GetDevice();
auto viewport = device->GetViewport();
DirectX::CommonStates states(device->GetDevice());
m_spriteBatch->Begin(DirectX::SpriteSortMode_Deferred, states.Additive());

for (auto& it : m_indicators) {
    const math::vector2& direction = math::vector2(it.direction.x(), it.direction.z());
    math::point p = m_ellipse.GetPointOnEllipse(direction);
    auto screenPoint = math::vector3(p.x() + viewport.Width()/2, p.y() +
viewport.Height()/2, 1.f);
    m_spriteBatch->Draw(*m_texture->GetView(),
math::vector2(screenPoint.x(), screenPoint.y()), nullptr, it.color, it.angle,
math::vector2(m_texture->Width()/2, m_texture->Height()/2));
}
m_spriteBatch->End();
```

We iterate over the list of indicators that we have accumulated during a frame, each indicator is an instance of damage received, the first thing we do it query the ellipse for a point on the ellipse given a direction (this is covered in detail in the section about ellipse) we will then offset the point so that it is centered around the viewport. Finally we draw the sprite, the Draw function allows us to provide a rotation angle and an offset within the sprite to use as the rotation pivot, we set the angle to the one we calculated when we received the damage direction $(\theta + \delta)$ and the pivot point will be the center of the sprite's texture.

5.5 World Space Markers

Often in games we want to display 2D information relative to objects in 3D space. We may want to display icons that represents targets, information about the game object such as its health, its distance to the player, whether it is friendly or not, or any other information we wish to present to the player.

For each entity in our world (or in the active section of the world if it is partitioned) we will compute the distance to the player.

$$\widehat{v} = p_{entity} - p_{player}$$

The direction from the player to the entity is calculated by subtracting the entity's position from the players'. Now we can use this vector to compute the *dot product* against the player's own *forward* vector.

$$d = \widehat{v} \cdot \widehat{f}$$

Recall the property of the *dot product*, if the dot product is equal to 0, the vectors are perpendicular, if it's less than zero, the angle between the vectors is greater than $\frac{\pi}{2}$ (*or* 90°) this information allows us to ignore or handle differently the case in which entities are not in front of the player. In fact we need to check if the dot product falls outside of the camera's horizontal field of view to make sure that as long as the entity is within the view frustum we consider it.

```
vector3 dirToEntity = (entity->Position() - playerPosition);
float distance = dirToEntity.Length();
dirToEntity.Normalize();

float horizontalFOV = camera.HorizontalFieldOfView() * 0.5f;
if (dot > horizontalFOV)
{
    screenPosition = math::vector2(device->GetViewport().Project(entity->Position(),
camera.Projection(), camera.View(), math::matrix::Identity));
}
```

Once we have determined that the entity is indeed within the camera's view frustum we project his world space coordinates into screen space. We do not need the distance to the entity for anything else than displaying this information to the user, if it's not required to display it we can avoid computing it. We can optimize this situation by providing a vector function that both computes the distance and normalizes the vector, as it is, we are currently computing the vector's magnitude twice. This is a reason why it is important to understand what the math functions are doing under the hood.

```
std::wstring distanceStr = helper::stringutils::FormatStringW(L"%.2f m", distance);
vector2 textExtents = vector2(m_font->MeasureString(distanceStr.c_str()));

m_spriteBatch->Begin();
m_font->DrawString(m_spriteBatch.get(), distanceStr.c_str(), screenPosition - (textExtents
* 0.5f), m_textColor);
m_spriteBatch->End();

m_iconSprite->Play(m_animations[Default]);

auto frameSize = m_iconSprite->FrameSize() / 2;
m_iconSprite->Draw(screenPosition - frameSize, entity->Color());
```

In our example, each game unit represents one meter, so we format a string to display a floating point value for the distance, we measure it in order to center the text on the projected screen position and finally we draw the icon's sprite centered as well.

This is the bare minimum code we need in order to render any type of information from the world space projected onto the screen. We can take this further by instead of simply ignoring items that are beyond the screen extents to constraining them either with a rectangle within the screen or an ellipse that encompasses the majority of the screen space. Depending on the type of game, this is a useful navigation aid for tracking targets or points of interest that is easier to follow than mini maps may be.

5.6 Grids

A grid is an organization framework of space in n-dimensions, in the context of user interfaces we are primarily interested in two dimensional grids, though there can be interesting uses for three dimensional grids. Grids are divided into m rows and n columns where each cell can be addressed by an index i, j in two dimensions or i, j, k in three dimensions.

For games we usually prefer Cartesian grids, grids in which cells are unit squares (or unit cubes in 3D) and vertices can be mapped by integer points.

The goal behind a grid system is to be completely logical, it should not be aware or even care about the data contained within, but it should provide an interface by which we can organize any type of data in a grid.

To create a very versatile grid system, we will take advantage of some template programming, it's not strictly necessary to do it this way, it can certainly be done by other means such as dynamic allocation of the grid array. However, when designing systems that may be reused several times and in general, it's best to avoid dynamic allocations.

Before we go into the specific functions of a grid we will create a grid object that gives us the flexibility of specifying the dimensions of the grid as well as the type of data each cell will contain.

```
template <int m, int n, typename T>
class grid {
...
};
```

This declaration of the grid class allows us to create a grid object and specify its dimensions, the following example shows a very simple example.

```
Grid<3,3,int> exampleGrid;
```

The *exampleGrid* object will be a 3x3 grid and each cell, or slot will hold an int. So in order to define the grid, we need to bring in the concept of a *slot*, the slot will be a cell in the grid that will hold an instance of the data type we specify. More than that, a slot can be configured to have a maximum number of instances of an object within it, and also to store information about how many instances there are.

```
class slot
{
public:

    slot()
        : m_count(0)
        , m_maximum(0)
    {}

    int& Count() { return m_count; }
    int& Maximum() { return m_maximum; }

    int Count() const { return m_count; }
    int Maximum() const { return m_maximum; }

protected:

    int m_count;
    int m_maximum;
};
```

The class *slot* will serve as the base class for a version of the class that will also contain the instance of the grid's parameter *T*.

```
class slot_item : public slot
{
public:
```

```cpp
    slot_item()
        : slot()
    {}

    slot_item(T&& item)
    {
        m_item = std::move(item.Item());
    }

    slot_item& operator = (slot_item&& rhs)
    {
        if ( &rhs != this )
        {
            m_item = std::move(rhs.Item());
        }
        return *this;
    }

    T& Item() { return m_item; }

    static slot_item Empty;

protected:

    T m_item;
};
```

The *slot_item* class is defined within the *grid* class, this allows us to use the *T* parameter to store the data for a given slot. When we store things in the grid, we will move the data into the grid. This simplifies certain grid operations, such as swapping between grid slots.

A swap operation between two slots can be performed with moves.

```cpp
void Swap(int m0, int n0, int m1, int n1)
{
    auto tmp = std::move(m_items[m0][n0]);
    m_items[m0][n0] = std::move(m_items[m1][n1]);
    m_items[m1][n1] = std::move(tmp);
}
```

Of course, this means we have to be very careful when constructing the grid. We do not keep any objects we add into the grid, these will be left in an indeterminate state by the move operation.

Having defined the representation of a slot of a grid, we should revisit the *grid* class declaration.

```
template <int m, int n, typename T>
class grid
{
public:

    T& operator ()(int i, int j) { return m_items[i][j]; }

    int Rows() const { return m; }
    int Columns() const { return n; }

protected:

    slot_item m_items[m][n];
};
```

Notice how by using the template parameters *m* and *n*, we declare a static two dimensional array of *slot_item* objects and thus avoided the need to dynamically allocate memory to hold the items. Furthermore, we can create some preset grid types through the *typedef* keyword, this simplifies the syntax when we create grid objects later on.

```
typedef ui::grid_game<4,4,ui::game_item> grid4x4;
```

We have two more core grid operations left to perform, we need the ability to add items into the grid, and to remove them.

Adding an item into the grid may mean different things, first, if the slot is empty, adding is straightforward.

Next, if the slot is not empty and the item within it is of the same type we are adding. In this case, we will increment the count of the item within that slot, if there is not enough space, we will add as many as we can and return the remainder count to the user. If there is not enough space available, we will just return false to indicate that the add operation did not succeed.

Finally, if we are trying to add an item into a slot already populated by a different item, we will return false to indicate adding is not possible.

The next operation we want to perform is removal of an item from the grid. Due to the fact that we created a static array for the grid and that we move items into it, we will need a way to represent an *empty* item. A way for us to test that a slot in the grid has nothing in it. What we will do is create a default initialized slot, with a default constructed item and we will use it as our *empty* slot.

```
static slot_item Empty;
```

Unlike addition however, we will not *move* this empty slot item, instead we will copy its value as to replace the item that was there.

```
void Remove(int m, int n, int count)
{
    slot_item& slot = m_items[m][n];
    if ( slot.Count() != 0 )
    {
        slot.Count() = math::Max(0, slot.Count() - count);
    }

    if ( slot.Count() == 0 )
    {
        m_items[m][n] = slot_item::Empty;
    }
}
```

At this point we have a complete, reusable, general purpose grid system that allows us to add, remove and swap items, and does not rely on dynamic allocations.

For our purposes, we want to implement a grid that draws an image at each of the grid's slots and some text to indicate the number of items within each slot.

We start by creating a derived grid class that will implement the drawing functionality.

```
template <int m, int n, typename T>
class grid_game : public grid<m,n,T>
{
...
};
```

To draw the grid, we will iterate over each row and each column, retrieving the item in each slot and then calling its own *Draw* function. This implies that we will create a specialized *grid_item* class that is able to draw itself.

```
void Draw()
{
    m_spriteBatch->Begin();
    {
        for (int i = 0; i < Rows(); ++i )
        {
            for ( int j = 0; j < Columns(); ++j )
            {
                auto& slot = m_items[i][j];
                auto& item = slot.Item();
                item.Draw(i, j, slot,
                    m_spriteBatch, m_font, m_position);
            }
        }
    }
    m_spriteBatch->End();
}
```

The *grid_item* class we will create will not only need to draw itself, but it will need to have some form of unique identifier. The identifier will allow us to test the grid to see if an item is already in a slot, in which case we increment its count. Normally, game items already have some unique identifier that we could leverage.

```
class grid_item
{
public:
    grid_item(unsigned int id, std::shared_ptr<render::texture> texture = nullptr)
```

```cpp
            : m_id(id)
            , m_texture(texture)
        {}

        void Draw(int m, int n, const slot& slot, std::shared_ptr<DirectX::SpriteBatch>
    spriteBatch, std::shared_ptr<DirectX::SpriteFont> font,
    const math::vector2& position)
        {
            if ( m_texture == nullptr )
                return;

            auto width = m_texture->Width();
            auto height = m_texture->Height();

            math::rectangle rc;
            rc.Left() = position.x() + (m * width);
            rc.Top()  = position.y() + (n * height);
            rc.Width()  = static_cast<float>(width);
            rc.Height() = static_cast<float>(height);

            spriteBatch->Draw(*m_texture->GetView(), rc);

            std::wostringstream ss;
            ss << slot.Count();
            std::wstring itemCount = ss.str();

            font->DrawString(spriteBatch.get(),
            itemCount.c_str(),
            rc.Position());

        }

        bool operator == (const grid_game_item& rhs) const
        {
            return (rhs.ID() == ID());
        }

        bool operator != (const grid_game_item& rhs) const
        {
            return (rhs.ID() != ID());
        }

        unsigned int ID() const { return m_id; }

    private:
```

```cpp
    std::shared_ptr<render::texture> m_texture;
    unsigned int m_id;
};
```

The important part about the drawing is in the calculation of the position where to draw. The slot's x_s, y_s position is given by:

$$x_s = x_g + mw$$

$$y_s = y_g + nh$$

Where x_g, y_g the top, left screen coordinates of the grid itself. The slot's index is given by m, n and the width and height of each slot by w, h. In this example the width and height are extracted from the texture, this means that we could have a problem if the texture sizes for each texture used is not the same. Ideally, the slot size should be configurable within the grid class itself, and on construction of every grid item, we pass a constant reference to the grid that owns it. Upon drawing, we can query the size from the grid, and scale our image accordingly. On interesting benefit of this approach is that if we were to move an item between grids of different sizes, the item would still draw correctly regardless of which grid it is on.

When we draw the grid, we pass a reference to the slot down to the items' draw function, this allows us to fetch some information from the slot in case we want to display it. After drawing the grid's item, we display on its top, left corner its count, or how many instances of the item are held by this slot.

```cpp
std::wostringstream ss;
ss << slot.Count();
std::wstring itemCount = ss.str();

font->DrawString(spriteBatch.get(),    itemCount.c_str() rc.Position());
```

First we use the *std::wostringstream* class to format a string that only contains the item count in that slot, then we draw the string at the top, left corner of the item.

5.6.1 Drag and Drop

One common feature to implement when working with grids is the ability to organize the items in the grid and to move items from one grid to another. In platforms that support and input device such as a mouse or touch, drag and drop is the familiar approach. Drag and drop using a gamepad is not as comfortable though it's certainly possible to do it. When using gamepads it's often best not to use drag and drop techniques but rather to add mechanics to select items in a grid's slot, move the cursor and give the player the ability to select a target slot into which to "drop" the item.

There are a few behaviors that are expected when developing a drag and drop feature.

Single Click

A single click on an item will set the item in focus, we will mark the item as in-focus and we will draw an outline to provide feedback to the player.

Click and hold

Clicking and holding will put the item into the drag mode. This means we will temporarily remove the item from its grid and place it in an intermediate object.

Click and drag

While the mouse button is held, as long as the input device moves, the item's position will be reflected to that of the input cursor.

Drop into empty grid slot

Dropping an item into an empty grid slot will result in the move of the item. We add the item into the new grid slot and remove it from the intermediate dragging object.

Drop into same grid slot

This has no effect, we return the item to its source grid slot and remove it from the intermediate dragging object.

Drop into different grid

This operation will result in the item being removed entire from the source grid and added as a new item of another grid.

Drop into non-empty slot

In this situation we have two possibilities, the non-empty slot may contain an item of the same type as the one we are dropping. In this case we will increment the item count in that slot, and remove the item from the source grid and slot. The other case is that the item is unrelated, in this case, we need to return the item to its source grid, as it is no longer being dragged.

Depending on the game mechanic there may be other possible situations, such as the ability to stack objects, having limits on the number of items per-slot, etc. There will be many subtle details that will ultimately need to be decided upon based on the direction and feel of the game being developed. For example, it's not strictly necessary to drag and drop while holding down the mouse button, an equally valid approach is to click once on an item and it becomes selected and will be dropped the next time a click is performed. These details are fairly straightforward to implement once the support for drag and drop is complete.

5.7 Mini Maps & Radars

Mini maps and radars are practically identical, the difference is that a mini map provides us with topographical data and the spatial relationship of nearby objects while a radar only provides the latter. Land based games typically will feature mini maps while space based games will generally only provide a radar.

There are many different features that make up a mini map or radar and different games will have different requirements. We will implement the most frequently used set of features for our minimap.

First it will feature a fixed image background, this will usually be a reasonably detailed texture that is either hand drawn by an artist or procedurally generated. We will only display a small portion of this texture. Next we will rotate the map according to the player's orientation. Not every game does it this way, but it does appear to be a popular approach so we will learn how to implement it. We will constrain the icons within the mini map using a circle (strictly speaking, an ellipse) this way even if there are elements beyond the range of the mini map, the player still has information about those objects of interest.

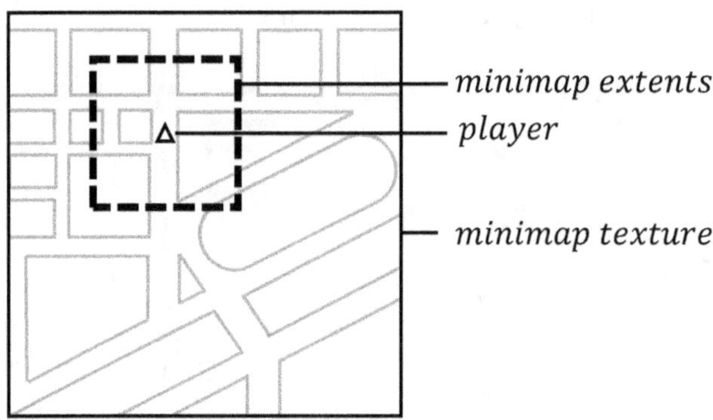

Figure 66 - A minimap as a window into a larger space.

There are many more features that can be implemented in a mini map, we can display the orientation of entities within the map by displaying their cone of vision, we can display different icons that represent whether entities in the world are at higher or lower plane than the player, fog of war, precise distance to entities, and a lot more.

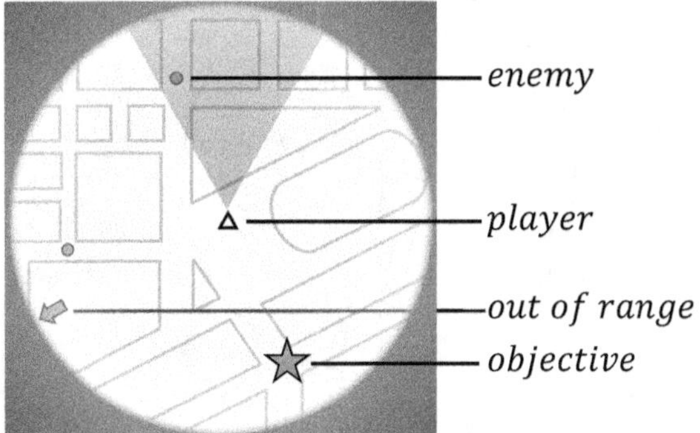

Figure 67 - Radially constrained minimap.

The first piece of information we will need is the player's orientation on a 2D plane, namely we want the player's orientation as if we were looking directly down at him from way up above his head. This will depend a lot on the type of game we are making. If we assume this is a 3D *first person* game we can get the forward vector of the camera's *world* transformation and calculate the angle in radians ignoring the up component of the vector.

Given the player's forward vector $\widehat{v}$

$$\theta = \frac{\pi}{2} + \tan^{-1}\frac{-\widehat{v}_z}{\widehat{v}_x}$$

We start by rotating the angle by $\frac{\pi}{2}$ to orient it up, then we use the *atan2* function to calculate the value of the arc tangent.

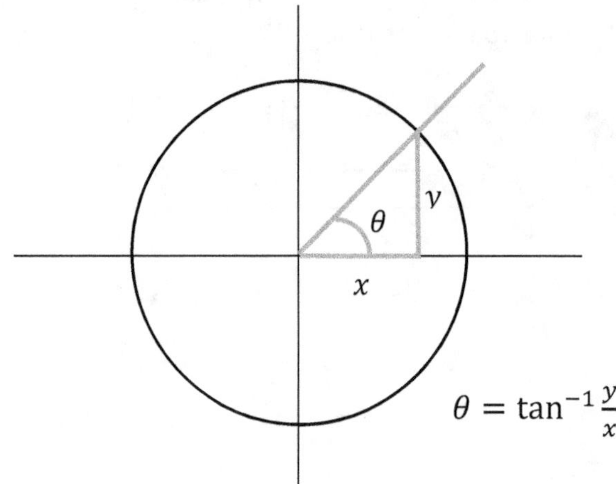

Figure 68 - The atan2() function returns the arc tangent of y/x, in the range [-pi, +pi] radians.

We will then use the player angle to create a 2D rotation matrix.

$$M = \begin{vmatrix} \cos\theta & -\sin\theta \\ \sin\theta & \cos\theta \end{vmatrix}$$

Which we will use to rotate each of our icons into an orientation relative to the player forward angle.

Now, there are two main parts that we need to implement, the first is the player's translation over our map, the conversion of world coordinates into map coordinates as the player explores the world. For the mini map we are implementing we need to know the extents of the world, even if the world was procedurally generated, we would need to know the size of the sector we are currently in.

We generally want to draw only a portion of our large mini map texture within the mini map's space, in order to do this we need to calculate a *source rectangle* which contains the coordinates in texels of the texture we wish to draw. We also will calculate a *destination rectangle* that is the actual screen real estate our mini map will use.

Our initial *source rectangle* will contain the width and height of the full map texture divided by some *zoom* factor. This *zoom* factor will determine how much of the map we will capture at a time, where a zoom factor of one means "no zoom" and the higher its value, the more zoomed in the mini map will be.

```
vector2 playerPos2D = vector2(playerPosition.x(), -playerPosition.z());

rectangle textureRect = rectangle(0.f, 0.f, m_background->Width(), m_background->Height());

float zoom = element.Zoom();
rectangle sourceRect = rectangle(0.f, 0.f, textureRect.Width() / zoom, textureRect.Height() / zoom);

auto halfTextureWidth = (textureRect.Width() / 2);
auto halfTextureHeight = (textureRect.Height() / 2);

sourceRect.Left() = halfTextureWidth + (playerPos2D.x() - (sourceRect.Width() / 2));
sourceRect.Top() = halfTextureHeight + (playerPos2D.y() - (sourceRect.Height()/2));
```

The *source rectangle*'s size will be the texture size divided by the zoom factor, this means that when the zoom factor is 1, the source rectangle has the same size as the texture and will be drawn in a 1:1 scale.

Calculating the *source rectangle's* top/left coordinates is slightly more complicated. If the player's world position is at the origin (defined by its 2D coordinates in a top-down view), we can calculate the top/left corner of the *source rectangle* by offsetting the player's position by half the size of the *source rectangle*, this gives us the top/left corner still in what would be world space coordinates. We then offset this coordinate by half of the texture's width (or height, respectively), this gives us the correct top/left coordinates within the map texture's space.

Having set the position of the player we will draw the background using the destination rectangle and the source rectangle we calculated, we will also rotate it using the player's angle.

```
auto destinationRect = m_rectangle;
destinationRect.Offset(m_rectangle.Width()*0.5f, m_rectangle.Height()*0.5f);

DirectX::CommonStates states(device->GetDevice());
```

```
m_spriteBatch->Begin(DirectX::SpriteSortMode_Deferred, states.NonPremultiplied());
{
    m_spriteBatch->Draw(*m_background->GetView(), destinationRect,
&((RECT)sourceRect), render::color::WHITE, playerAngle,
DirectX::XMFLOAT2(sourceRect.Width()*0.5f, sourceRect.Height()*0.5f));
}
```

Now that we have drawn the background we will begin iterating over all the entities in our world in order to gather enough information from them and draw them in our mini map.

```
for (auto& entity : element.World().Entities())
{
    if (entity->Type() == game::entity::EntityType::Player)
        continue;

    vector2 entityPos2D = vector2(entity->Position().x(), -entity->Position().z());
    vector2 directionToEntityXZ = (entityPos2D - playerPos2D) * (zoom/4);

    directionToEntityXZ = rotationMatrix.Rotate(directionToEntityXZ, playerAngle );

    auto frameSize = m_iconSprite->Animation()->CurrentFrame().Region().Size();
    auto halfSpriteSize = math::point(frameSize.x() / 2, frameSize.y() / 2);

    vector2 screenPosition = directionToEntityXZ;
    screenPosition = m_ellipse.GetPointInEllipse(directionToEntityXZ) - halfSpriteSize;

    m_iconSprite->Play(m_animations[Default]);
    m_iconSprite->Draw(screenPosition, entity->Color());
}

m_iconSprite->Play(m_animations[Player]);
auto frameSize = m_iconSprite->Animation()->CurrentFrame().Region().Size();
auto halfSpriteSize = point(frameSize.x()/2, frameSize.y()/2);
m_iconSprite->Draw(m_rectangle.Center() - halfSpriteSize);
```

We start by calculating the direction from the player's position to the entity, we then convert this direction into a 2D direction only taking the X and -Z axes. We need to scale our direction vector by a fourth of our zoom factor, consider that the zoom factor is scaling our *source rectangle* in all four directions, yet the direction we calculate to our object is only affected once by our zoom.

We now use the rotation matrix we had previously calculated to rotate our 2D direction vectors by the player's angle θ, this ensures that as the mini map rotates, so do the entity icons on it.

Finally, we constrain our mini map icons on a circle on top of the map, this gives a very nice effect as we are moving closer or away from entities.

```
float radius = (m_rectangle.Width()/2);
m_ellipse = math::ellipse(m_rectangle.Center(), math::vector2(radius, radius));
```

The ellipse is centered using our element's rectangle boundary by using half its width as the radius. This makes our circle fit snuggly within the mini map. Calling the ellipse's *GetPointInEllipse* function on the *directionToEntityXZ* will give us the final screen position for our icon, finally we need to make sure we center our sprite by half of its size.

At this time we could use the information we have to select a different sprite animation if the player is below or above the entity, we could rotate the entity's icon itself to represent its own view direction and possibly draw the entity's field of view.

The player is also an entity yet we skip doing any calculations for it, the player is a special case as all other entities are being drawn relative to it and even the mini map itself is being rotated according to its own rotation.

5.8 Optimization Opportunities

One thing many of our HUD elements share in common is the fact that many require iterating over the list of entities in the world and performing the same calculations, we calculate the distance from each entity to the player, we compute the dot product, in some cases we compute the relative angles. For our examples we iterate over the entities within each of our elements, this gives us an algorithmic complexity of O(mn) where m is the number of elements that require iterating over the list of entities (locators, mini maps, radars, etc.). We can create a base class for any elements that require iterating over entities and in it we can create a cache of visible entities, their distance relative to the player, relative angles and any other information we may need during this game frame. This brings back the complexity to O(n) for the iteration over the game entities.

5.9 Analog Gauges

Altitude, fuel, RPM, there are many indicators that still use analog gauges as their way to communicate important information to the user, sometimes they need to be functional, displaying accurate information while other times they may be purely aesthetic, but still must look real enough to be convincing.

To simulate an analog gauge we will need to work on the rotation of a quad. For this example we will not use a *SpriteBatch* which already has built-in support for sprite rotation, instead we will see how to implement a diegetic (world space) quad. The concept applies equally whether we are using 2D or 3D.

If our analog component uses a needle pointer, rotating the quad around the center as it is the default case in the *quad* object will not yield the correct result.

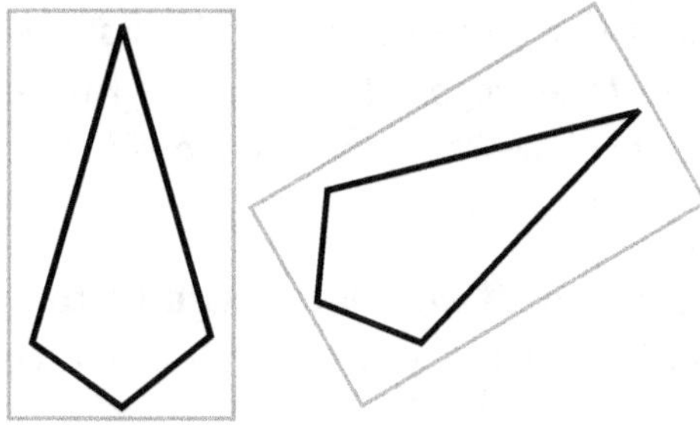

Figure 69 - Rotation about the center of the quad produces incorrect translation of the pivot.

What we need is a way to change the point relative to which the rotation is applied. This is called the *pivot*. By default, the *pivot* is on the center of the quad, this means the rotation is done relative to a point p in the quad's local space.

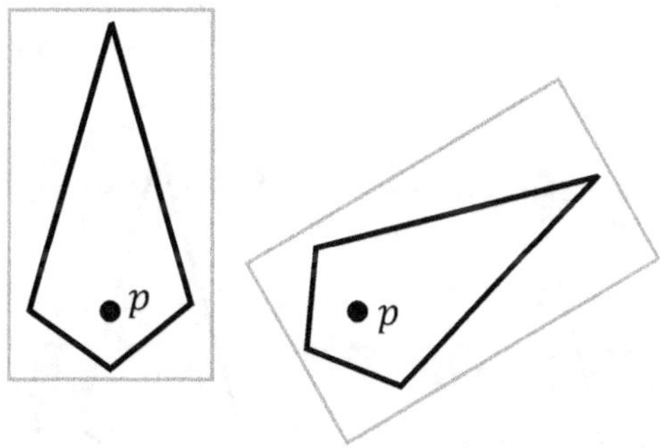

Figure 70 - Rotation about a pivot p.

We will add a vector to the *quad* object which we will call *m_pivot*. Recall from the section

Matrix Concatenation that the order in which we apply transformations will affect the end result. In order rotate the quad around a given pivot, we first will want to translate the quad by that pivot's vector, and after apply the rotation transform.

Since rotating a quad by a pivot is an operation we will likely want to do often, we will add the feature to the *quad* class. We will add a *vector3* member to the class called *m_pivot* which we will initialize to zero, this will preserve the default behavior of rotating the quad, which is to rotate about the center of the quad.

Before rendering the quad, we will calculate its transform, first we will create a pivot transform, which we will then transform by the user provided world transform.

```
matrix transform = matrix::CreateTranslation(m_pivot) * world;
```

In our example, our arrow image is taller than it is wider, the pivot transformation will define how much we translate the image from its origin, so in order to bring the pivot to the point at which the arrow needs to rotate, we need to move it about ¾ of its height in the y-axis. That is to say, the pivot is relative to the center of the quad, where -0.5,-0.5 would be the top left corner, and 0.5,0.5 the bottom right.

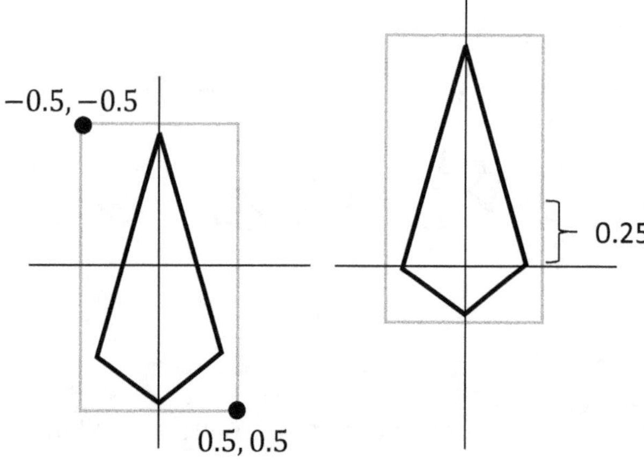

Figure 71 – The pivot transformation is relative to the center of the quad.

Once we are able to rotate our quad with a proper pivot, we need to implement the behavior of our analog control. Since this could be anything, speed, altitude, fuel, etc. We will implement a general version that can be customized or extended as needed.

```cpp
class analog
{
public:
    analog(render::device_direct3d* device)
    {}

float& Ratio() { return m_ratio; }

private:
    render::quad m_quad;
    std::unique_ptr<render::texture> m_texture;

    float m_minimum;
    float m_range;
    float m_ratio;
};
```

Some analog meters will have their resting position on the left and rise towards the right, the needle artwork we are using is facing up, this means we will initially need to rotate the quad by $\frac{\pi}{2}$ to bring it into a resting position on the left and then . the rotation angle within a range. It is also possible to not constrain the display, in which case it will cover the full 360 degrees possible, and continue winding around.

We will usually constrain the angles because not everything we represent with an analog display can be negative, or exceed some predetermined maximum. Speed for example is not represented as a negative value but altitude may be negative if the aircraft should fly below sea level (or the altitude at which the ground is calibrated).

The implementation of the display will vary on its use-case but the goal is to calculate a ratio, the ratio is used to calculate the angle from its resting position (the lower bound of the range) to its maximal position (the upper bound of the range).

If we are trying to simulate a car's odometer, the needle may range from its resting position on the left side which corresponds to the angle π to the maximum on the right which is at the angle 0.

In order to constrain the speed at some maximum, we will need to define what the maximum speed possible will be, for simplicity we will say it is 100 km/h, if the car is travelling at 33 km/h, the ratio will be:

$$\frac{33}{100} = 0.33$$

This ratio translates to *how much has the needle moved within its range.*

We need two parameters to simulate our analog display, the *m_minimum* parameter will be used to define the starting resting position of the need, and *m_range* will define how much can the needle move. Thus for a car odometer display, the needle needs to rest on the left side. Given that our artwork is initially facing up, this means we will need to set its rotation to $\frac{\pi}{2}$ and in order to move it to the right side, on the upper quadrants of the circle we will subtract the interpolated range.

```
float angle = m_minimum - ( m_ratio * m_range );
```

This is important to remember, as different gauges will need to follow this convention. For an aircraft's altitude display for example, the minimum would remain the same to make the needle's resting point on the left, but the range will be 2π to allow the needle free movement along the entire circle.

Having calculated the rotation angle for our quad, we can create a rotation matrix along the *z* axis.

```
matrix rotation = matrix::CreateRotationZ( angle );
```

Since we are using a world space quad to simulate our analog gauge, we will take the opportunity to project it into screen space.

```
vector3 worldPosition = m_device->GetViewport().Unproject(vector3(320.f, 360.f, 0.05f),
camera.Projection(), camera.View(), matrix::Identity);
```

We are *unprojecting* the screen coordinate 320, 360, 0.05 as the position at which we want to display the analog gauge (the coordinate was arbitrarily chosen for this example), *unprojecting* will give us the corresponding world space coordinate at which we will draw the quad. The Z component of the position is very small, this is to offset the projection so that it's just slightly in front of the near clipping plane.

The next step will be to align the quad to the camera as we saw in **Screen Aligned Quad** and then apply the rotation matrix on it.

```
auto transform = matrix::CreateViewAligned(camera.View(), worldPosition);
transform = matrix::CreateUniformScale(m_scale) * rotation * transform;
```

And finally we can draw the quad using our calculated transformation matrix.

```
m_quad.Draw(transform, camera.View(), camera.Projection(), m_texture);
```

With all the pieces in place, the analog gauge is driven by the ratio provided and constrained within the specified range. This means that if we have another ratio, a speed, acceleration, altitude, pressure, etc. we can map it to the analog gauge.

5.10 Subtitles

Subtitles can be fairly straightforward to implement and are rarely given much thought or attention, however, aside from being useful for localization, allowing the game to be translated and sold in multiple territories, they also provide accessibility to players that may have disabilities, such as hearing impairment.

In addition to localization and accessibility, subtitles are a useful development tool for certain games. Many games are written and developed well before audio is recorded by voice actors, after the final audio has been recorded, there may be some additional time before the audio is available as a game asset; the game text, however, may be available early in the production cycle and we may wish to display it, even if the final voice audio is not available.

When a subtitle is displayed concurrently with its audio, it is displayed for the duration of the audio, when the audio finishes playing, the subtitle is removed. If the audio is not playing, but we still wish to see the subtitle because it allows us to playtest the game, we will need to estimate some amount of time for the subtitle to remain visible. We can do this by assigning some small amount of time, in seconds, to each character that makes up the subtitle, by making the time dependent on the length of text, we guarantee that short texts will remain visible a small amount of time, while longer texts will remain visible long enough to allow the text to be read.

$$t = \text{length}(\text{subtitle}) * 1.15$$

In practice this provides a reasonable amount of time to keep the subtitle visible.

Subtitle text is often not enough, sometimes, subtitles should also convey the intention of the writers. A poorly timed subtitle could mean that all the effort by the writer to conceal the some element of suspense would be lost. The solution is in encoding time information within the subtitle itself; parsing the subtitle before displaying it will allow us to take any custom timings and split the subtitle so that we display it piecewise over the specified amount of time.

There is no unified standard subtitle format, this could be due to the fact that unlike movies and television, game subtitles cannot be stored as a single, continuous file of text that follows some set timing, except for pre-rendered cinematics. Games are typically dynamic and unpredictable, an NPC may speak a random line of text as the player walks by and the only way to display the subtitle is if it is linked in some way to the audio file that is played.

As a result, each team implements their own subtitle format. Some subtitle formats may use XML, which is a good solution, especially if the rest of the game data already uses XML. Other games may choose to provide an .ini style file that is purely structured text, ultimately the format chosen for the subtitles is not as important as following some guidelines when implementing a subtitle system. Television has developed general standards that media companies must follow, it is prudent for game companies to begin doing the same. (Griffiths, 2009)

The key things that a subtitle system must provide are:

Clean, readable font, must not get lost with other UI elements.

The font selected for subtitles should be crisp and readable, avoid choosing a font that will get lost or can be easily confused with other elements in the UI.

Text styling to allow for emphasis, bold, italics.

Allow writers to convey emphasis or emotion, provide means for them to stylize the text within subtitles.

Ability to include timing information within text.

Allow writers some control over the duration subtitles need to remain on-screen, it helps synchronize them better with the audio track.

Support for different aspect ratios (4:3, 16:9) will ensure proper subtitles across devices.

Ensure that subtitles are drawn within the title safe areas of the screen with a reasonably sized font that remains readable even when scaled down.

Give subtitles their own background.

Game environments may vary in brightness, for example a white subtitle in front of snowy landscape may be difficult to see. Providing an alpha blended background behind the subtitle text improves visibility.

Use Unicode encoded files to store subtitles.

Unicode is a character encoding standard designed to provide a unique number for every character regardless of platform, application or language. It supports three forms of encoding, UTF-8, UTF-16 and UTF-32 each form has different advantages, the number in the encoding refers to the number of bits used to represent each character. UTF-8 has the advantage of sharing the same byte values as ASCII, allowing for some degree of compatibility. UTF-16 is a reasonably compact form and is typically used when storage or memory space is not plentiful, yet it allows access to the full range of Unicode characters by using 16-bit code pairs. UTF-32 is suitable when memory space is not an issue, and fixed width, single code access to characters is desired.

Allow subtitles to be easily turned on or off.

Not every player needs or likes having subtitles visible, provide an accessible way to turn them off.

There are other considerations to take into account when developing a subtitle system. Depending on the type of game it is possible that multiple subtitles may be sent for display (imagine the game's protagonist walking into a crowded bar). In this case we could use a priority queue to process subtitles as they come in, the priority can be determined on different criteria such as the distance to the speaker, the importance of the dialog, background chatter is less important than a main character addressing the player.

5.11 Development Tools

A user interface programmer often has the opportunity to provide the development team with useful tools that can greatly improve the development and debugging of features, making the team more efficient. It's important to speak with other team members and identify how we can use the user interface to make their work easier. The key thing to remember is that the development and debugging features we implement must be straightforward and intuitive to use. If a feature is difficult or convoluted to use, it will not be used or worse, it will pollute the game code with development or debugging code that may have to be disabled or removed once the game is shipped.

5.11.1 Development Console

The development console has been around for a very long time, it's a useful development tool used to input commands directly from within the game. Some game engines are advanced enough that allow you to write game scripts directly within the development console. Here we will create a flexible console that will allow us to change the value of runtime variables, execute predetermined commands, it will feature auto-completion and it will maintain a history of the commands that have been entered. We will also allow the ability to send messages to the console for the purpose of runtime logging and a smooth scrolling that will allow us to review the contents of the console.

Rendering the console may be the simplest part of this system, as it will consists primarily of text, a background and a cursor. We will add support for colored text as it will allow us to distinguish at a glance notifications, warnings or errors.

5.11.1.1 Runtime Variables

Runtime variables are valuable development tools that allow us to expose properties that can change at runtime, usually through an in-game console or through a network interface, the latter is typically used when the game editor is bound to the game process or when running the game on a console. Runtime variables can also be serialized to file, making them useful for any number of properties that may differ depending of the target platform.

The goal of a runtime variable is to provide a very straightforward way to create them in code and automatically make them available for use externally.

```cpp
runtime_variable_float g_windowTransparency("window_transparency", 1.f, 0.0f, 1.0f);
```

The first part is creating a base runtime variable object that will hold all the common properties for any runtime variable type. We will implement a template based approach in which we will specialize each runtime variable by the type they represent.

```cpp
class runtime_variable
{
public:

    runtime_variable(const std::wstring& name, const std::wstring& description);
    virtual ~runtime_variable();

    virtual const wchar_t* Type() const = 0;
    virtual void Parse(const wchar_t* text) = 0;

    const std::wstring& Name() const { return m_name; }
    const std::wstring& Description() const { return m_description; }

    static runtime_variable_database& GetDatabase() { return s_database; }

private:
    std::wstring m_name;
    std::wstring m_description;
```

```
    static runtime_variable_database s_database;
};
```

The base runtime variable class will then hold descriptive properties, but not the type nor facilities related to the type.

We will talk about the runtime_variable_database a bit later, the rest of the class is straightforward, we keep the name and description.

Optimization hint: The description string is only useful for documentation, such as providing a "help" command that displays, for systems with strict memory requirements this could be stripped out using a preprocessor directive (e.g. #if BUILD_SHIPPING), however, if the game design allows the player to use the in-game console, then we would want to keep the description as it's useful documentation for players or modders to access.

The Parse function needs to be implemented by the specialized classes, this function will receive a string and from it, it must be able to recognize the value and apply it on itself. This is the function that will translate what the player typed in the console into the value we apply on the runtime variable itself.

We will define a templated base class that will be the foundation for any runtime variable type we chose to implement.

```
template <typename T, runtime_variable::eType type = Undefined>
class runtime_variable_type : public runtime_variable
{
protected:
    T m_value;
    T m_minValue;
    T m_maxValue;
    T m_defaultValue;


runtime_variable::eType m_type;


};
```

The first template argument T will determine the internal type the runtime variable will represent, the simplest kind to implement will be the fundamental data types, int, float, bool or any other basic type, however we will also implement a specialization that supports an std::function in this sense, some runtime variables will in fact behave like runtime functions or commands that we can invoke from a console, or remotely.

The second template argument is not strictly required, the system could exist without it; at the cost of an increase in code maintenance, we get the ability to filter runtime variables by type, as well as create a self-documenting system which would allow us to dump a listing of all runtime variables, including their type.

The goal of the runtime variable type base class is to simplify as much as possible the implementation of the specialized runtime variable types, for this reason we provide the ability to set limits on a variable type, though the *m_minValue* and *m_maxValue* members. Given that only numeric types will need to take advantage of this feature we can create two specializations of the Set function.

```cpp
template <typename T>
typename std::enable_if<std::is_arithmetic<T>::value, void>::type Set(T value) {
    m_value = value;
    math::Clamp(m_value, m_minValue, m_maxValue);
}

template <typename T>
typename std::enable_if<!std::is_arithmetic<T>::value, void>::type Set(T value) {
    m_value = value;
}
```

What this translates to is, if the type of T is an arithmetic type, mainly integers and floats, then the version of the function that performs a clamp on the value within the limits will be a member of the *runtime_variable_type* class. However, if the type of T is not an arithmetic type, then the function that only does a clean assignment will be a member of the class. This is not necessary, it's definitely an option to pass the responsibility of applying limits to the different specialized types, and in that case a simple virtual Set function may suffice.

In some cases, we will want to give variables a default value, a starting value and maybe after some tweaking, we may find that we're not satisfied with the values we've changed and would like to restore, or revert a value to its default value. It is for this that the *m_defaultValue* member variable exists, and a Revert function which restores *m_value* to *m_defaultValue*.

```cpp
virtual void Set(T value) = 0;
```

The Set function does not need to be called directly, it's useful to wrap it around the operator =, this gives us the ability to use our runtime variables as regular variables.

```cpp
runtime_variable_type<T,type>& operator = (const T& value)
{
    Set(value);
    return *this;
}
```

It is also convenient to provide a type operator that will allow us to access our runtime variable's value as its internal type, as well as a getter that gives us a reference to the internal value, as we may not always want to rely on automatic type conversion or force the user to cast.

```cpp
operator T()
{
    return m_value;
}

T& Get()
{
    return m_value;
}
```

With the base templated *runtime_variable_type* class in place, we can begin creating the different specializations we may need, int, float, bool, string, vector and *std::function* would provide the functionality for the vast majority of situations, though it's possible to specialize types that are more specific to your games.

Runtime Variable Database

In order to be able to search for runtime variables when we type their name in the console we will have to keep track of them somewhere. We will create a database and anytime we create a runtime variable we will automatically register it to the database. We only need a single database for all runtime variables, so we can make it a static member of the runtime variable, this makes it straightforward to register runtime variables as they are constructed.

```cpp
runtime_variable::runtime_variable(const std::string& name, const std::string description)
: m_name(name)
, m_description(description)
{
    s_database.Register(this);
}
```

Now, it could be enough if the database held a vector of all the registered runtime variables, but this doesn't give us a lot of flexibility or performance if we want to implement some nice features, like auto completion.

Auto Completion

We can implement auto completion for runtime variables by creating a trie that holds all the names of every runtime variable we create, the runtime variable database will keep this trie and whenever we register a runtime variable we will add its name into it.

The auto completion feature is implemented within the Text Box control, we will then just need to pass in our database's trie to the console's text box and it will magically work, for reference, here is where the magic happens.

```cpp
void textbox::AutoComplete(bool reset = false)
{
```

```cpp
    if ( reset || m_currentResult == nullptr )
    {
        m_currentResult = m_trie->find_prefix(m_text);
    }

    if ( m_currentResult != nullptr )
    {
        m_autocompleteText.clear();
        m_trie->get_from_prefix(m_currentResult->next(), m_autocompleteText);
    }
    else
    {
        m_autocompleteText.clear();
    }
}
```

We store the result of a query to the trie in m_currentResult using the text that the user has typed into the text box m_text. If there is a valid result, we will clear the auto completion text and attempt to get a new result using get_from_prefix passing in the next child of m_currentResult, each call to AutoComplete will cycle the next available entry in the trie that matches the prefix, unless the reset parameter is true, we use this when we know that the prefix has changed, for example when backspace is pressed.

To wrap up the runtime variable database, we need to implement the function that registers runtime variables, it needs to add the name of the variable into the trie, and add keep a pointer to it. However, it is not enough to keep a pointer to it, should the variable be released (and it will during the game's shut down) we would have problems. Most of the time our runtime variables will be static objects, and here we are using shared_ptrs to them, this means that if at some point during execution the runtime variables are released, the underlying object will be destroyed, and we would be hanging on to an invalid pointer.

Fortunately, *std::shared_ptr* allows us to specify a callback function to be invoked should the underlying object be destroyed, we take advantage of this to provide a function that will unregister the pointer from the database and prevent any catastrophes.

```cpp
void runtime_variable_database::Register(runtime_variable* variable)
```

```
{
    m_trie->add(variable->Name());
    m_variables.push_back(std::shared_ptr<runtime_variable>(variable,
OnRuntimeVariableDeletion));
}

void runtime_variable_database::OnRuntimeVariableDeletion(runtime_variable* variable)
{
    variable->GetDatabase().Unregister(variable);
}
```

Text Entry

There does not need to be any custom text entry done for the console, we just need to add a ui::textbox control to the console class and let it do its magic. As mentioned before, the important requirement is that when constructing the textbox control we provide it with the trie that we have created in the runtime variable database.

```
m_textBox = std::unique_ptr<textbox>(new textbox(m_core, m_font, m_spriteBatch));

m_textBox->SetPosition(textRectangle.Position());
m_textBox->SetSize(textRectangle.Size());
m_textBox->SetBackgroundColor(m_backgroundColor);
m_textBox->SetForegroundColor(render::color::WHITE);
m_textBox->OnTextEntered() += [this](void* sender, const std::wstring text) {
Execute(text); };

m_textBox->SetAutoCompleteSource(runtime_variable::GetDatabase().GetTrie());
```

What is important is what happens when text has been entered and we need to take some action with it. There are three things that may happen:

The player typed in the name of a runtime variable, but did not provide a value to set.

In this situation, it is useful to print into the console the variable name and the value it is currently set to, ideally, we should also display the description this allows the user to get more information about a particular variable.

The player typed in the name of a runtime variable followed by some value.

In this case we want to change the value of the variable, we will need to parse the text typed in by the player and convert it to the appropriate data type.

The player typed in some text that does not correspond to any runtime variable.

While not an error condition, we should notify the player that no such variable exists, our auto-completion implementation makes this case less likely to happen, however, accidents do occur and we all make typos or hit the occasional random key just before we press enter.

```cpp
void console::Execute(const std::wstring& text)
{
    if ( text.size() == 0 )
        return;

    console_parser params(text.c_str());

    auto& database = runtime_variable::GetDatabase();
    if ( !database.GetTrie()->contains_word(params.GetString(0).c_str()) )
    {
        AddHistory(text);
        AddItem(text + L" not found.", render::color::RED);
        return;
    }

    for ( auto it : database.GetVariables() )
    {
        if ( wcscmp(it->Name().c_str(), params.GetString(0).c_str()) == 0 )
        {
            if (it->Parse(params.GetParametersFromIndex(1).c_str()))
            {
                AddItem(text, m_textBox->GetForegroundColor());
                AddHistory(text);
            }
            else
            {
                auto color = m_textBox->GetForegroundColor();
                AddItem(it->Name() + L" " + it->Value(), color);
```

```
                AddItem(it->Description(), color * 0.75f);
            }

            break;
        }
    }
}
```

The goal of the console is to take a string of text and translate it into parameters we can apply on a runtime variable or find a function to execute. When we call Execute we pass the input text into a helper class called *console_parser*. This helper class does some preliminary parsing of the input text, it will split the string of text into separate string objects by space.

```
console_parser(const wchar_t* text)
    : m_source(text)
{

    helper::stringutils::SplitW(text, ' ', m_split);

}
```

Having split the input text into separate strings in a vector, we will implement a function that allows us to get any individual parameter by index *GetString*, and a function to get all the parameters starting from some index, *GetParametersFromIndex* we use this function to pass only the parameters to the runtime variable, to allow it to parse them and apply them if they are valid.

```
const std::wstring GetParametersFromIndex(size_t argIndex)
{
    size_t index = m_source.find_first_of(L' ');
    if ( index != std::wstring::npos )
    {
        return m_source.c_str() + index + 1;
    }
    return std::wstring();
}

const std::wstring& GetString(size_t argIndex)
{
```

```cpp
    if ( m_split.size() > argIndex )
    {
        return m_split[argIndex];
    }
    throw new std::out_of_range("index argument is out of range");
}
```

The first step is to query the database's trie and verify if the variable name exists in the database, this allows us to exit the function early in case it does not exist. Knowing that it exists, we need to find the variable in the database, once we find it we will call Parse on it, passing in only the parameters; no need to pass the variable's own name. Parse is a pure virtual function of the class *runtime_variable*, it's required that any deriving classes provide their own implementation, it will return true if parsing was successful and false if the parameters did not meet the expectations of the variable.

If the *Parse* function returns true, we can add the text into the console as-is, otherwise we display the name of the variable and the current value, we can also display the description of the variable providing users with some built-in documentation. Finally, any text entered into the console needs to be added to the input history, this allows us to recall previously typed entries by pressing the up or down keys.

Runtime Commands

One of the specializations that we provided was for *std::function*, unlike runtime variables, these allow us to execute a code function rather than change the state of some variable. This is useful when you want to provide certain code that may execute regardless of the game state, for example one such command would be *take_screenshot*, when you type this command, we can execute a function in code that will briefly hide the console, take a screenshot (save the current frame buffer to file) and restore the console, other useful commands may be to quit the game, clear the console, and even game specific code such as kill all enemies, or teleport to a new location.

As an example, let's see at how to implement a *runtime_variable_function* that will clear the console. The first part is to declare a runtime variable function as a member of the console class:

```
class console
{
...
private:
    runtime_variable_function m_clear;
};
```

We need to initialize our variable during the console's construction:

```
console::console(std::shared_ptr<core> core)
    : m_core(core)
    ...
    , m_clear(L"clear", L"Clears the console.", [&](std::vector<std::wstring>) -> bool {
Clear(); return true; })
```

As with all runtime variables the first parameter is the name of the function, the second one is a description, the difference is the value, in this case we provide a lambda that uses the function signature required for all *runtime_variable_function* objects, and internally it calls the console's Clear() function which does the actual work of clearing it.

At this point, if the player were to bring down the game console and type the text "clear" and press enter, the lambda we provided in the constructor would be called and the console will be cleared.

It is also possible to bind a *runtime_variable_function* to a class' member function, we can do this using *std::bind*.

```
// .h
runtime_variable_function m_memberFunction;
bool OnMemberFunction(std::vector<std::wstring> parameters);

// .cpp
ctor()
```

```
: m_memberFunction(L"test", L"function to test parsing arguments",
std::bind(&example_game:: OnMemberFunction, this, std::placeholders::_1))
```

History

It is very useful to allow users to recall their last typed commands without requiring them to type them out again, it allows for quick iterations while tweaking the value of a runtime variable and also can be useful to correct mistakes we may have made while typing the name of the variable. We can implement a history function that allows us to cycle back and forth between anything that has been typed. We will keep a list of strings, and anytime a new string is typed, we will push the text to the front of this list, this way, whatever is at the front of the list will be the most recently typed text, while the back of the list will have the oldest text entered. Having a list we can also keep an iterator from this list, if the user presses the up key, we will decrement the iterator, grab the text from the history at this position and insert it into the console's text box.

Recall that *ui::textbox* has an event handler that we can access with *OnTextEntered*, the first part of this system is to provide a function to call when this event happens, and we do this during the initialization of the text box.

```
m_textBox->OnTextEntered() += [this](void*, const std::wstring& text) { Execute(text); };
```

For simplicity we provide a lambda function that captures this object to allow us to call the Execute function directly within. The Execute function will attempt to execute the runtime variable, and after we can push the newly entered text to the front of the history's list and reset the iterator to the front.

```
void console::AddHistory(const std::wstring& text) {
    m_history.push_front(text);
    m_currentHistoryItem = m_history.begin();
}
```

We add the text to the front of the list because we want to iterate the list in reverse order as we press the up key, showing the last added item first and so on.

5.11.1.2 Rendering the Console

To render the game console we can take advantage of the UI controls we have already developed. We need two controls, a listbox and a textbox, the textbox will serve as user input and we will take advantage of the auto completion feature we developed. The listbox will allow us to keep the history of commands that we have entered and will also serve as the place to provide the user with information related to the commands or variables they have entered.

In our console class we will add our UI controls.

```cpp
std::unique_ptr<textbox> m_textBox;
std::unique_ptr<listbox> m_listBox;
```

In the console's constructor we will initialize the console UI controls to the size and position we want, typically this is the top of the viewport and extending about one third of the screen.

```cpp
auto viewport = m_core->GetDevice()->GetViewport();
m_rectangle = math::rectangle(viewport.Left(), viewport.Top(), viewport.Width(),
viewport.Height() * 0.4f);


m_backgroundColor = render::color::DARKSLATEGRAY;
m_backgroundColor.A() = 0.4f;


math::rectangle textRectangle = m_rectangle;
textRectangle.Top() = m_rectangle.Bottom() - m_font->GetLineSpacing();
textRectangle.Height() = m_font->GetLineSpacing();


m_textBox = std::unique_ptr<textbox>(new textbox(m_core, m_font, m_spriteBatch));
m_textBox->SetPosition(textRectangle.Position());
m_textBox->SetSize(textRectangle.Size());
```

```cpp
m_textBox->SetBackgroundColor(m_backgroundColor);
m_textBox->SetForegroundColor(render::color::WHITE);
m_textBox->OnTextEntered() += [this](void*, const std::wstring& text) { Execute(text); };
m_textBox->SetAutoCompleteSource(runtime_variable::GetDatabase().GetTrie());

m_listBox = std::unique_ptr<listbox>(new listbox(m_core, m_font, m_spriteBatch));
m_listBox->SetPosition(m_rectangle.Position());
m_listBox->SetSize(math::vector2(m_rectangle.Size().x(), m_rectangle.Size().y() - m_font->GetLineSpacing()));
m_listBox->SetBackgroundColor(m_backgroundColor);
m_listBox->SetForegroundColor(render::color::WHITE);
m_listBox->Mode() = ui::listbox::Ascending;
```

Having initialized the controls we have the advantage that not much else is left to do but to draw them in the console's *Draw* function.

```cpp
m_listBox->Draw();
m_textBox->Draw();
```

Some settings in this example are hardcoded, such as the white foreground color, these things are easily exposed as runtime variables themselves as we did in the case of the console's transparency and height, or as part of the console class itself to allow some amount of customization by the user.

5.12 Heat Map

Heat maps are gaining popularity in games, though often not in a way players can see. Many games gather a lot of statistical data regarding anything that happens while we are playing, how many times we died, where we died, what was our weapon of choice, which paths did the players take, what are the most significant choke points in a map, etc. All this information is invaluable to game designers, level designers, it helps analyze and determine which decisions made during game production where correct, which ones need to be reconsidered, we may also find some surprising results.

Recording positional data is useful because it allows us to reconstruct a visual map of what happened, using a heat map we can see the areas where some significant activity took place. We will generate a heat map by drawing a gradient texture at every recorded point, our goal is to draw the cumulative of the events we are interested in tracking, this means that we will not only draw the gradient, but in order for the heat map to correctly display the accumulation, we need to draw each point additively, this means the more points in the area, the more the area will tend towards white as the pixel intensity increases.

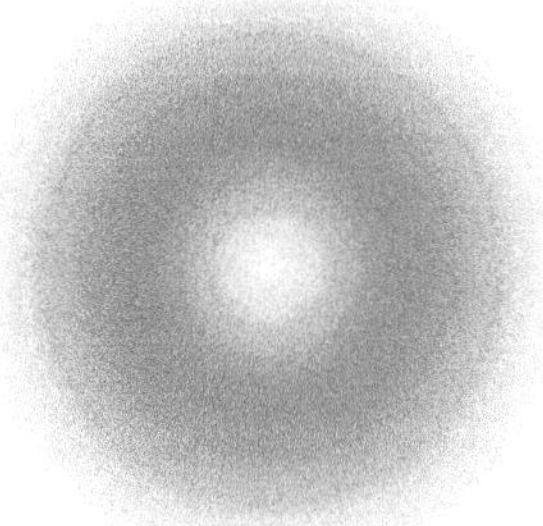

Figure 72 - Radial gradient.

The addition of all the gradients at the points of interest will generate an intensity map, ranging from transparent to full white. The intensity map will then look as a heat map, but it will lack any color information.

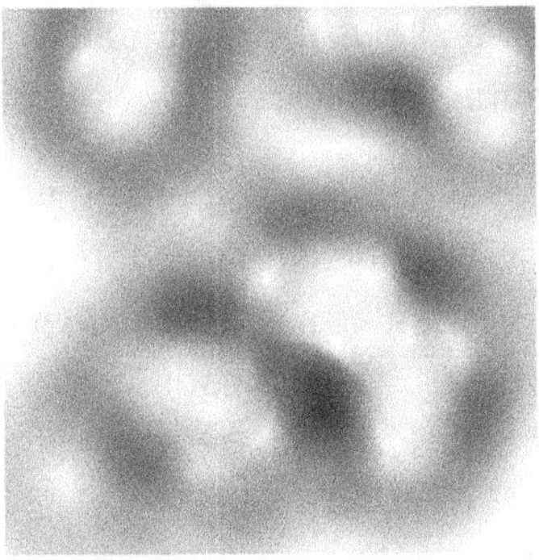

Figure *73* - Intensity map.

It's very useful to separate the heat map generation into intensity map and a colorization pass because this allows us to change the colors of the heat map on the fly. The heat map colorization can be provided by a color look up table, a one dimensional texture with a gradient, the most familiar of which would range from blues for the lower values, towards reds as values grow in intensity, and then towards yellow and finally white.

Figure *74* - Heat map color look-up table.

The look up table is a texture 256 pixels wide and 1 pixel high, each pixel in the table is used to represent a height value. The value of each pixel in the intensity map we previously generated is in the range 0..255, where 0 is black and 255 is white, if we then use this value as an index into the look up table we can apply that color, creating our finalized heat map.

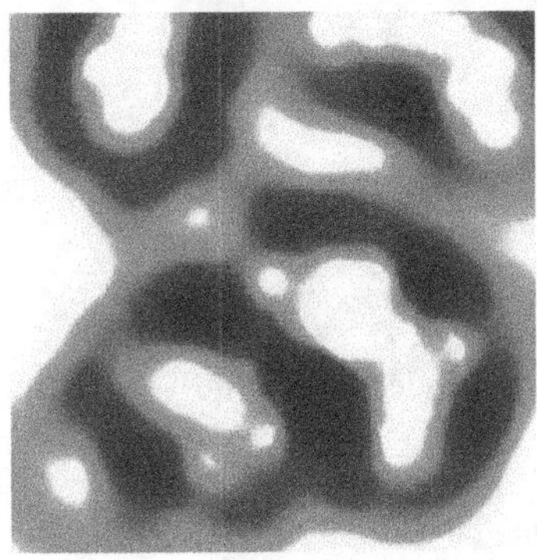

Figure *75* -Colorized heatmap.

Changing the look up table allows the heat map to acquire a different look and it can be used to represent different types of data.

In 3D games, the positional data we will record will, of course be in three dimensions, heat maps as we have described them so far are 2D images, so how can we represent 3D data as a heat map? One possibility is to ignore the up component, grab only the x, z coordinates and generate the heat map, we can then overlay this heat map over a top-down view of the game world, such as the game's mini-map and we would be able to have a birds-eye view of the areas of the game where players die the most, or the most often taken paths. Another option is to take the heat map system into the 3D world, all the recorded world space positions will give us a point cloud, we can render a sprite in world space, mapped with the radial gradient texture with an additive blend mode enabled at each point in the point cloud then colorized according to the look up table, the result will be a three dimensional heat cloud that we can study as we move around the actual game world; the more data available, the better the heat cloud will look.

To create a 2D heatmap we will need a buffer large enough to contain the data we want to record, a buffer of a size that is representative of an area of the game world we are interested in analyzing. Often we will want to overlay our heatmap over the game's minimap if one is available. Ultimately the size will depend on the game and the way we choose to display it.

```cpp
class heatmap
{
public:

    heatmap(render::device_direct3d* device, int size, int pointSize, const std::wstring
colorMapPath)
        : m_device(device)
        , m_size(size)
        , m_gradient(pointSize, render::color::TRANSPARENT, render::color::WHITE)

    {
        m_data = new unsigned int[size*size];
        memset(m_data, 0, sizeof(unsigned int)*size*size);
```

```cpp
        m_colorLUT = std::unique_ptr<color_lut>(new color_lut(device, colorMapPath));
    }

    ~heatmap()
    {
        delete [] m_data;
    }
```

On construction we allocate the buffer into which we will write the heatmap pixels and clear it to all black, including the alpha channel, we also create the radial gradient for the intensity map, it ranges from black to white, we will draw this gradient onto our heatmap buffer at any point in the data we sample.

There are two ways we could consider generating the heatmap, the first would be to generate it in immediate mode, by adding one point at a time or deferred by iterating over a list of points. If the heatmap is being generated in realtime we'd want to do it in immediate mode, if it is being generated from collected data then deferred would work well. When generating the heatmap in immediate mode, it's important to understand the game engine's rendering architecture, in particular if it is multithreaded, we need to be certain that we don't write into the heatmap data while it is being accessed by the rendering thread.

We will see how to generate the heatmap in immediate mode, the algorithm is the same in deferred mode except we iterate over the list of points, but we avoid using the function *AddPoint*.

```cpp
void heatmap::AddPoint(const math::point& point)
{
    const unsigned int* gradient = m_gradient.Data();

    const auto gradientSize = m_gradient.Size();
    float gradientRadius = gradientSize * 0.5f;

    unsigned int offsetX = static_cast<int>( point.x() - gradientRadius );
    unsigned int offsetY = static_cast<int>( point.y() - gradientRadius );
    math::Clamp(offsetX, 0U, m_size);
    math::Clamp(offsetY, 0U, m_size);

    for (unsigned int y = 0; y < gradientSize; ++y )
```

```cpp
    {
        for (unsigned int x = 0; x < gradientSize; ++x )
        {
            unsigned int indexX = (offsetX + x);
            unsigned int indexY = (offsetY + y);
            math::Clamp(indexX, 0U, m_size-1);
            math::Clamp(indexY, 0U, m_size-1);

            auto& sourcePixel = m_data[indexY * m_size + indexX ];

            const color source = color(sourcePixel);
            const color grad = color(gradient[y * gradientSize + x]);

            const color destination = (source) + (grad * grad.A()) ;

            sourcePixel = destination.ToU32();
        }
    }
}
```

We will draw a radial gradient at each point's position, we start by offsetting the starting position by the radius of the gradient, this will ensure that the center of the gradient will be at the point's position. If the offset should fall outside the boundaries of the heatmap, we will clamp it to the edge.

Now we will begin drawing the gradient image into the heatmap image, we iterate over each pixel in the gradient and we calculate the corresponding pixel index to the position to which we want to draw, index and *indexY*.

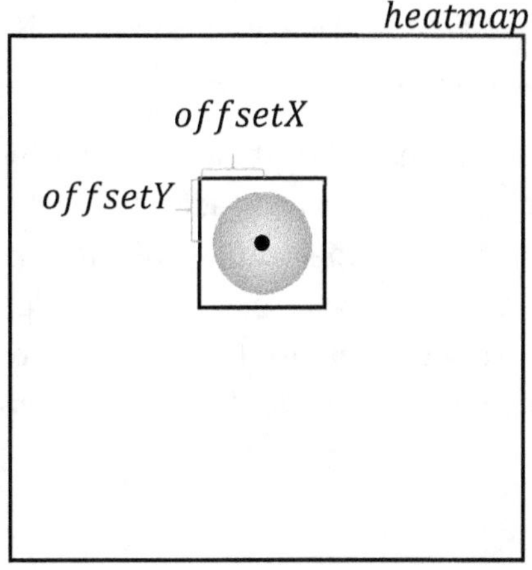

Figure 76 - The offset calculated for the radian gradient.

We start by sampling the pixel at the heatmap image, we do this because we will want to blend the colors additively to achieve the heat effect.

```
auto& sourcePixel = m_data[indexY * m_size + indexX ];
```

We get a reference to the pixel in the heatmap, it is important to make it a reference as we will write into it later. The *sourcePixel* is 32-bit type that holds color information, we will use it to construct a color entity in order to be able to perform some color arithmetic on it. We also sample the gradient color data, and create a color entity for it.

```
const render::color destination = (grad * grad.A()) + source;
```

The final step is to do an additive blend between the color in the heatmap and the color in the gradient, if you recall from the **Blend Modes** section, the additive blend is:

$$f(a, b) = (a * \{A_s, A_s, A_s, A_s\}) + (b * \{1,1,1,1\})$$

Which is precisely what we are doing, where a is the gradient's color grad and b is the heatmap's color. Finally, we write this color back into the heatmap's source pixel reference.

Once we have added as many points as we need we will have built an intensity map, recall that the radian gradient we used had colors ranging from black to white, the next operation we want to perform is to colorize this intensity map. For this we will create a small helper class that will take some texture and extract its data into the same format as we used to generate the heatmap, this will make the calculations easier to do.

```cpp
class color_lut
{
public:
    color_lut(render::device_direct3d* device, const std::wstring& path)
    {
        std::unique_ptr<render::texture> texture = std::unique_ptr<render::texture>(new render::texture(device, path) );
        if ( texture->Width() != 256 && texture->Height() != 1 )
        {
            throw std::out_of_range("The color look up table texture must be 256x1");
        }

        auto& image = texture->GetImage();
        const auto& pixels = image.GetPixels();
        memcpy(m_data, pixels, image.GetPixelsSize());
    }

    unsigned int operator [](const unsigned char i) const
        { return m_data[i]; }

private:

    unsigned int m_data[256];

};
```

This is a *Direct3D* specific example, however it should illustrate well the idea behind it, we need to load a texture, access its color data, its pixels and make a copy of them for ourselves, we can then discard the texture, we won't need it anymore. The requirement that the texture should be 256x1 is in the interest of keeping things simple though it could be removed with some slight modifications if desired. Once we have captured a copy of the pixel data into our 256 element array, we implement the [] operator to let us access it by index.

```cpp
void heatmap::Colorize()
{
    for (int i = 0; i < m_size*m_size; ++i )
    {
        auto& source = m_data[i];

        unsigned char a = ( source >> 24 );
        unsigned int finalColor =  (*m_colorLUT)[a];
        finalColor = ( (*m_colorLUT)[a] & 0x00ffffff) | ( a << 24 );
        render::color c = render::color(finalColor);
        source = c.ToU32ABGR();
    }
}
```

To colorize the intensity map we will iterate over every pixel in the heatmap, read its alpha channel (at this point, all pixels are grayscale we could take any channel except that we want to keep the value of the alpha channel and apply it towards our final color), the alpha channel's value will range from {0..255} which is convenient if you remember that our color_lut class holds a 256 value array with color information. We will use the value of the alpha channel to index into the *color_lut* and retrieve the color we wish to use for that particular height. None of the colors in the *color_lut* have any alpha information of their own (or if they do in the source texture, we will ignore it), the line:

```cpp
finalColor = ( (*m_colorLUT)[a] & 0x00ffffff) | ( a << 24 );
```

Translates to clear out only the first 8 bits, then add in the alpha value shifted into those first 8 bits. Having our final color value as a 32-bit value, we build a color entity and we assign it to our source pixel reference variable.

NOTE: The color is converted to a 32-bit ABGR to conform to the DDS file format used, this may vary depending on the platform used.

And that's it, the heatmap has been generated and colorized and is ready to be rendered and/or saved to file.

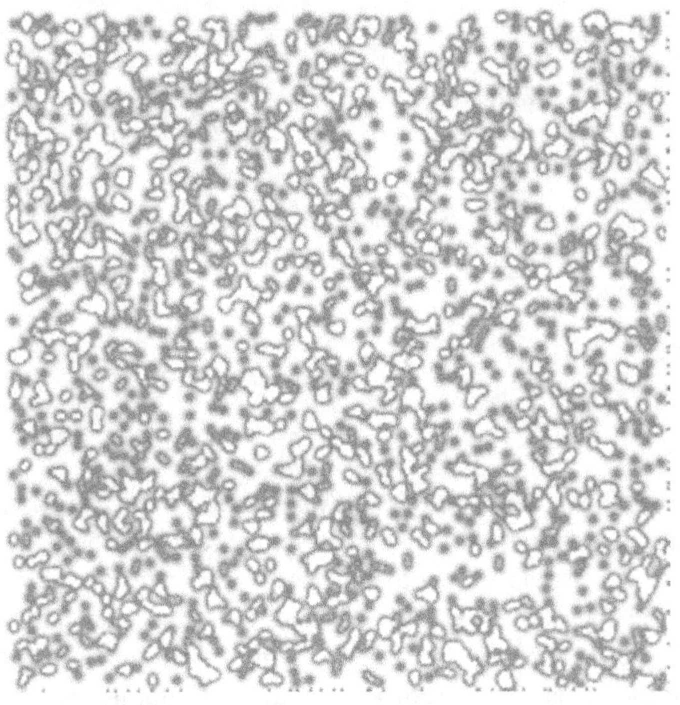

Figure 77 – 3,000 points on a 256x256 heatmap with an 8x8 radial gradient.

The color images for this topic are available online at http://uipg.sempemedia.com/heatmap.

5.13 GRADIENTS

In the previous section we talked about generating heat maps to represent different types of statistical information. At the core of the heat map generation algorithm is the use of radial gradients that when drawn additively will produce the desired intensity that represent the accumulation of some data at some location. In many situations we could just run our favorite image editing software and create the gradient we need, save it as a file and load it when needed, often it is useful to generate the data procedurally at runtime, based on parameters from the user or from the data being received, heatmaps are one such use case.

The gradients we implement are linear and radial, though more are definitely possible. We start by implementing a base class that holds the interface any implemented gradients must provide and we'll put the shared functionality in the base class which is a way to access the gradient's data.

```cpp
class gradient
{

    gradient(unsigned int size, const color& startColor, const color& endColor, bool
reverse=false);
    virtual ~gradient();

    const unsigned int* Data() const { return m_data; }
    const unsigned int Size() const { return m_size; }

protected:

    unsigned int m_size;
    unsigned int* m_data;

    color m_startColor;
    color m_endColor;
    bool m_reverse;

};
```

We will build the gradient within the class' constructor, notice that the base class was left clear of anything but the actual gradient data, this is deliberate to avoid adding platform specific code in a class that stands well enough on its own. To provide a mechanism to store a gradient into a texture we can implement a class that will receive a reference to a gradient, this class can perform platform specific operations, or ideally provide an interface to per-platform implementations.

```cpp
class gradient_texture
{
public:
    gradient_texture(device_direct3d* device, gradient& gradient)
        : m_device(device)
        , m_gradient(gradient)
    {
        m_texture = std::shared_ptr<texture>( texture::Create(device, gradient.Size(),
gradient.Size(), 1));

        auto context = device->GetImmediateContext();
        auto resource = m_texture->GetTexture2D();
        D3D11_MAPPED_SUBRESOURCE res;

        context->Map(*resource, 0, D3D11_MAP_WRITE_DISCARD, 0, &res);
        memcpy(res.pData, gradient.Data(), m_texture->Size());
        context->Unmap(*resource, 0);
    }

    std::shared_ptr<texture> Texture() const { return m_texture; }

private:

    device_direct3d* m_device;
    gradient& m_gradient;
    std::shared_ptr<texture> m_texture;
};
```

The *gradient_texture* class is a *Direct3D* specific example that given a gradient, it will create the texture object necessary to render the gradient and also provides a way to save the texture to file. In a multi-platform project it would be advisable to create a base class or interface and derive classes that do the platform –specific operations.

5.13.1 Linear Gradient

A linear gradient creates a smooth pattern from a start color to some end color, gradually blending both colors using linear interpolation. To create a linear gradient we begin by providing a start color and end color, we will use the size of the image to determine the gradient, or ramp between the two colors. Additionally, we can provide an angle, allowing us to create the linear gradient in any orientation we specify.

Figure *78* - Linear gradient.

To generate the gradient we need to iterate over the x and y axes of the image we are generating, for simplicity we will assume the image is square, x and y both are in the range $[0..\text{size}]$. For each point in x, y we will calculate a rotated point.

$$x' = x \cdot \sin\theta$$
$$y' = y \cdot \cos\theta$$

This will become the point of reference for the gradient, next we need to calculate the distance to the pixel x', y' using the Pythagorean theorem:

$$d = \sqrt{x'^2 + y'^2}$$

Finally we will normalize the distance by dividing it by the size of the image.

$$r = d\,/\,\text{size}$$

To compute the final color we need to consider that for each pixel we want to apply the amount of the starting color as given by r and the inverse proportion of the ending color amount $(1 - r)$, this ensures we blend just the right amount of each of the colors.

$$\text{finalColor} = \text{startColor} \cdot r + \text{endColor} \cdot (1 - r)$$

We can also reverse the gradient by doing the opposite calculation.

$$finalColor = startColor \cdot (1 - r) + endColor \cdot r$$

The linear gradient class derives from the gradient class and calculates the gradient data in the constructor.

```cpp
class gradient_linear : public gradient
{
public:

    gradient_linear(unsigned int size, const color& startColor, const color& endColor, float
angle, bool reverse=false)
        : gradient(size, startColor, endColor, reverse)
        , m_angle(angle)
    {
        m_data = new unsigned int[size*size];

        const float angleSin = sinf(angle);
        const float angleCos = cosf(angle);
        for ( unsigned int y = 0; y < size; ++y ) {
            for ( unsigned int x = 0; x < size; ++x ) {
                float xx = x * angleSin;
                float yy = y * angleCos;

                float r = sqrtf(xx*xx + yy*yy) / size;

                color c =  reverse ? (startColor * (1-r)) + (endColor * (r)) : (startColor * r) +
(endColor * (1 - r));

                m_data[y * size + x] =  c.ToU32();
            }
        }
    }

private:

    float m_angle;

};
```

5.13.2 Radial Gradient

A radial gradient creates a smooth circular pattern in which the edge is in a starting color and it blends smoothly towards the center into a target color. Generating a radial gradient is not very different from the linear gradient, the difference is that instead than calculating the distance of each pixel to the origin and rotating the point, we calculate a radius from the center of the image to the pixel, we again apply the Pythagorean theorem to calculate the distance from each pixel to the center and normalize it by the radius.

$$\{cx, cy\} = \left\{\frac{size}{2}, \frac{size}{2}\right\}$$

$$radius = \sqrt{c_x * c_x + c_y * c_y}$$

$$x' = x - c_x + 0.5$$

$$y' = y - c_y + 0.5$$

$$d = \sqrt{x'^2 + y'^2}$$

$$r = d/radius$$

The final color calculation is done the same as with linear gradients, we apply r amount of the starting color and the inverse proportion of the ending color.

$$finalColor = startColor \cdot r + endColor \cdot (1 - r)$$

It is also possible to reverse the gradient, as we did with linear gradients.

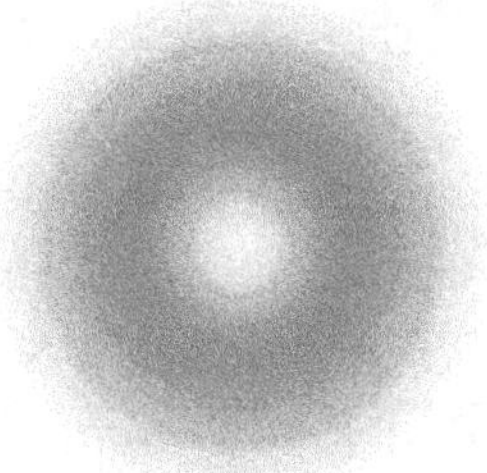

Figure *79* - Radial gradient

We may also want to control the size of the gradient; by decreasing the radius we will reduce the size of the gradient, leaving a larger empty edge around it.

```cpp
class gradient_radial : public gradient
{
public:

    gradient_radial(unsigned int size, const color& startColor, const color& endColor, float
sizeRatio=0.75f, bool reverse=false)
        : gradient(size, startColor, endColor, reverse)
    {
        m_data = new unsigned int[size*size];

        const math::vector2 center(size/2, size/2);
        const float radius = center.Length() * sizeRatio;

        for ( unsigned int y = 0; y < size; ++y ) {
            for ( unsigned int x = 0; x < size; ++x ) {
                float xx = x - center.x() + 0.5f;
                float yy = y - center.y() + 0.5f;
                float r = sqrtf(xx*xx + yy*yy) / radius;

                color c =  reverse ? (startColor * (1-r)) + (endColor * (r)) : (startColor * r) +
(endColor * (1 - r));

                m_data[y * size + x] = c.ToU32();
            }
        }
    }
};
```

There are more optimal methods to calculate gradients, and it is also possible to add more features to the linear and radial gradients presented here, for example, we can provide the center point of a radial gradient as a user defined parameter, allowing the radial gradient to be centered about any point within the image. Another useful feature would be to allow more than just a start and end color, but rather to add color ranges, this would be a useful feature to generate more complex gradients, such as the look up texture gradient used to colorize heat maps. For further reading, see (Lomont, 2002).

6 Useful Patterns & Techniques

There are many recurring problems in user interface development that can be solved by certain techniques and patterns.

6.1 Enum Flags

This section is intended as an introduction to bitwise operations using flags, it's a useful idiom that can greatly simplify code that allows for multiple conditions to be satisfied or excluded. Many beginner programmers fall into the trap of writing very complex conditions using Boolean flags, in many cases this leads to unwieldy code. During production as features evolve and more variables come into play, the condition tests become more and more complicated to the point that it takes more time to understand how to test for a new condition without breaking the existing tests than it would be to implement the feature. Enum flags provide a way to test for single or multiple conditions without a great deal of complexity for the user.

BIT 31   BIT 0

```
00000100 10010010 01110100 01100110
```

BYTE 3   BYTE 2   BYTE 1   BYTE 0

An enum by default represent an int, C++11 gives us the ability to specify the size of the type we wish it to be, it can be signed or unsigned. For our discussion on enum flags, we will be using a 32-bit unsigned integer as the size of the enum. The first part to understand is which values need to be assigned to the elements of the enum in order to have the ability to perform bitwise operations on them.

There are three different ways in which an enum could be constructed to be used as flags, they are all equivalent and usually are chosen by programmer preference or coding convention.

```
enum {                  enum {                  enum {
FLAG0 = 0x01,           FLAG0 = 1,              FLAG0 = (1<<0),
FLAG1 = 0x02,           FLAG1 = 2,              FLAG1 = (1<<1),
FLAG2 = 0x04,           FLAG2 = 4,              FLAG2 = (1<<2),
FLAG3 = 0x08,           FLAG3 = 8,              FLAG3 = (1<<3),
FLAG4 = 0x10,           FLAG4 = 16,             FLAG4 = (1<<4),
FLAG5 = 0x20            FLAG5 = 32              FLAG5 = (1<<5)
};                      };                      };
```

If we see the binary representation of the flags, we see that they are all one bit apart.

```
FLAG0 = 00000001
FLAG1 = 00000010
FLAG2 = 00000100
FLAG3 = 00001000
FLAG4 = 00010000
FLAG5 = 00100000
```

This is precisely what we need because it will allow us to combine flags as needed, first let's do a quick review of the bitwise operations.

6.1.1 AND Operator &

The AND operator is applied on each of the bits of two values and will return a value that has its bits set to 1 if and only if both values have their corresponding bits set.

```
1 & 1 = 1
1 & 0 = 0
```

```
0 & 1 = 0
0 & 0 = 0
```

We will use the AND operator to verify if one or several flags we are testing for are enabled.

```
   0101 (0x5)
 & 1100 (0xC)
   ----
 = 0100 (0x4)
```

In code we use the AND operator to verify if a particular flag or combination of flags are set within a value.

```
unsigned int value = (FLAG0 | FLAG2 | FLAG4);
if ( value & FLAG4 == FLAG4 )
{
    // bit at position 4 is set.
}
```

6.1.2 OR Operator |

The OR operator is applied on each of the bits of two values and will return a value which has its bits set to 1 if one or both of the bits are set.

```
1 | 1 = 1
1 | 0 = 1
0 | 1 = 1
0 | 0 = 0
```

We will use the OR operator to ensure that the bits for a particular flag is set.

```
   0101 (0x5)
 | 1100 (0xC)
```

```
    ----
  = 1101 (0xD)
```

In code we use the OR operator to create a value that holds a combination of bits, this is what allows us to concatenate the different flags into a single value.

```
unsigned int value = (FLAG0 | FLAG2 | FLAG4);
// FLAG0 = 00000001
// FLAG2 = 00000100
// FLAG4 = 00010000
// value = 00010101
```

6.1.3 XOR Operator ^

The XOR operator is applied on each of the bits of two values and will return a value which has its bits set to 1 if one or the other value has its bits set to 1, but not both.

```
1 ^ 1 = 0
1 ^ 0 = 1
0 ^ 1 = 1
0 ^ 0 = 0
```

We can use the XOR operator to toggle certain bits.

```
  0101 (0x5)
^ 1100 (0xC)
  ----
= 1001 (0x9)
```

In code we can use the XOR operation to unset a bit in a value.

```
unsigned int value = (FLAG0 | FLAG2 | FLAG4); // 00010101
value ^= FLAG2;
```

```
// FLAG2 = 00000100
// value = 00010001
```

6.1.4 Inversion Operator ~

The operator ~ is the ones complement or inversion operator, it flips the value of a bit, if it's 1 it will become 0, if it's 0 it will become 1.

```
0101 (0x5)
~(0101) = 1010 (0xA)
```

We can use the inversion operator to clear a particular bit or bits from a value, if we combine the inversion operator with the AND operator.

```
unsigned int value = FLAG0 | FLAG1 | FLAG2 | FLAG4; // 00010111
const unsigned int mask = ~(FLAG4); // 11101111
value &= mask; // 00000111
```

6.1.5 Left Shift <<

The shift operators move bits by the number of positions specified, the left shift operator will shift the bits from the low bit to the high bit, bits below the shift will be set to 0 and the bits shifted beyond the type's size are lost.

```
  00000001 << 2
 = 00000100
```

Left shifting can be used as an efficient way of performing multiplications by powers of two. Shifting a value left by n bits has the effect of multiplying it by 2^n.

6.1.6 Right Shift >>

The right shift is exactly the same as the left shift, except a right shift operator will shift the bits from the high bit towards the low bit

```
00001101 >> 2
= 00000011
```

A right shift by n bits can be used to perform division by 2^n.

The **Alignment** section has an example use case in which enum flags are useful. Alignment is an operation which can be combined, for example it is possible to align one element to both the top and the left edges of some rectangle. Using enum flags allows us to reduce the amount of code that would be necessary if each possible combination were to be implemented individually, and the duplication of code would make it difficult to maintain and understand.

6.2 BEWARE OF SINGLETONS

A singleton is a design pattern in which only one instance of an object should ever exist. Singletons may appear like a great solution when you first think about certain types of systems. Quite often high level *manager* type systems are quickly considered as singleton candidates. In practice however, the decision to use a singleton should not be made lightly, given some shortcomings and potential problems we will discuss.

One of the biggest problems with singletons is that they do not evolve well when the project requirements change. In many cases singletons will end up as a repository of special case tests because the singleton ends up in use in unexpected places; often polluting the codebase in which it needs to be included.

Many problems that seemingly require a singleton to work can be solved by a more diligent analysis of the situation. Given that a singleton guarantees a single instance of an object in existence, it also provides a global access to the object. But many times a global object is not needed, the object just needs to be accessible from a place that is already well distributed throughout the game codebase. In games a problem that may occur is when the technology is being developed assuming it will only power single player games, so singletons are used for a variety of game and UI systems. When the concept of multiple players is implemented the singleton pattern begins to break, at best the singletons will be refactored to be a member of another high level system, such as the player object itself, but this may represent a significant amount of work and in many cases the singleton is retrofitted to work in the new architecture, and this can lead to a nightmare to maintain.

That said, there are valid use cases for singletons, good candidates are abstract code factories, these are code constructs that create instances of other objects. Another possible candidate for a singleton is the localization system, the benefit of which is that we have a single repository in which all localized text is stored, this makes storage and retrieval of text global and straightforward.

A very common but very weak implementation of the singleton pattern makes use of a local static object to ensure only one instance is ever created.

```cpp
template <class T>
class singleton
{
public:

    static T& Get()
    {
        static T instance;
        return instance;
    }

protected:

    singleton() {}
    singleton(const singleton&) {}
    singleton(const singleton&&) {}
    singleton& operator = (const singleton&) { return *this; }

};
```

This singleton implementation is meant to be used as a base class for any object we wish to make a singleton.

Calling *Singleton::Get()* gives you a reference to the one instance of the object, the fact that the constructor, copy constructor and assignment operator are private makes it impossible for the singleton to be instances multiple times.

One of the most significant problem with this implementation is controlling the lifetime of such a singleton. First, the singleton will be constructed on the first *Singleton::Get()* call, depending on what it does on construction, if it has dependencies on any resources, it would need to ensure they are ready and available but it has no way to guarantee it. The next significant issue is if the singleton creates or references any resources, it will need to release them and itself at the right time. In a large game engine, this is not always as clear cut, many resources often have dependencies that must be released at different stages of the pipeline. Finally, this implementation is not thread safe, a singleton implies global access, it is conceivable that a user may unknowingly try to access a singleton from different threads and run into problems with resources that may not be available when expected. There are strategies to deal with all of these problems, but this results in a more complex singleton pattern implementation.

So in conclusion, beware of singletons, in game development they are often overused and rarely robust enough to handle many of the complex situations that arise often in game code.

For a very thorough description of singletons and how to address many of the complexities that we run into when using them, see (Alexandrescu, 2001).

6.3 Model View Controller (MVC)

A *model view controller* (MVC) pattern is useful when developing user interface systems because it separates the data being presented to and manipulated by the user from the user's control or input and the presentation of said data.

An MVC pattern consists of three objects, the model is the most live data such as the player's inventory or a tech-tree. The *view* is the object that will render or present the information on the screen by querying the latest snapshot of the model. And the controller is responsible for providing an interface between the user and the model, communicating user input that will modify the model's state.

By decoupling the view from the model, we gain the advantage of providing multiple views for any given model, this allows us to create different ways to visualize the state of the data without rewriting or duplicating the model's code. For example in an MMORPG auction house, thousands of players will have a different view of the large database of items depending on what they wish to buy. Player's do not own a local copy of this data, they only see a snapshot of it.

The same applies to the controller, being disconnected from the model, we can have multiple controllers, or swap controllers as needed, effectively changing the way the model reacts depending on the type of user input it receives. A great example is the case of multiplatform games, a game that runs on a PC typically will have a physical keyboard for the user to input text, if the game is then compiled to run on a console or a mobile device, the input is still available but it will come from a gamepad or a virtual keyboard displayed on-screen, in this situation we can detect the platform and use the corresponding controller.

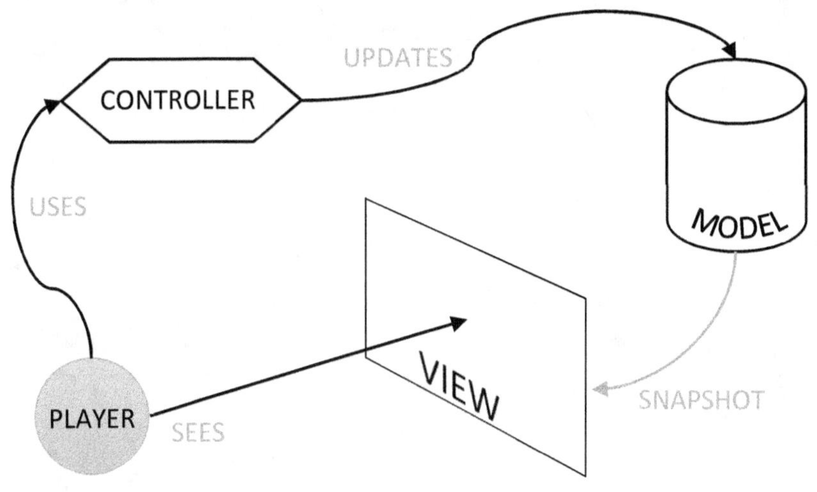

Figure 80 - Model View Controller relationship.

A very important trait of the MVC pattern in modern game UI is that by separating the data, the controlling and the rendering of a UI element, we open the door towards having a multithreaded architecture. Multithreaded games will usually run the rendering of the game on its own thread and the game update will run in another or several other threads, we can update the model continuously in a thread and at some point in the game's execution we will synchronize the data with the rendering thread, displaying the latest state of the data model.

The *model view controller* is used in the example code to create different user interface elements, health bars, counters, damage feedback, etc. There is no explicit *model* class because in a game the model is the player's data, the view may query or poll a snapshot of the data and the controller will update the data according to the player's actions.

7 Advanced Topics

7.1 Animation with Interpolation Curves

To make dynamic, visually and functionally pleasing user interfaces, we want things to move, fade, change colors, expand or contract; we want these things to appear to work in ways we are familiar with, that feel natural. We can accomplish this by animating elements of our user interfaces with a variety interpolation curves. This concept is often referred to with a popularized, if desultory term tweening, ostensibly derived from "in-betweening", as in the generation of an intermediate frame "in-between" two frames to create the appearance of a smooth transition, between said frames.

The idea is to create a collection of mathematical curves from which you can select the one that creates the most aesthetically pleasing result, whether you are fading in/out a menu, bouncing text on the screen, creating animated particles, the list of use cases is endless. These curves are often called easing functions and are generally described as ease-in, ease-out or ease-in/out which refers to the behavior we might expect from the curve.

7.1.1 Ease Functions

There are three types of easing curves we will use, ease in, ease out and ease in/out. These functions are applied over the curves. The functions we will use are designed to receive the curve function as a template argument, this allows us to reuse the same behavior with a different curve without triplicating the same code for each of the ease types we will use.

Ease In

Ease in is the first and most straightforward case, it starts slow and gradually speeds up over the curve, the curve itself will drive the behavior.

```cpp
template <double (*function)(double)>
double ease_in(double t)
{
    return function(t);
}
```

Ease Out

Ease out is the inverse behavior of ease in, the curve starts off slow and gradually speeds up, following the provided curve.

```cpp
template <double (*function)(double)>
double ease_out(double t)
{
    return 1.0 - ease_in<function>( 1.0 - t );
}
```

Ease In/Out

Ease In/Out combines both previous ease functions, during the lower half of the curve traversal the ease in behavior will be applied, since we are applying it to only half of the function we bias the parameter by two and scale it down by 0.5, and on the upper half of the curve, the ease out behavior will be applied, this time we apply the bias to ensure the curve starts from 0.5 and fits the remaining space up to 1.

```cpp
template <double (*function)(double)>
double ease_in_out(double t)
{
    if ( t < 0.5 )
    {   return ease_in<function>( 2.0 * t ) * 0.5; }
    else
    {   return 0.5 + ease_out<function>( 2.0 * t - 1.0 ) * 0.5;        }
}
```

There are a number of well-defined curves used by different libraries and applications, we will implement the most popular ones, it is definitely possible to provide custom curve functions and extend the library of animation effects as needed.

7.1.2 Ease Curves

The following few pages provide a reference for the different type of ease curves that we will implement. This is not an exhaustive list of curves, but enough to develop a large variety of effects.

Having this library of curves is useful, but there needs to be a system that can be used to animate parameters over the different set of curves, over a specified amount of time, parameters that will control movement, colors, fades, etc. In the next section we will implement a system to interpolate values along the curves presented here.

7.1.2.1   Quadratic

$$y = x^2$$

```
double quadratic(double t)
{
    return t * t;
}
```

Curve	Example
Ease In	animation anim(m_alpha, 0.f, 1.f, curves::ease_in<curves::quadratic>);
Ease Out	animation anim(m_alpha, 0.f, 1.f, curves::ease_out<curves:: quadratic>);
Ease In/Out	animation anim(m_alpha, 0.f, 1.f, curves::ease_in_out<curves:: quadratic>);

7.1.2.2 Cubic

$$y = x^3$$

```
double cubic(double t)
{
    return t * t * t;
}
```

Curve	Example
Ease In	`animation anim(m_alpha, 0.f, 1.f,` `curves::ease_in<curves::elastic>);`
Ease Out	`animation anim(m_alpha, 0.f, 1.f,` `curves::ease_out<curves::elastic>);`
Ease In/Out	`animation(m_alpha, 0.f, 1.f,` `curves::ease_in_out<curves::elastic>);`

7.1.2.3 Quart

$$y = x^4$$

```
double quart(double t)
{
    return t * t * t * t;
}
```

Curve	Example
Ease In	`animation(m_alpha, 0.f, 1.f, curves::ease_in_out<curves::quart>);`
Ease Out	`animation(m_alpha, 0.f, 1.f, curves::ease_in_out<curves::quart>);`
Ease In/Out	`animation(m_alpha, 0.f, 1.f, curves::ease_in_out<curves::quart>);`

7.1.2.4 Quint

$$y = x^5$$

```
double quint(double t)
{
    return t * t * t * t * t;
}
```

Curve	Example
Ease In	`animation(m_alpha, 0.f, 1.f, curves::ease_in<curves::quint>);`
Ease Out	`animation(m_alpha, 0.f, 1.f, curves::ease_out<curves::quint>);`
Ease In/Out	`animation(m_alpha, 0.f, 1.f, curves::ease_in_out<curves::quint>);`

7.1.2.5 Sine

$$y = 1 - \cos(\pi x)$$

```
double sine(double t)
{
    return 1 - cos(t * math::HalfPi);
}
```

Curve	Example
Ease In	`animation(m_alpha, 0.f, 1.f,` `curves::ease_in<curves::sine>);`
Ease Out	`animation(m_alpha, 0.f, 1.f,` `curves::ease_out<curves::sine>);`
Ease In/Out	`animation(m_alpha, 0.f, 1.f,` `curves::ease_in_out<curves::sine>);`

7.1.2.6 Exponential

$$y = \begin{cases} 0, & x = 0 \\ 2^{10(x-1)}, & x\,!=0 \end{cases}$$

```
double expo(double t)
{
    return t == 0 ? 0 : pow(2, 10 * (t - 1));
}
```

Curve	Example
Ease In	`animation(m_alpha, 0.f, 1.f,` `curves::ease_in_out<curves::expo>);`
Ease Out	`animation(m_alpha, 0.f, 1.f,` `curves::ease_in_out<curves::expo>);`
Ease In/Out	`animation(m_alpha, 0.f, 1.f,` `curves::ease_in_out<curves::expo>);`

7.1.2.7 Elastic

$$x' = x - 1, k = 0.3$$

$$y = -2^{10x'} * \sin\left(x' - \frac{k}{4}\right)\frac{\pi}{k}$$

```
double elastic(double t)
{
    const double v(t - 1.0);
    const double p(0.3);
    return -pow(2, 10. * v) * sin( (v - p / 4.) * math::TwoPi / p);
}
```

Ease In	Ease Out
 Ease In	animation(m_alpha, 0.f, 1.f, curves::ease_in<curves::elastic>);
 Ease Out	animation(m_alpha, 0.f, 1.f, curves::ease_out<curves::elastic>);
 Ease In/Out	animation(m_alpha, 0.f, 1.f, curves::ease_in_out<curves::elastic>);

7.1.2.8 Circular

$$y = \sqrt{1 - x^2}$$

```
double circular(double t)
{
    return 1 - sqrt(1 - t * t);
}
```

Curve	Example
Ease In	animation(m_alpha, 0.f, 1.f, curves::ease_in<curves::circular>);
Ease Out	animation(m_alpha, 0.f, 1.f, curves::ease_out<curves::circular>);
Ease In/Out	animation(m_alpha, 0.f, 1.f, curves::ease_in_out<curves::circular>);

7.1.3 Interpolator

The interpolator is the object responsible for performing the interpolation of any running animations. It's reasonably straightforward, it maintains a list of user added animations and updates them each frame.

```cpp
class interpolator
{
public:

    void Add(animation& anim)
    {
        m_activeAnimations.push_back(std::move(anim));
    }

    void Update(float deltaTime)
    {
        auto anim = m_activeAnimations.begin();
        while ( anim != m_activeAnimations.end() )
        {
            anim->Update(deltaTime);

            if ( anim->IsFinished() )
            {
                anim = m_activeAnimations.erase(anim);
            }
            else
            {
                ++anim;
            }
        }
    }

private:

    std::list<animation> m_activeAnimations;

};
```

When an animation is added to the interpolator, it takes ownership of it by way of *std::move* there is no need for animations to exist outside of the interpolator.

Updating each animation is trivial, the only thing to notice is that if after an animation's update we determine that it has finished, we will erase it from the list.

7.1.4 Animations

Animations will hold the parameters that describe how an interpolation will behave. The main properties will be the starting value, the ending value and the duration of the animation. We will also specify which of the ease curves we wish to use, and finally we will provide a way for users to know when an animation has finished.

An animation will provide users the ability to specify three functions, an update function, this function will be called each frame during an animation. Users may want to inject custom behaviors at precise points in an animation's lifetime. The ease function, this will be one of the ease and curve functions we have defined in our curves library. And a finish function, this is a function called when the animation is finished. Alternatively, instead, or in addition to, we could trigger an event *OnFinished*, it would provide another way of achieving the same result. The function approach may be favorable because it results in more concise code when constructing an animation, as we will see.

```
typedef std::function<void(float)> update_function;
typedef std::function<float(float)> ease_function;
typedef std::function<void()> finish_function;
```

The next important properties of an animation define its behavior, and keep its state.

```
float m_start;
float m_end;
```

```
float m_duration;
float m_time;
```

There are two types of animations, those that start from some value and end in another where the user is responsible for providing an update function by which we can use the results of the interpolation. And, an animation that operates on a reference to an existing value, external to the animation. The latter will be used more often as we generally have a value we wish to interpolate.

The constructor for the second type of animation takes a reference to the value, it will then bind a swap function that will swap the resulting value of the interpolation with the value in the reference.

```
animation(float& value, float end, float duration, ease_function easeFunction,
finish_function finishFunction = nullptr)
        : m_start(value)
        , m_end(end)
        , m_duration(duration)
        , m_time(0)
        , m_easeFunction(easeFunction)
        , m_finishFunction(finishFunction)
{
    using namespace std::placeholders;
    m_updateFunction = std::bind( &swap, std::ref(value), _1);
}
```

Finally, the animation must be updated, this is the main function in the system, it is where the ease curves are used and the interpolation takes place. It is also where we determine if the animation has finished, and if it has, we invoke the finish function just before the animation is removed from the interpolator.

```
void animation::Update(float deltaTime)
{
    const float dt = math::Min(m_duration - m_time, deltaTime);

    m_time += dt;

    const float t = m_easeFunction( m_time / m_duration );
```

```cpp
    const float result = math::Lerp(m_start, m_end, t);

    m_updateFunction(result);

    if ( m_time >= m_duration )
    {
        m_finishFunction();
    }
}
```

The parameter *dt* is the time remaining to advance the animation, or if the frame's time is larger than what is needed to complete the interpolation, we take the lesser amount.

Calling the ease function requires a parameter from 0.0 to 1.0, for this we divide the present animation's time by its intended duration, and we then do a linear interpolation between the starting value and the ending value, with the t from the curve function.

We call the update function to make sure our calculated values are used, whether to update the reference that the user provided, or to perform a custom update function.

Finally if the time is greater than the duration, if a finish function was provided we use it.

Using the system requires creating an interpolator object and adding animations to it.

```cpp
ui::animation anim(m_currentAngle, targetAngle, 5.f,
ui::curves::ease_in_out<ui::curves::quadratic>,
[&]{ m_animating=false; } );

m_interpolator.Add(anim);
```

In this example an animation is created which will interpolate from *m_currentAngle* to *targetAngle* over the course of five seconds. It will use an ease in/out quadratic curve and once the animation is finished, it will reset a flag that indicates that the object was animating.

It is also possible to chain animations together, the finish function of one animation could add a new animation into the interpolator. This can be used to achieve varied effects.

This system is very versatile and choosing interesting curves when moving, fading or changing colors will result in much more lively and interesting user interfaces. The best part of it is that it is powerful, yet lightweight enough to be integrated into existing systems or to be used early in a project's lifetime.

7.2 Transformation Hierarchies

Transformation hierarchies are a way to organize and manipulate data such that by changing one part of the hierarchy, any dependent parts will be transformed accordingly, a familiar example of a transformation hierarchy is seen when animating game characters using skeleton hierarchies. A root bone exists somewhere within a model, and one or many child bones are attached to it, creating parent/child relationships, as a parent bone's position or rotations changes, so do its children.

The same concept can be brought to user interfaces, we can create transformation hierarchies that bind user interface elements to "bones" in the way animation systems do, and then we can achieve control movement of many UI elements, respective to each other by moving or animating a single transformation in the hierarchy.

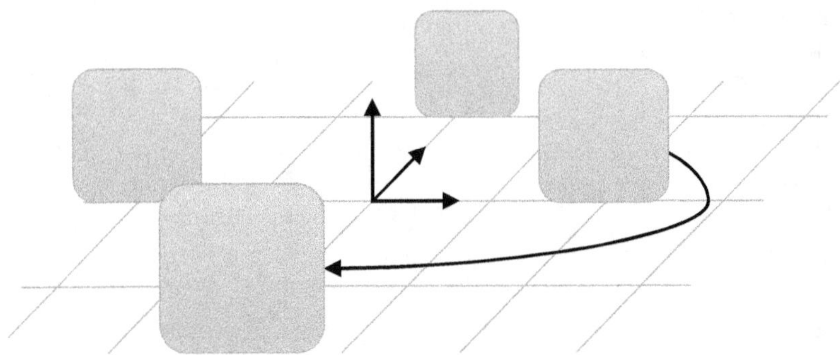

Figure *81* - Transformation hierarchy, the rotation of the parent node in the center rotates the child elements sorrounding it.

The concepts apply to both 2D and 3D user interfaces, in 2D, an object may be the parent of other objects, causing them to move, rotate, and even scale in relation to their parent.

One interesting application of a hierarchical animation system is to create a 3D radial menu, it is a good system to illustrate the idea of creating transformation hierarchies for user interfaces elements without too much complexity.

We will create an object called menu_3d, this will be the class that will hold the main functionality for the menu, it will handle user input and with it, control the animation parameters of the menu. It will also contain the hierarchy of objects, which we will define as an internal class of the menu_3d called item. The menu object will only need one item, this will be the root item and it may have as many items as needed.

```
class menu_3d
{

...

private:

    float m_currentAngle;
    float m_targetAngle;
```

```
        float m_animationTime;
        bool m_animating;
        int m_currentItem;

        std::unique_ptr<item> m_root;

        ui::interpolator m_interpolator;

        std::shared_ptr<DirectX::SpriteBatch> m_spriteBatch;
};
```

The goal of the menu_3d class is to rotate a root item about its y axis, this in turn will make all of its child items rotate in relation to it. The current angle will be the animated parameter used to create the rotation matrix during each frame, the target angle will be set as a result of user input.

```
void CycleLeft()
{
    if ( m_animating )
        return;

    for (auto& item : m_root->Children() )
    {
        item->Selected() = false;
    }

    if ( m_currentItem - 1 < 0 )
    {
        m_currentItem = m_root->Children().size() - 1;
        m_currentAngle = math::TwoPi;
    }
    else
    {
        --m_currentItem;
    }

    m_root->Children()[m_currentItem]->Selected() = true;

    const float step = math::TwoPi / m_root->Children().size();
    m_targetAngle = m_currentItem * step;

    ui::animation anim(m_currentAngle, m_targetAngle,
        m_animationTime,
```

```
        ui::curves::ease_in_out<ui::curves::quadratic>,
        [&]{ m_animating=false; } );

    m_interpolator.Add(anim);

    m_animating = true;
}
```

For simplicity, during the time we are animating either left or right, we disallow any further changes to the menu. This is not necessary if a more advanced system is developed to queue up, or interrupt animations. We first do a pass on the menu items, clearing any of them that have been previously marked as selected, this is done as a simpler alternative than tracking the currently selected item more closely, which would have better performance results. The next part is to determine which the next item is, or which the target item we will animate towards is. If the next item goes beyond the scope of the list, we will loop around to the last element and the target angle will be 2π. Otherwise, if we are single stepping from one item to the next item, we can calculate the step by partitioning a circle into the number of items in the menu, just like slicing a pizza. The target angle will be the index of the item we wish to animate to times the step angle we calculated.

This is a perfect opportunity to make use of the interpolation curves for animation we saw in **Animation with Interpolation Curves**. We will animate the *m_currentAngle* parameter towards *m_targetAngle*, over the duration specified by *m_animationTime*. In this example we will use an ease in/out quadratic curve, this will give it a nice feeling of acceleration as the animation begins and a nice smooth deceleration as the item reaches its target, and we provide a finish function that resets the *m_animating* flag to false once the animation is done. It's fun to change the selected curve to see the difference each ease curve makes and find the one that gives the best responsiveness and fluidity to the menu.

Updating the menu is straightforward, we will update the interpolator to make sure the animations we create are updated. We then set the root item's world transform to a rotation matrix at *m_currentAngle*. And finally we update the root item, this will internally propagate the transformation to all of its children items.

```cpp
void menu_3d::Update(float deltaTime)
{
    m_interpolator.Update(deltaTime);
    m_root->SetWorld(matrix::CreateRotationY(m_currentAngle));
    m_root->Update(deltaTime);
}
```

The parts of the system that handles the hierarchy is within the item class,

```cpp
class item
{
private:
    math::matrix m_localTransform;
    math::matrix m_worldTransform;
    std::vector< std::shared_ptr<item>> m_children;
};
```

An item will have two transforms, the world transform defines its position, rotation and scale relative to the world's origin {0,0,0} and the local transform that will be relative to its parent's world transform.

```cpp
void item::ApplyWorldTransform(const math::matrix& world)
{
    m_worldTransform = world;
    for ( auto& child : m_children )
    {
        child->SetWorld( m_worldTransform * child->Local() );
    }
}
```

When we apply a world transform on an item, we will recalculate each of the children's world transform by multiplying their local transform with the parent's new world transform.

During an item's update we can iterate through all the children and apply the world transformation on them.

```cpp
void item::Update(float deltaTime)
{
    if ( m_applyTransform )
    {
        for ( auto& child : m_children )
        {
            child->ApplyWorldTransform(m_worldTransform);
        }
        m_applyTransform = false;
    }
}
```

To avoid unnecessary matrix multiplications, we keep a flag, *m_applyTransform* which is set anytime we modify the local or world transforms. This ensures that we only propagate a matrix down the hierarchy if it has been modified, it would be a potentially costly waste of CPU cycles to be transforming the hierarchy every frame.

To draw a menu item, we simply draw the item itself, then draw each of its children.

```cpp
void item::Draw(const render::camera& camera)
{
    if ( !m_visible )
        return;

    if ( m_texture != nullptr )
    {
        m_quad.Draw(m_localTransform * m_worldTransform, camera.View(),
camera.Projection(), m_texture);
    }

    for ( auto& child : m_children )
    {
        child->Draw(camera);
    }
}
```

If an item is not visible, none of its children should be visible either, so we return early. Otherwise we will draw the item's quad, applying the item's local transform to its computed world transform. Recall that the world transform was applied from the parent, but each item still contains its own local transform, now is the time to apply it.

Some interesting things we can do with this hierarchy, first, if we set the quads to be view aligned, they will always face towards the camera, no matter what, this is generally good if you want to see the quads that have gone behind. Another option is to rotate them using their local space position as a direction vector, this makes the quad always face away from the direction it is coming from. In the case of our circle this will give us an almost cylindrical type shape, depending on how many items the menus has.

The best part about a system such as this is how we can achieve such seemingly complex animation of multiple objects by simply animating one variable, the angle of the root item, which is a lot easier than tracking angles for each menu item.

7.3 Virtual Reality

7.3.1 Stereo Rendering

Stereoscopic rendering provides a method for simulating how our brain perceives the 3D world. We can do this by rendering from two cameras that represent each of our eyes into separate frame buffers; typically these two renders are then combined to generate a single stereoscopic image.

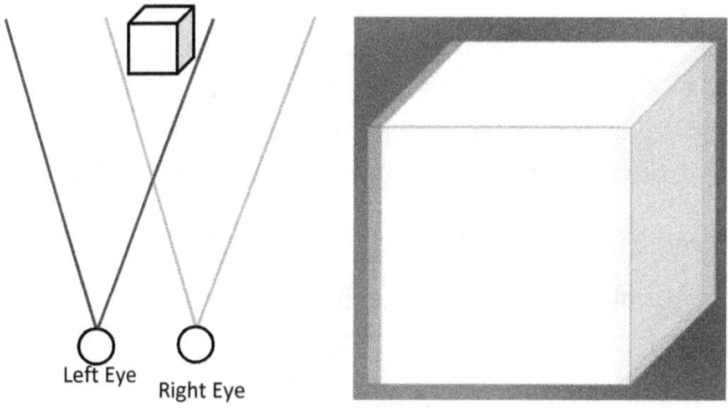

Rendering for Head-Mounted Devices (HMD) such as the *Oculus Rift* work off of this same concept; however, rather than merging the left and right frame buffers into a single stereoscopic image (which can result in significant artifacts at the edges of objects), the Rift uses half the screen for each eye; our left eye will see the left side of the screen while the right eye will see the right side of the screen, using a different projection matrix and applying distortion correction to account for the shape of the Rift's optics.

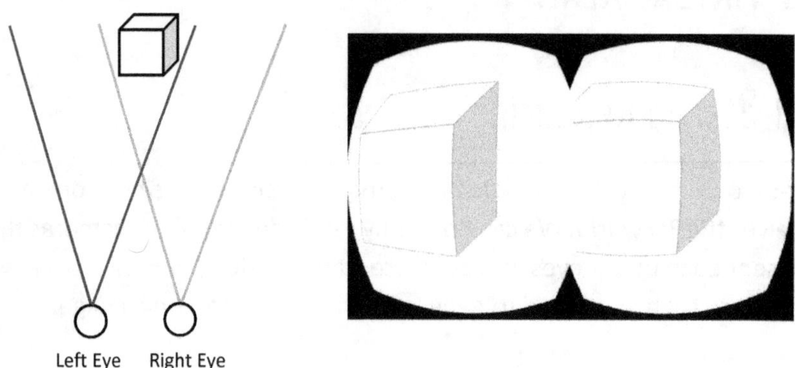

Our rendering setup needs to change in order to support the Rift, as mentioned before we will need to render the game twice, one for each eye. We will start by setting up the viewport for the area covered by the left eye.

```
SetViewport(0, 0, HorizontalResolution / 2, VerticalResolution);
```

We then need to calculate the half-screen's aspect ratio α and vertical field of view (FOV) θ_{fov}.

$$\alpha = \frac{HorizontalResolution}{2 \cdot VerticalResolution}$$

$$\theta_{fov} = 2 \cdot atan\left(\frac{VerticalScreenSize}{2 \cdot EyeToScreenDistance}\right)$$

With these values we are able to build a non-distortion corrected projection matrix.

$$P = \begin{bmatrix} \dfrac{1}{\alpha \cdot \tan(\frac{\theta_{fov}}{2})} & 0 & 0 & 0 \\ 0 & \dfrac{1}{\alpha \cdot \tan(\frac{\theta_{fov}}{2})} & 0 & 0 \\ 0 & 0 & \dfrac{z_{far}}{z_{near} - z_{far}} & \dfrac{z_{far} \cdot z_{near}}{z_{near} - z_{far}} \\ 0 & 0 & -1 & 0 \end{bmatrix}$$

This will give us a projection matrix with a projection center in the middle of each screen, however for HMDs we need the projection center to be the center of the eye, we can create a matrix that will translate the projection center for each eye into the correct position.

We will calculate an absolute offset to apply on the horizontal direction h in meters to correct for different screen sizes, and then rescale into viewport coordinates.

$$h_{meters} = \frac{HorizontalScreenSize}{4} - \frac{InterpupillaryDistance}{2}$$

It is important that the offset is applied by half the interpupillary distance in world units, you will need to convert real-world units back into game-units.

$$h = \frac{4 \cdot h_{meters}}{HorizontalScreenSize}$$

The value of h is now the absolute horizontal offset we need to apply to our projection matrix such that:

$$H = \begin{bmatrix} 1 & 0 & 0 & 0 \\ 0 & 1 & 0 & 0 \\ 0 & 0 & 1 & 0 \\ \pm h & 0 & 0 & 1 \end{bmatrix}$$

Where h will be positive for the left eye correction and negative for the right eye correction.

$$P' = HP$$

P' is the final non-distortion corrected projection matrix. The game's view transform also has to account for the eye position shift, similarly we will create a transform matrix that will apply the interpupillary distance correction for each eye.

$$V' = \begin{bmatrix} 1 & 0 & 0 & 0 \\ 0 & 1 & 0 & 0 \\ 0 & 0 & 1 & 0 \\ \pm\dfrac{ipv}{2} & 0 & 0 & 1 \end{bmatrix} V$$

Where V is your game's non-stereo view transform centered between the eyes, V' is the final stereo correct view transform.

7.3.2 Distortion Correction

The next step is to perform distortion correction to account for the Rift's optics. The lens used by the Rift magnifies the image, increasing the field of view. It will generate a radial pincushion distortion that will increase the image magnification with distance from the optical axis, this results in a visible effect in which lines that do not go through the center of the image are bowed inwards, towards the center of the image.

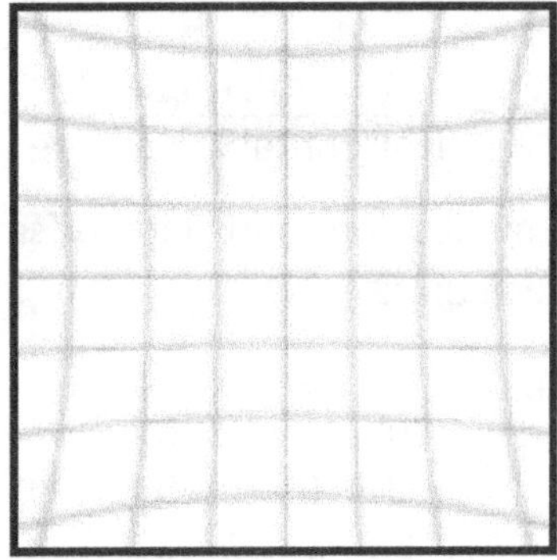

This distortion can be corrected by applying a mathematically inverse effect, a barrel distortion. A barrel distortion, will decrease magnification with distance from the optical axis, the visual effect is that of an image that has been mapped on top of a sphere, or a barrel. By combining the distortions, the pincushion effect is neutralized resulting in straight lines.

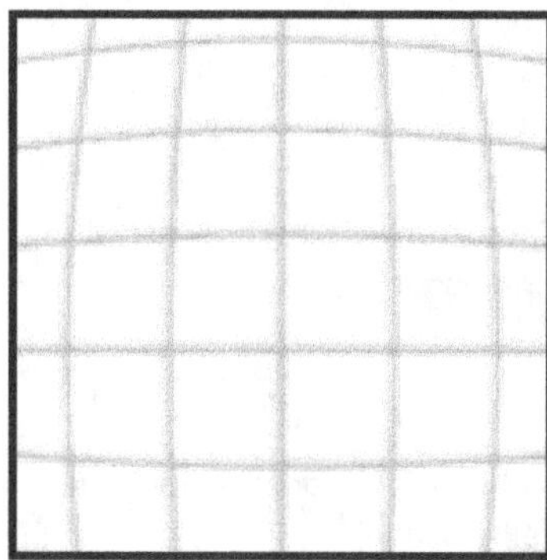

Mathematically, barrel and pincushion distortions are quadratic, they increase as the square of the distance from the center.

Radial distortion can be corrected using the radial distortion correction from Brown's distortion model, of which we are only interested in the radial distortion, and can ignore the tangential distortion component.

$$r' = r(k_0 + k_1 r^2 + k_2 r^4 + k_3 r^6)$$

Where r is the radius of the distortion effect (from the center of the image), and $k_{0...n}$ are the radial distortion coefficients, which will be positive for barrel distortion and negative for pincushion distortion.

The resulting radius r' is used to calculate the sample location in the render surface generated during rendering, this will result in pixels being pulled towards the center of the lens; the amount of displacement will increase with the radius.

The distortion correction can be applied on the GPU using a pixel on the final image. This means that to support the Rift, the game must be rendered into a render target which we will then use to draw a quad onto the frame buffer using a pixel shader that performs the distortion correction.

The following pseudocode explains the rendering flow necessary for a rendering a game on the Rift.

```
SetRenderTarget(RT)

// Left eye
SetViewport(0, 0, HorizontalResolution / 2, VerticalResolution)
SetProjectionMatrix(LeftEyeProjection)
Render(RT)

// Right eye
SetViewport(HorizontalResolution / 2, 0, HorizontalResolution, VerticalResolution)
SetProjectionMatrix(RightEyeProjection)
Render(RT)

// Render screen quad using distortion correction pixel shader to frame buffer
T = SetTexture(RT)
SetPixelShader(DistortionCorrection)
DrawFullScreenQuad(T, fullscreen);

// Finished rendering, present the frame buffer
Present
```

The render target will need to be larger than the final viewport to account for the distortion pulling pixels towards the center, and finally, the field of view and image scale will need to be adjusted to accommodate for the distortion.

Modern VR headsets give us an exciting opportunity to research and develop new forms of user interaction. The techniques described in this book for projecting user interface elements into world space, *augmented reality* are immediately useful as they allow us to provide users with information about the world they are immersed in. Using transformation hierarchies with augmented reality rendering techniques we can create a user interface that is as immersive and responsive as the virtual world. It's an exciting time for virtual reality technologies.

8 Localization

Localization is the process of preparing a game for distribution in different locales or regions, it is an important part of a game's development cycle and is something that user interface programmers must be familiar with. Localizing a game means enabling the replacement of text, audio, video and images to a version prepared for the target locale. This section is an introduction to many localization concepts and strategies used to bring games into many locales.

The localization for the user interface is something that should not be left as an afterthought, it is far easier and more cost efficient to design and develop user interfaces with localization in mind than it is to retrofit a user interface to support localization when the game is nearing completion. It cannot be stressed enough how important it is to be certain that the user interface is using the localization pipeline from the start.

Unfortunately, there is no universal way to perform localization, each team develops their own localization pipeline to best utilize its resources, from very simple approach that uses either a large text file, possibly generated from a spreadsheet to complete localization packages that run as a service, an application or as ideally, as an internal web application.

8.1 Text Localization

Text replacement is the most common localization strategy used, it means that all text used in the game and all of its user interfaces will be replaced by the text translated to the language of the target locale. As with film, some games may not have the resources to localize audio, providing localized subtitles may be a less expensive alternative for in-game dialogs and videos.

Any text fields that require localization should not contain the text that is to be translated, instead it should use a unique identifier, a key. Not only is it far easier to match a key to text in multiple languages than it would be to translate word for word, but this allows linguistic and cultural references to be applied to make the game more appealing and relevant to the target locale. This implies that a key may represent a word, a phrase, or even a block of text. With a key and a locale, we are able to query the localization database for the text that needs to be displayed.

When designing a localization system, consider that you should only ever load or stream in the data for the locale the game is currently running on. We don't need to keep a large amount of localization data for each language in memory. When changing the locale, an infrequent operation usually done from the main menu; it is best to release the data for the current locale from memory and load in the new locale data, recreating our localization database.

The localization key should not be a string, as we want to avoid unnecessary and computationally expensive string comparisons. Instead, each key should be a unique identifier that we can use to query from the database. In terms of the unique identifier, some game engines will already provide a mechanism for identifying resources, this is perfectly fine to use as it will be consistent with the rest of the game systems. That said, we can also implement a more straightforward solution. Localized text is not something that can change dynamically, we can use an auto incrementing unsigned int as the key every time we add a string to the database. The downside to using a numeric identifier for text is that when we reference keys we lose the context.

```cpp
const std::wstring label = localization::get_string(20); // ID 20 maps to "Open Chest"
const std::wstring label = localization::get_string("OpenChest");
```

This situation is less of an issue when you have a game editor or tools that are able to build or package the game data such that you may use a string comparison during development, while an automated system will convert these strings to their respective numeric identifiers with the goal that during the game's execution no string comparisons are performed.

There are different methods that may be used to store the localization data. It is important to understand the implications of the method you choose. While one approach is to use XML to store the raw localization data, this can have performance issues, higher than necessary memory use or even logistical complications.

```
<id>1</id>
<en>Hello World!</en>
<fr>Bonjour tout le monde!</fr>
<sp>Hola todo el mundo!</sp>
```

Depending on the game and the amount of localized text, this approach can quickly take up a lot of memory and we would incur the processing cost of parsing this XML data. The XML data should only be used as an intermediate format, the data should be converted to a binary format during the build or packaging process. One logistical issue that may arise is at the time of delivering data to be localized. If all the data is stored in a single, very large XML file, it may become difficult to send out this data to multiple localization agencies or to multiple translators, have them apply their translations and then ship the file back to you. You may find yourself having to merge multiple revisions of the file as work is delivered.

A more flexible approach is to create a simple file format using UTF-8 files, one file per localization string. The format of the file may look something like this:

```
1
en: Hello World!
fr: Bonjour tout le monde!
sp: Hola todo el mundo!
jp: こんにちは この世!
```

This file may follow a naming convention to make it easy to know what the files are, *1_helloworld.loc.* Now, these files can be easily shipped to the different translators or agencies, they may be passed around and if ever a file needs to be merged for some reason, it is a lot simpler to do so. During build packaging we can collect all these files and create a binary database per language. As we discussed earlier, having one database per language will allow us to only ever load the active locale's text and nothing more.

The database should be loaded into a hash table. We have designed the system so that each entry has a unique key thus we do not have to worry about key collisions, in other words, our hash table has a perfect hash function and no collision resolution needs to be implemented. Given a key, we can query our database in constant time, O(1).

In the context of user interfaces, there are some important considerations when it comes to different locales, not all words in different languages have the same size, the user interface must be flexible enough to scale to fit the text, or in some cases be restrictive and force translators to closely match as close as possible the number of characters to the original text to maintain the artistic direction. This is not something that is clearly defined as every user interface is unique, some will be more suitable for a flexible dynamic rescaling of labels and dialogs, while others may prove more challenging if the user interface space is limited. As user interface developers it is important to discuss localization with the artistic direction team early in the process to make sure their vision and goals are met without hindering the ability to localize the game or sacrificing the visual quality of the game in other markets.

8.2 Image Localization

Image localization is not as common as text localization, however, it is no less important. It's worth mentioning that the goal behind image localization should not be to localize text that has been "burned" into images or textures, at least, it's something that should be avoided. It is far more work for translators to modify images especially if they don't have the source data readily available, which may be the case when the localization is outsourced than it is for them to modify text and for the text to be rendered.

However, there are legitimate situations in which image replacement is absolutely necessary, many times it is to meet many different game rating guidelines established by different countries, depending on the subject matter of the game it may be necessary to remove or replace imagery that may be considered offensive to some countries.

8.3 Audio Localization

Audio localization is an important part of preparing a game for distribution in different locales, and it is a significant undertaking, the game text and dialogue will be written then sent to an agency, or an in-house localization department where voice actors for the different locales will be hired for recording. As the audio for different locales becomes available, it will be sent back to the team and will need to be integrated into the game's asset database.

This is another reason why separating text localization data into individual files pays off. We can associate a localization string file to a sound file in the game engine (primarily in the case of speech audio), with the goal that when the audio system plays a given sound we will know the respective localized text for it. The sound playback would then prompt the subtitle system to display the associated text for the current locale.

8.4 Asset Localization

The best strategy for game asset localization, be it images or audio is one that is global for any asset in the game's data. This is because, whether it is an audio file, an image file or any other custom data file, it is not always possible to predict precisely which assets will need to be localized, if localization is supported by any type of asset in the game, then it becomes straightforward to localize any asset should it need to. For example, some animation packages have facial animation features that are stored as custom files, if the resources are available and facial animation is localized to match the locale's language, then doing so will be immediately supported by this global strategy.

One approach that is straightforward to implement and is generally compatible with build automation systems is given a game asset file, say an image file called image00.png. Should a locale replacement be available, a locale-specific folder can be created in the same location as the file. This folder will contain the localized version of the file. When the build automation system prepares the data for each locale, as it scans each file, if it finds a locale-specific folder in the file's folder it can check for a locale override. If it finds one, it will ignore the source file and integrate the locale-specific file into the build.

It is important to be mindful of how the game's final builds will be generated, stored and distributed. Game certification and distribution requirements may vary depending on the company, publisher and hardware vendors as well as physical limitations in bandwidth, disk space and resources. The packaging system should be designed so that it can package custom builds and output different SKUs (stock keeping units) which will be distributed to different regions. North American SKUs typically are produced with English, French and Spanish while European SKUs may also include Italian, Polish, German, Russian and possibly others, while Asian SKUs will vary as they often require more specialized localization support.

8.5 Cinematic Localization

Cinematics are video sequences that are usually used to tell the game's story. Cinematics are usually encoded using video formats that will vary in quality, performance and cost. There are some special considerations to have when preparing cinematic assets for localization.

Most video formats have built in support for multiple audio tracks to be encoded into a single file, some may also provide support for encoding text subtitles into them. The advantage of using this support, in particular for localized audio is that the audio and video will generally have very good synchronization, the video may be played using the audio as the driver of the streaming such that if there is a lack of synchronization the audio will have higher priority while the video may drop some frames to compensate. Other configurations may opt for using the video as the master, unfortunately this approach may result in audible skips. Our ears are far less forgiving than our eyes, we may not notice if a video interpolates between two or more frames depending on the visual coherence of the cinematic, however and audio skip is hard to ignore.

Video encoding may be a time consuming process. And videos may need to be encoded multiple times during a game's production, especially closer to the end of the development cycle. Consider that every time a new audio track is delivered by the localization team the video will be need to be encoded to include the new track. If subtitles are encoded within the video, fixing a small typographical error in the text would require a full re-encoding of the video. The problem becomes more severe when the game is being released in multiple platforms, videos are generally encoded using different quality settings depending on the platform they will run on.

8.6 Localize Early

Localization and internationalization are important parts of game development and are too often neglected and like homework, done at the very last minute. This creates very difficult, stressful and costly situations.

Plan for localization early! Use the localization pipeline even if no localization has been done, any string that is put off until after will require time and effort to find and fix, a tedious thing to do when there are so many more important issues to fix. Understand how localization agencies will need to receive the source files to be localized and make sure your systems can import or export data if necessary.

Make localization a simple, unobtrusive part of your game and automate as much as you can, no one wants to spend eight hours manually encoding videos for days or weeks on end. Create scripts or tools that will encode in batches with minimal or no direct human involvement.

CONCLUSION

This is not the end, we are only getting started!

We have seen many techniques and algorithms that will allow us to create the core functionality for most game user interface systems, the next step is to venture outside the code and create data driven tools to give artists and designers the power to create game user interfaces.

Creating a powerful user interface authoring tool is a significant undertaking and worthy of its own book. There are many subjects that we have yet to cover in areas of data serialization, tool development, user experience, scripting languages, data definition languages and much more.

User interface programming is growing field with endless possibilities. The topics and the techniques we discussed are the first stepping stone onto greater features and more advanced ways of interacting with players. The future of user interface programming is very exciting, games and devices continue to evolve allowing us to discover new ways to interact with our virtual worlds and the real world.

A great example of user interface technology extending beyond the game world is augmented reality. With the advent of new wearable mobile devices, many of the user interface concepts we apply in games are becoming real world applications.

BIBLIOGRAPHY

Alexandrescu, A. (2001). *Modern C++ Generic Programming and Design.* Addison-Wesley.

Anderson, S. E. (n.d.). *Bit Twiddling Hacks.* Retrieved from http://graphics.stanford.edu/~seander/bithacks.html#RoundUpPowerOf2

Chen, G. (n.d.). *The Truth Behind Homogeneous Coordinates.* Retrieved from http://deltaorange.com/2012/03/08/the-truth-behind-homogenous-coordinates/

Eberly, D. H. (2004). *Game Physics.* Morgan Kaufmann Publishers.

Gregory, J. (2009). *Game Engine Architecture.* A K Peters/CRC Press.

Griffiths, G. (2009, February 5). *Subtitles: Increasing Game Accessibility, Comprehension.* Retrieved from http://www.gamasutra.com/view/feature/3922/

James M. Van Verth, L. M. (2004). *Essential Mathematics for Games & Interactive Applications.* Morgan Kaufmann Publishers.

Lomont, C. (2002). *A Fast Gradient Fill Algorithm.* Retrieved from http://www.lomont.org/Math/Papers/2002/FinalPaper.pdf

Paeth, A. W. (1986). A Fast Algorithm for General Raster Rotation. In *Graphics Interface 86* (pp. 77-81). Vancouver, British Columbia, Canada. Retrieved from http://www.leptonica.com/rotation.html

Stanley B. Lippman, J. L. (2013). *C++ Primer (Fifth Edition).* Addison Wesley.

Tomas Akenine-Moller, E. H. (2008). *Real-Time Rendering (3rd Edition).* A K Peters, Ltd.

PIRACY

I would love if everyone buys a copy of this book and proudly displays it on their desk or bookshelf, but I live in the real world. I understand not everyone can, wants to or will see the value of investing in books. So you downloaded this book, now what? Well, get to work! Read the book, download the sample code, apply the concepts into your game's UI and learn as much as you can. One day, when you bask in your creation, when you receive a well-deserved promotion or when your indie game is a breakout success, remember this book was there to help you along the way, buy a hard copy and display it proudly on your desk.

INDEX